POWER AND SELF-CONSCIOUSNESS IN THE POETRY OF SHELLEY

St. Martin's Press Studies in Romanticism:

COLERIDGE AND THE SELF: Romantic Egotism
Stephen Bygrave

WORDS AFTER SPEECH: A Comparative Study of
Romanticism and Symbolism
Paul Coates

WORDSWORTH: Play and Politics, A Study of Wordsworth's
Poetry, 1787–1800
John Turner

POWER AND
SELF-CONSCIOUSNESS
IN THE POETRY
OF SHELLEY

Andrew J. Welburn

St. Martin's Press   New York

All rights reserved. For information, write:
Scholarly & Reference Division,
St. Martin's Press, Inc., 175 Fifth Avenue, New York, NY 10010

First published in the United States of America in 1986

Printed in Hong Kong

ISBN 0–312–63371–8

Library of Congress Cataloging-in-Publication Data
Welburn, Andrew J.
Power and self-consciousness in the poetry of
Shelley.
1. Shelley, Percy Bysshe, 1792–1822 – Criticism
and interpretation. I. Title.
PR5438.W45   1986   821'.7   85–22145
ISBN 0–312–63371–8

For Mona

And from her lips, as from a hyacinth full
Of honey-dew, a liquid murmur drops,
Killing the sense with passion; sweet as stops
Of planetary music heard in trance.
In her mild lights the starry spirits dance,
The sunbeams of those wells which ever leap
Under the lightings of the soul – too deep
For the brief fathom-line of thought or sense.

Contents

viii   *Contents*

List of Illustrations

Preface

This book is an attempt to sketch a new way of understanding Shelley's poetic achievement. Earlier studies have stressed the individually very different facets of Shelley's imagination, in particular drawing attention to the opposition between his scepticism and his 'visionary', idealist leanings – or simply devoting themselves, often in illuminating detail, to his political, scientific, philosophical, religious or literary interests as the case may be. The poet who emerges from these studies can easily appear an extremist; and certainly the straining after extremes was a part of Shelley's nature. But it was no more than a part, and it has been my aim to delineate the controlling central consciousness which any serious reader of Shelley soon encounters in his work, and which exists in paradoxical and vital dependence on the lure toward the heights and depths. It is only in attempting to define that consciousness, I believe, that the full integrity and value of Shelley's achievement becomes clear.

The attempt to define it involves the consideration of all Shelley's major interests; indeed it soon emerges that to discuss Shelley is to explore the great currents of art, science and myth which shaped his world – and continue to shape ours today. His project is still one where we may follow a profound mind entering into little-explored territory, and the achievement he brought back from the outer bounds of awareness, as well as his feeling for the human centre, is still an exciting subject of consideration; it is perhaps still more important for us today, in our own world of extremes, than it was in his own time.

Inevitably I have neglected some aspects of Shelley to concentrate on others. I have said little on the explicitly biographical dimension of his poetry, although it might certainly be possible to relate the dominant 'landscapes' of Shelley's imagery to his travels and experiences in Europe. The contrast between the bare mountains of the Alps and the sunny paradise of Italy or the Mediterranean isles appears to have made contact with deep and contrary intuitions in his soul, and no doubt without his European experience that great blossoming of a lyric poet after 1815 could not have taken place. The suicide of Harriet, his first wife, too, was a blow whose submerged effect can be felt in the subsequent greater maturity of his verse, despite his new life with Mary and his brightening prospects. And for that matter, the 'daemonic' energies which figure in Shelley's thought were to be found embodied in the colourful characters who at various times thronged around him: Trelawney with his fantastic lies, the disturbing Lord Byron, the ironic and obscurantist Peacock, the occultist John Frank Newton. Yet in the end Shelley's journey was, more importantly, an inward one where we can all follow, a mental voyage still more fascinating than the restless pursuit of his external biography.

This study has had the advantage of friendly comment and criticism over a number of years. I am especially grateful to John Beer, Owen Barfield and Anne Barton, whose responses have all affected the book substantially for the better; I should like to thank also the late Sir Christopher Cox for his diligence in drawing my attention to the more intelligent commentators on Shelley and politics. Mona Bradley typed the manuscript from my jigsaw puzzle of drafts and emendations: my thanks to her for her patient wrestling with the minutiae of the text – a gift freely given and with a grace not every author has the privilege to know. Invaluable advice and help at the stage of publication came from Frances Arnold of Macmillan Press, and the text had the advantage of attention from Valery Rose, so that only the most obstinate of my own errors remain. Further thanks go to Hedley Teale for his support, and for conducting me on a memorable tour of Shelley's Italy and the Alps. My mother continued to believe in the book in what seemed to her the long time between my first talking of it and the moment of its appearance, and supported it during the several stages in-between.

The book was written during my time as a Research Fellow at New College, Oxford. It was a Fellow of New College – the Revd John Walker – who in 1811 initiated the train of events which led to the author of *The Necessity of Atheism* being promptly sent down. Moreover, an earlier member of the Shelley family, Thomas Shelley who was a Fellow of New College in the sixteenth century, was 'removed' in 1567 for refusing to attend divine service. I am grateful to New College for enabling me to make a positive contribution to Shelley studies.

A.J.W.

Outline Chronology of Shelley's Life and Works

1817   Beginning of friendship with Leigh Hunt and Keats.
        Completes *Laon and Cythna* (later called *The Revolt
        of Islam*) composed in friendly rivalry with Keats'
        Endymion.
1818   Shelley *ménage* leaves for Italy. Translates Plato's
        The Banquet (Symposium), etc. Writes 'Painted Veil'
        sonnet. At Venice with Byron. Starts *Prometheus
        Unbound*. Death of daughter Clara. Writes *Julian
        and Maddalo*.
1818–19 Tours Rome, Naples, Pompei and Vesuvius.
1819   Writes *Ode to the West Wind*. Completes *Prometheus
        Unbound* (published 1820). Writes *The Cenci, The
        Mask of Anarchy* and *Peter Bell the Third*.
1820   Engaged in alchemical and meteorological studies.
        Writes *Letter to Maria Gisborne, The Cloud, To a
        Skylark, Ode to Liberty, The Witch of Atlas, The
        Sensitive Plant* and *Swellfoot the Tyrant*. Meets
        Emilia Viviani. Writes *Hymns of Apollo and Pan*.
1821   Interest in 'Magnetism'. Writes *Epipsychidion,
        Adonais* and *A Defence of Poetry* (published 1840).
        Relationship with Jane Williams. Writes *Hellas* and
        On the Devil and Devils.
1822   Writes *The Triumph of Life* (fragment). Death of
        Shelley (8 July) by drowning in the Gulf of Spezia,
        near Lerici.

Introduction:
the Painted Veil

Fear & Hope are – Vision.
(William Blake, *The Gates of Paradise*)

Perhaps no poem from the mature body of Shelley's work comes closer to announcing the poet's central preoccupations – expounding with a directness that is almost programmatic the fundamental movements of mind he sought to articulate in his briefest impassioned lyrics, in his uniquely internalised or 'lyrical' drama, and in his sustained, reflective philosophical verse – than does the sonnet written in 1818: 'Lift not the painted veil'.

It is, as a poem, unmistakably Shelleyan. Yet it is also a poem that reveals starkly enough a number of the deep paradoxes and disquieting contradictions with which Shelley's poetic thought seems always to be hedged about, and which have done so much to call in question his reputation as a major English poet. It entangles us immediately, too, in some of the more salient difficulties thrust on us by Shelley's highly individual concept of the nature of poetry, above all in the treatment of traditional poetic forms; of which few can conceivably have been harder to recreate with new and individual interest than the historically hard-worked and internally intricate sonnet. We must concede that from all three perspectives – exemplary, philosophical and formal – the poem does not represent the pinnacle of Shelley's achievement. But it is also very far indeed from being a mere 'problem poem', and if from each of his difficulties the poet wrests a somewhat less-than-total victory, his struggle may yet be of profounder interest than an outright success on easier terms. We shall attempt to prove in the course of this book that Shelley's poetry is written on terms which (contrary to a still popular though declining myth) are well nigh the most demanding it is possible to conceive. For this reason, a brief and

1

idiosyncratic sonnet forms a more revealing point of departure than many a more famous climactic achievement or startling lyrical flight.

It may be as well, therefore, to allow the poet to have the first word (or almost the first word) to himself:

> Lift not the painted veil which those who live
> Call Life: though unreal shapes be pictured there,
> And it but mimic all we would believe
> With colours idly spread, – behind, lurk Fear
> And Hope, twin Destinies; who ever weave
> Their shadows, o'er the chasm, sightless and drear.
> I knew one who had lifted it – he sought,
> For his lost heart was tender, things to love,
> But found them not, alas! nor was there aught
> The world contains, the which he could approve.
> Through the unheeding many he did move,
> A splendour among shadows, a bright blot
> Upon this gloomy scene, a Spirit that strove
> For truth, and like the Preacher found it not.

With the image of the 'painted veil' itself in the opening line Shelley proclaims himself among the ranks of the visionary poets.[1] He is not one who can be content to celebrate the everyday world as it lies all about us. He is no observer even of the raw complexities of human life, in the inexhaustible variety of relationships that have afforded material to so many poets, dramatists and novelists. He is a poet of ultimates. He casts all the varied experiences of life as a tapestry of unreal shapes, mimicking all we would like to believe but yielding us no final truth. He appears, in the lines which follow, to resent the inconclusiveness which follows from the very diversity, the infinite multiplicity of life which makes its meaning hard, perhaps impossible, to fathom.[2] Its colours are spread before our gaze indeed, richly but idly.

To probe behind the phantom images of ordinary life-experience, the 'painted veil', however, is a dangerous undertaking. A 'veil' can be torn aside, or lifted to reveal what lies beyond. But when that veil has been identified by those who live with 'Life' itself, who can tell us what we will uncover on the other side? We might find there the grand Truth we failed to discern in the ebb and flow of our confusing life; but we might also be made aware of ultimate absurdity, the meaninglessness of everything. Shelley poses explicitly both alternatives, of Hope and Fear, 'twin Destinies' of this dangerous and shadowy undertaking. Of a final goal he can see nothing, only an abyss – 'sightless', 'drear', inconclusive. Beginning with a warning and ending with the fate of one 'lost heart' who ignored it, Shelley's visionary and exploratory sonnet does not envisage, like Wordsworth in his own programmatic Prospectus to the projected poem *The Recluse*, passing unalarmed Jehovah's thunder and the empyreal thrones;[3] nor is Shelley a committed visionary in the mould of Blake, impatient of doubts and doubters, longing 'to converse with my friends in Eternity, See Visions, Dream Dreams & prophecy & speak Parables unobserv'd & at liberty from the Doubts of other Mortals'.[4] Shelley is of a mottled temper, and shares all the uncertainties of contemporary sceptics, so that his visionary poem is shot through with paradox. In the very act of imaginatively parting the illusory veil, he solemnly warns us not to look. None the less, the poem only exists by scorning its own admonition and, with its uncertainty confessed, it offers us a tentative but powerful vision of the forces beyond the veil.

In the 'lost heart' of the latter part of the poem we recognise, of course, Shelley himself. Less obviously, Shelley makes here an implicit comparison between his own attempt to gaze beyond mundane reality and traditional Christian mystical ecstasies, for he echoes the phraseology going back to Paul ('I know a man in Christ, fourteen years ago, whether in the body, I know not, or whether out of the body, I know not, God knoweth, such a one caught up even to the third heaven'), phraseology in which Paul is also traditionally taken to be referring indirectly to himself.[5] To Paul, his vision was deeply significant, perhaps also deeply disturbing. What is striking is how little he can say about it: he does not know whether his experience was bodily or incorporeal; he heard words in Paradise – but they cannot be repeated. All these are marks of authenticity. But to the religious outsider they emphasise how much is necessarily obscure and ambiguous, as is in a still greater degree Shelley's personal and less committed vision of transcendent possibilities. Indeed, lacking Paul's commitment to a Christian interpretation of his experience, Shelley's poem might seem to be becoming lost in obscure and ambiguous speculations. The poet's introduction of himself into the poem, however, serves as an important counter-weight to the initial speculative tendencies. Shelley did have such tendencies, as his prose *Speculations on Metaphysics* will confirm; but in his poetry we have something different. There Shelley keeps faith with experience. His sonnet, as its personalised second part makes clear, is not concerned with realms beyond human knowledge, but with the human self in its search for truth and beauty, its hopes and fears about ultimate realities. And in its intensest form that search is the search of love for an answering love.

'Lift not the painted veil' turns upon the double nature of our response to the world we inhabit. On the one hand, we feel trapped if our experience should ever settle into a dull round, ceasing to excite our curiosity or stimulate our interest. Indeed, however wide that experience may be, the long-term evidence from poetry and art seems to be that it never will satisfy us completely. The very existence of the arts already testifies to man's need to go beyond whatever is given, to extend, to deepen and transform. If in life we ever do stand still, our world will sink down to a strange half-reality, a veil of unreal forms through which some deep and unsuppressable part of us will always long to penetrate. Shelley therefore, like other Romantic poets, undertakes to 'startle the reader from the trance of ordinary life', much as Coleridge and Wordsworth had more famously aimed 'to excite a feeling analogous to the supernatural, by awakening the mind's attention from the lethargy of custom'. In that way they hoped to disperse 'the film of familiarity and selfish solicitude' from before our eyes.[6]

But at the same time Shelley is aware of dangers which the first generation of visionary Romantics only discovered through bitter disappointment and disillusion. He is profoundly aware that objectivity and practical judgement, together with the psychological stability that goes with them, is intimately bound up with human confidence in a dependable world. Our inner balance is largely built out of our reliance upon a steadfast outer world-order – that very world of custom and selfish solicitude which Coleridge mentioned to dismiss so disparagingly. So that to look beyond it, bracketing the whole of normal life together under the emblem of a 'painted veil' of unreal shapes, is to risk grave psychical disruption, perhaps permanent damage to the moral self. And yet the desire to transcend, to move on, to look beyond his immediate situation, seems inherently human and drives Shelley, with his radical and uncompromising nature, to insist upon asking the ultimate questions.

Thus the sonnet is not a verse essay in metaphysics at all, despite first appearances. It chronicles Shelley's resentment at the cruel paradox of human existence, his consciousness trapped between the threat of alienation when experience dwindles into a depressing round and nothing in earth's 'gloomy scene' offers human satisfaction or even abstract truth, and the threat of inner dissolution of the self with its objective values when every outer support is torn away, in the metaphysical quest to which man is so mysteriously urged. It is the poem of a visionary by temperament who does not know how far to believe his own vision.

Wordsworth and Coleridge, in casting off the restraints of custom, trusted themselves to the spirit of Hope.[7] They began as revolutionaries in philosophy, poetry and politics. But they learnt that the world teaches a hard lesson to those who hope too much, that Hope is but one of the 'twin Destinies'. Both came to know disappointment and dejection:

> We poets in our youth begin in gladness;
> But thereof comes in the end despondency & madness.[8]

A generation later, Shelley tries to incorporate the painful lessons they learnt into his Romantic aspiration from the start. His formulation of the visionary need to dissipate the film of custom and familiarity is much more cautious than theirs – in his prose statements as well as in poems like 'Lift not the painted veil'.

It is true that he begins by saying in his essay *On Life* that: 'Life and the world, or whatever we call that which we are and feel, is an astonishing thing. The mist of familiarity obscures from us the wonder of our being.'[9] Yet only a few lines later he concedes what Wordsworth and Coleridge would not have liked to allow, at least in their early careers, namely: 'It is well that we are thus shielded by the familiarity of what is at once so certain and so unfathomable, from an astonishment which would otherwise absorb and overawe the functions of that which is its object.'[10] Here in his prose we find the same ambiguity as in

Shelley's poetry: even if we escape the stultifying restrictions of everyday life and perception, and the half-reality they entail, we still face the further threat of a dazzling, overwhelming fullness in which our human consciousness would equally be absorbed and annihilated. It is clear that the intense awareness typical of Shelley's poetry does not spring, as used widely to be thought, from self-indulgence; it is intimately related to his sense of danger. Consciousness survives precariously against a backdrop of huge perspectives, reminding us of the dwarfed human figures in some Romantic landscapes.[11] But survive it does.

Shelley's treatment of verse-forms, moreover, reflects these same tensions on a different plane. Certainly the closed, disciplined structure of the sonnet may not seem the most natural vehicle for poetry of such far-reaching and uncertain explorations at the limits of awareness. Shelley moves consciously toward the periphery of thought where normal patterns of language and syntax begin to break down – it seems extraordinary to construct such speculative verse within a firm scheme of five rhymes and fourteen lines. It is true that Shelley's sonnet is somewhat bizarre in form. It breaks with the whole history of acquired technique in the careful balancing and inner movement of the classical sonneteers, and corresponds to none of the major recognisable types (Spenserian, Shakespearean, etc.). Having set out on his flight of imagination, Shelley finds that he needs his greater scope in the drawing out of possibilities, and thus departs from the kind of form whereby an extended problem is resolved or given clear definition in the tight organisation of the sestet. Rather 'Lift not the painted veil' divides naturally by subject-matter and rhyme into six lines followed by eight, not the usual octave and sestet at all. The final effect, however, is triumphantly and uniquely Shelleyan. It is a recurring phenomenon in Shelley that the actual proclaims its own abolition; a substantial form dissolves away upon close reading to unleash a hidden sense of infinitude. The process resembles that fiercely dissolving method of artistic creation described in Blake's *The Marriage of Heaven and Hell* – although Shelley's irony is generally less corrosive in feeling than that of Blake.[12]

The last lines of 'Lift not the painted veil' are remarkable as they are elusive. There is no final couplet, and correspondingly no sense of ultimate definition. The unexpected and striking rhyme with 'blot', coupled with the absence of a full rhyme in the preceding lines ('move' – 'strove'), brings the sonnet oratorically to a conclusion – or lack of one – with an oddly resounding 'not'. Then again, the disparity between the final cadence of negation and the assertive tone perplexes us. The resonance, and the rhetorical piling of phrases before the final release, persuades us of a committed voice. We sense that something is being urged upon us, but we are strangely baffled as to what it might be.

In matters of form, equally as in philosophical content, then, Shelley's yoking of radical commitment and intellectual scepticism creates a poetry of contradictions – a self-effacing poetry that is often deepest when it seems to disappear. Common things turn inside out. In the sonnet he momentarily likens himself to a preacher: but he turns out to mean the supremely sceptical author of Ecclesiastes, for whom all life was vanity and grasping at the wind.[13] In the last lines he creates a world like that in a photographic negative, with the poet as a 'bright blot' on the dark page of things, a redundant splendour in a world of shadows.[14]

'Lift not the painted veil' remains in the mind as an artefact of conscious verse beneath whose wrought surface infinities open. It begins and ends in negation. But between the warning and the actuality of failure, between 'lift not' and 'find not', Shelley admits the grandeur and the importance of the quest. Fear in the visionary undertaking balances uneasily with hope. Neither response is revealed as final or absolute, and Shelley remains profoundly agnostic about the ultimate reality they overlay.

The mysterious chasm remains, unsearchable and unapproachable.

1   Contrary Landscapes

Although philosophers have long debated the relationship which subsists between mind and the world it perceives, as if this were something unchanging and immutable, a little reflection will show that our mind's transactions with the world are inconstant, like our apprehensions of its beauty. At one time we may scarcely be aware of what is happening around us, abstracted in our own concerns. At another we may be drawn into intense involvement with our surroundings, as for example when we read a book intently, or scrutinise something that engages our whole attention, or when we cope with a situation where all our faculties are fully occupied.

It can sometimes be a very striking experience, even a disturbing one, to become aware of these states. Suppose, in the one case, we are rapt in our own thoughts when something happens that recalls us to ourselves. We may discover that the objects surrounding us have taken on an effect of alienness, externality, with even a hint of menace that may take several moments to overcome. We may see our own hands and limbs with a slightly hallucinatory foreignness.

The second case is of rarer occurrence. But if we do become self-aware during a state of close involvement with, say, reading a book, we may feel that the printed words have ceased to be opaque markings on the page: they may appear for the moment to have fused with our consciousness in an inseparable reality, scarcely to be differentiated from our own mental activity. We glimpse a condition in which the ordinary 'otherness' of things is overcome, making us conscious of a startling sense of unity – a coalescence whereby the common duality of mind and external object seems to have been resolved completely into ideal content. This state is (at least so I find) not only of rarer occurrence than the former one, but also much harder to sustain when it does occur. Self-awareness usually succeeds in restoring the ordinary impression of objective distance almost

8

instantaneously. Often, however, as in the former case, a lingering aura of disturbance may remain for a short time afterwards. A sense of unreality or hyper-reality persists as an undercurrent in our experience until normality is gradually restored in full.

It is worthwhile attending to these unusual but by no means unfamiliar conditions of experience, I believe, at the outset of our reading of Shelley, for several reasons. In the first place: because Shelley's imagination suggests them, or settings and situations where we feel either one of them as an undertone, with remarkable frequency. Sometimes indeed he describes them explicitly, both in his poetry and in his speculative prose. More often they make their impact through the suggestive power of imagery and the emotional resonance of his poems. They will serve us as useful coordinates in our attempt to map out the main lines of Shelley's poetic development. Yet I think it is also a valuable exercise to study these states briefly first of all outside the immediate context of poetry, and to make an initial attempt at self-observation: for in this way we begin to acquire some sense of the reason why certain fringe phenomena in the psychology of perception should have retained their fascination for Shelley all through his short but densely packed literary career. In both cases the key is to be found in the way that the ordinary conditions of commerce between the mind and the world are disturbed or interrupted. And the result of this is that they temporarily undermine the usual sense that we have of the limits of our being.

Both extremes, occupying though they do opposite poles of conscious experience, take away our usual assurance of standing as individuals in an objective world. For it is not only that we are made aware, at such times, of peculiar aspects of ourselves; the world around us also seems for the moment a differently constituted place. If, to take the first instance, our mind is suddenly confronted with the fact of its own abstractedness, our experience is liable to be of a world pressing in upon us with a perceptible degree, greater or lesser, of hostility. We feel almost attacked by an environment that appears to us wholly external, alien. The sheer, brute fact of existing things seems implicitly to deny our right to a conscious 'space' in the world. If at the other extreme we become self-conscious in the moment of total involvement, we will most probably be left with a strong sensation of the potential boundlessness of our inner being, our kinship with infinity. We may feel ourselves inwardly pervading our whole environment, making it the expression of our cognising self.

Of course, virtually the whole of mental life falls comfortably somewhere between the two poles. Objective awareness of the boundaries dividing the self from its world is normally, therefore, unproblematic. But Shelley is a visionary poet. He is a Romantic who strives to experience everything in life in its greatest possible intensity, and as such he is constantly probing the outermost limits of ordinary awareness. Hence it is that his style, as one critic has put it, is a continual 'gamble with the limits of poetry'.[1]

When the dominant mood of either pole becomes an established temperament, it may generate a philosophy. Both extremes of perception seem to point beyond ourselves to an ultimate foundation of experience, and prompt the invention of a metaphysic. They point, however, in diametrically opposite directions.

The mood of the first, 'alienated' pole will generally find expression in a world seen as external, independent of the cognising mind, governed by laws of inflexible outward necessity. Such was Shelley's prevailing philosophy in his youth, although it co-existed in his mind with many alarmingly inconsistent elements suggesting a very different view of the world. His juvenile poem *Queen Mab* is a propaganda piece in which he was determined to force together his opinions into a scheme of dogmatic materialism.[2] He gladly hailed there the

Spirit of Nature! all-sufficing Power,
Necessity! thou mother of the world![3]

He found a first intellectual vocabulary in the writings of the French materialists of the Enlightenment, in the work of rationalist thinkers like La Mettrie and the Baron d'Holbach, who argued that the world was a vast machine.[4] In such a universe the destiny of human consciousness, of man's desires and hopes, can only be a final submission to the existing: an ideal which slowly made the materialist world-conception come to look to Shelley somewhat less than 'all-sufficing' for a fully human vision of life. Indeed, already in *Queen Mab* the imagination cuts through the didactic flow of the propaganda with a powerful glimpse of industrialised, mechanised humanity, 'living pulleys of a dead machine, / Mere wheels of work and articles of trade'.[5] The picture of a living figure trapped in an inanimate landscape was to persist into his mature poetry. Above all there was to be the grand metaphor of Prometheus, shackled to the 'icy rocks' in an inert universe, a landscape

> Black, wintry, dead, unmeasured; without herb,
> Insect, or beast, or shape or sound of life.[6]

His body is pierced by the 'crawling glaciers', benumbing his human warmth and vitality. In Shelley's last poetry, too, there is the writhing figure in *The Triumph of Life*, who projects with 'strange distortion' like an old root from the bank at the roadside. He occupies another landscape of estrangement, 'where flowers never grew', under a 'cold glare, intenser than the noon, / But icy cold'.[7]

At the time when he was an enquiring student in Oxford and wrote, with such calamitous effect, his brief pamphlet on *The Necessity of Atheism* (1811), Shelley believed that the materialism of the French Encyclopaedists had been proven philosophically by Locke's empirical analysis of knowledge. All human knowledge was based, Shelley then supposed, on sensations which impinge upon the passive surface of the mind and make it conscious of the objects spread around it in space and time.[8] At this period he would still cheerfully have concurred with Holbach's prayer: 'O Nature, mistress of all being, and you, her daughters, Virtue, Reason and Truth, may you be forever our only divinities!'[9] For although he had strong instincts to the contrary, urging him to believe in a beneficent God steering the universe with a fatherly hand, he saw in the Enlightenment creed of materialism the only way of undercutting the claims of kings and priests to a tyrannical superhuman authority. He was therefore prepared to follow Locke in explaining away what looked at first like an 'innate' disposition to a belief in God. Shelley wrote to Miss Hitchener in 1811:

Locke *proves* that there are no innate ideas, that in consequence there can be no innate speculative or practical principles, thus overturning all appeals of *feeling* in favour of Deity. . . . Since all ideas are derived from the sense, this *feeling* must have originated from some sensual excitation.[10]

For a certain period, at any rate, Shelley managed to cope with his ambivalent feelings and followed outwardly the dictates of his reasoning mind.

The darker aspects of the materialist vision were the easier to accept, in that it offered several advantages and reassurances. It furnished the universe with reliable material objects which behaved predictably, in a scientifically investigable and practically useful manner. It presented man as a material being, suited by nature to his environment and able to manipulate that environment to a considerable extent in order to achieve his own purposes. Above all it gave man freedom from supernatural domination, and for that alone Shelley would no doubt have been more than willing to pay the price of a degree of alienation. Much more disturbing, however, was his realisation in the years following the writing of *Queen Mab* that dogmatic materialism already far exceeded the conclusions which could validly be drawn from a Lockean theory of perception. Under the influence of Locke's disciple–critic David Hume, and even more under the impact of Sir William Drummond's *Academical Questions*, Shelley soon came to adopt a more radically sceptical position. This new phase of his thought was completed somewhere around 1815.[11] He now felt, after absorbing the arguments of Drummond and Hume, that his confidence in reason and its power of searching out the causes of perception had been excessive.

He enquired more deeply into the all-important notion of 'cause'. For what is it that we mean by 'cause', he asked, following Hume, if not a constant and recurring conjunction of certain experiences in our field of perception? But if that is so, how could the idea of 'cause' possibly enable us to arrive at anything outside that field of experience? Even if we admit that experience seems somehow to point to 'causes' outside of experience, it soon seems clear that we could not actually know anything about them. Shelley concluded that the materialist dogma about the ultimate material nature of the causes of experience had really been too easy an assumption. It now appeared to him that human cognition simply could not know what lay beyond human perception.[12] The world of phenomena became a painted veil, and behind it lay the dark unfathomable.

This had serious consequences for the imaginative search of man, in Shelley's poetry, for an answering reality outside himself. Shelley was forced pessimistically to conclude: 'It is infinitely improbable that the cause of mind, that is, of existence, is similar to mind.'[13] Pursuing this direction of thought to its conclusion, even the sinister world of inert matter gave way to a greater threat, an infinite darkness in which it was infinitely improbable we should find anything we can understand. Any mind which, like Shelley's, searches itself and looks to its ultimate destiny must face with a certain fear the conviction that the world is in this way finally unaccommodating to man. In Shelley's writing an image surfaces ever more insistently: from the youthful novel *St Irvyne, or The Rosicrucian*, where a chasm is constantly felt to yawn at the hero's feet, threatening to swallow him up; to the 'dark and water depths' which the poet-hero of *Alastor* senses behind the reflected mountains in the mirror of a lake. Later it grows into the fabulous, formless darkness of Demogorgon's Cave in *Prometheus Unbound*.[14]

At all these moments in Shelley's work we push against the bounds of possible awareness: beyond lies self-extinction in the unknowable – perhaps insanity. We are brought, in Shelley's famous phrase, to 'that verge where words abandon us, and what wonder if we grow dizzy to look down the dark abyss of how little we know!'[15]

The mood of the second, 'involved' pole of experience finds its characteristic expression in a type of philosophy that is very different – though it is also one which strongly engaged Shelley's sympathies. For what we feel as a result of our moments of temporary coalescence with the surrounding world suggests the validity of some form of idealism. Such moments intimate that the world must ultimately be a unity, and the chief tenet of the various kinds of philosophical idealism is that the intractability and otherness of things can be overcome, and resolved into the content of thought. The idealist apprehension of the world offers the self a hope, in its quest for final belonging, of eventual fulfilment and realisation.[16] The underlying reason for the attraction of the mind to idealism emerges strongly in the following passage from the modern idealist A. E. Taylor, who argues openly that the universe must be such that it meets man's fundamental demands – for example his sense of justice, his sense of his own immortality. 'If it is the fundamental principle of a sound philosophy', he writes,

> that all existence forms a harmonious unity, then, if we can discover what are the essential and permanent features in the demands made by art, morality, and religion upon the world, we may be sure that these demands are somehow met and made good in the scheme of things. For a world which met our ethical, religious, and aesthetic demands upon life with a mere negative would inevitably contain aspects of violent and irreconcilable discord, and would thus be no true world or systematic unity at all.[17]

Despite his highly evolved intellectual scepticism, Shelley was also inclined to think that something like this must at the same time, somehow, be true. We may suspect that his temperamental indulgence in reverie and states of contemplation made the foundations in experience of the idealist hope especially clear to him. At any rate, something in Shelley's nature impelled him to fashion poetry quite as much out of idealist philosophisings as out of his materialism and scepticism – which leaves those who see Shelley as a 'philosophical poet' to untangle the conceptual knots as best they may!

Idealism to the Romantic poets meant primarily Plato.[18] For Plato, reality had consisted ultimately of Ideas (Forms) akin in nature to the 'ideas' of ordinary thought, though existing apart from any individual mind. Nowadays we know in considerable detail about Shelley's Platonic reading and the way it shaped his poetry and thought. We know, for example, that he read not only the master himself, but also Plato's followers (the Neoplatonists) and some of his critics. In due course Shelley translated some of the Platonic dialogues, notably the one on love, *The Symposium* (or *The Banquet of Plato* as his version is more sumptuously entitled). The task of translation was indeed still an outstanding one: Plato was not highly regarded in educational and university circles at that time and was not widely read; moreover, the renderings done into English in the eighteenth century by the intellectual heretic Thomas Taylor (the 'English pagan') left a great deal to be desired, to say the least, in literary quality.[19]

Yet we also know that Shelley's leaning toward idealism was not formed by his reading of Plato, but antedates it; for that leaning is clearly present even in some passages of *Queen Mab*, written at a time when Shelley could still dismiss, in a conventional phrase, the 'reveries of Plato'.[20] Certain critics have appealed to the shadowy notion of a 'natural Platonism' to help explain Shelley's development, but it is difficult to evaluate so complex and question-begging a concept as the starting-point for literary criticism.[21] More pertinent to a broader understanding is an underlying tendency of Shelley's imagination: his preference for huge prospects that strain to the bounds of the conceivable; his urge to imagine his scenes *sub specie eternitatis*, from a vantage-point beyond the humanly attainable, so that his sceptical conviction of the limits of knowledge seems temporarily lost to sight. In *Queen Mab* itself he appears determined to soar not just above the Aonian mount, as Milton had claimed, but to extend his imaginative gaze as 'far as the remotest line / That bounds imagination's flight'.[22] Indeed, there is a remarkable and violent discrepancy between the fanciful, magical, Spenserian machinery of *Queen Mab* and its resolutely materialist message. It is more than a little odd that Shelley chooses to proclaim his rationalist message from the vantage of Mab's Fairy Palace, an allegorical abode described as being outside of 'matter, space and time'.[23] For Mab's fairy realm Shelley posits, in fact, an idealist absolute world in which all is wisdom. There the human self, freed from the constraints of mundane life, happily

o'erbounds
Those obstacles, of which an earthly soul
Fears to attempt the conquest.[24]

Queen Mab presides over her world of intrinsic wisdom in plain defiance of Shelleyan materialism. It is nevertheless reached by an essentially Shelleyan movement of imagination. If you were to watch the Sun sinking over the western horizon and strain your gaze after its disappearing light, Shelley explains, at the instant when the material light vanishes altogether and you reach with your gaze into the invisible, 'Then has thy fancy soared above the earth' and brought you to the visionary, absolute world of the Fairy Queen.[25]

The title-page of *Queen Mab* bears as an epigraph a quotation from Archimedes which perhaps helps explain Shelley's inconsistent philosophy in the poem: 'Give me somewhere to stand, and I will move the world.'[26] Now Archimedes presumably knew that no one could actually conduct him to a leverage point from which to make his assertion good; yet he held none the less that his principle was sound. Likewise Shelley wants to project for the purposes of his poem an absolute realisation of man's potential for knowledge, even though he denies in cold fact the possibility of man's ever attaining to it. He did not at any time of his life believe that one could ascend the scale of intelligible reality from particular sense-impressions up to the Absolute.[27] Nevertheless, in his later work the imaginative leap into a transcendent world assumed a more and more important role after Shelley's readings in scepticism had effectually knocked the foundations away from under his youthful dogmatic materialism. And the philosophy of Plato recommended itself to him primarily as an intellectual weapon with which to defend that imaginative leap, since it suggested that one could as coherently understand the universe by working down from transcendent principles to particulars as by attempting to work from particulars up to general truths. To an Archimedes of the imagination, Platonism provided rational ways of articulating the irrepressible hopes of the imagination in its striving for unity and ultimate belonging.

To that recurring image of a cold, inanimate scene with a living figure trapped in torture, we must therefore add a contrary landscape: the landscape of complete realisation, complete spiritual transparency. Sometimes it may fuse with a natural landscape in the mind's eye, like the vista of unbroken sand and sea in *Julian and Maddalo*:[28]

> where we taste
> The pleasure of believing what we see
> Is boundless, as we wish our souls to be.[29]

This landscape does not oppress us with the sense of its otherness. It unleashes our sense of psychic infinity, mirroring our desires and hopes, becoming a landscape of the mind whether or not it is also outwardly visible. Often it appears as a landscape of dream or reverie, an imagined Paradise or island of the blest. In Shelley's imagery after *Queen Mab* it is associated especially, not with the sun disappearing over the hard edge of the horizon, but with the last star of morning fading into invisibility as morning light grows.[30]

It is not true – although it is how some influential critics have presented his development – that Shelley progressively abandoned his scepticism for an increasingly Platonic view of reality. What does appear to be the case is that in maturing as a poet he jettisoned that dogmatic rejection of the heart's instinctive desires which we noted in his remarks to Miss Hitchener. *Queen Mab* is at once a consolidation and a transcending of Shelley's cruder materialistic ideas. Thereby he opened his imagination to an exploration of the human, poetic significance of both philosophies, scepticism and idealism alike. The result is a body of poetry, sometimes immensely subtle, sometimes bafflingly elusive, sometimes unsurpassed in its lyrical power. But it shows Shelley as in essence a poet. He is always as passionately concerned with the human implications as with the logical truth of his philosophical speculations.

Our background sense of the modes of experience which underpin opposing philosophies will thus help make it clearer how, in Shelley's mature poetry, certain patterns of ideas become conditions of awareness; how Shelley's often subtle discriminations of thought are also poetic discriminations of feeling and tone. His imagination responds most powerfully at a deeper psychological level than that of ideas. He is stirred by the hidden desires, hopes and fears which give to philosophies their appeal and their danger. And it is just because of his poet's commitment to the whole range of experience that he refuses to accept either scepticism or Platonism as in itself absolutely or ultimately true. He is too great a poet – as he was too honest a man – to allow thought to deny life. He embodies in his poetry both the scepticism of Hume and the idealism of Plato, identifying life and thought.[31]

In Shelley's prose philosophy his indecision makes for an 'inchoate metaphysic', a crossbreed which he did not quite succeed in making the start of a new philosophical species. Since the closer studies of his thought by philosophically minded critics it has become harder to catch the poet in undeniably flat contradiction; but his essays and speculative fragments are generally disappointing in comparison with the scope and subtlety of his verse. I find it on the whole more profitable to read the prose in the light of the poems than the other way around. To develop further as a philosopher, he would have needed to evolve a dialectical method like that which Coleridge learned from the Germans (Kant, Fichte, Hegel) – and that Shelley did not do. *A Defence of Poetry* stands as a solitary prose masterpiece, distilled from much that Shelley had touched upon elsewhere.[32] But the *Defence* should perhaps really be regarded as a rhapsodic prose-hymn to Poetry, rather than as a strictly logical essay in aesthetics.

To say this is not to denigrate Shelley's capacity for clear-headed analysis or to deny the insights of the *Defence*. It is to say that the constructive elements in Shelley's thought were evidently able to unfold more freely in the context of imaginative creation than within the strict confines of philosophical reasoning. And by his own imaginative route Shelley arrived at many of the radical thoughts that Coleridge and the German Romantics reached with the dialectical aids of post-Kantian philosophy.[33] His is therefore a valuable independent testimony in the study of Romanticism – and in many ways his is the uniquely English voice, representing a confluence of Romanticism with specifically English literary traditions, though also touched by the influence of European writing in Spain, France and Italy.[34] When Shelley did come to read and translate Goethe, in the latter part of his life, he recognised a companion spirit; but the path Shelley had taken was his own.[35]

Shelley is remarkable among the English Romantics, as we intimated in our Introduction, in his concern for self-awareness. He is the poet of self-conscious imagination in Romantic England, as Coleridge was its theorist.[36] And this is the key to Shelley's ambivalent attitude toward the opposing world-conceptions. He must admit the foundation of both in human experience; but what makes him turn back from either of them is an intuition that they both deny the self-consciousness which for him is the centre of imaginative life. The abyss of the unknowable to which scepticism leads forms one threat to the spirit by leaving no real place for human consciousness, isolating it from any possible contact with the real. It is in vain that we seek for a sufficient intellectual explanation of why Shelley abandoned this view of the world as an ultimate creed. Much more revealing is a passage like that in another letter to Miss Hitchener, where he speaks of the personal unhappiness it has meant to him.[37] Likewise the Platonic speculations of the essay *On Life* often appear tenuous as argument; but they have greater relevance when read as an index of Shelley's poetic sensitivity to the human dimension of a direction of thought. Take for example his difficult response to the Platonic notion of a universal mind. He follows the unifying implications of idealism to the stage of admitting that:

> The difference is merely nominal between those two classes of thought, which are vulgarly distinguished by the names of ideas and of external objects. Pursuing the same thread of reasoning, the existence of distinct individual minds, similar to that which is employed in now questioning its own nature, is likewise found to be a delusion.[38]

The linguistic distinctions 'I', 'you', 'they', are merely marks denoting 'the different modifications of the one mind'. Thus Shelley arrives at the central idealist position. But having arrived there, he appears disturbed. It is not that he objects to anything in the argument. What makes him uneasy is a submerged sense that, far from having won through to a cosmic truth, he has been tricked into solipsism, unable now to know anything at all outside himself.

In the following paragraph he rejects the idea of solipsism with sudden and exaggerated indignation, betraying the sense of threat: 'Let it not be supposed that this doctrine conducts to the monstrous presumption that I, the person who now write and think, am that one mind.'[39] Yet he is now in a region where the usual contrast between the self and the world, between outward and inward reality, has disappeared. Accordingly, at the very moment of fulfilment he is thrown into uncertainty. He cannot articulate his thoughts, and resorts lamely to excuses: 'It is difficult to find terms adequate to express so subtle a conception as that to which the Intellectual Philosophy has conducted us.'[40] He has expanded his consciousness to embrace the universe, and the status of knowledge – especially linguistic knowledge –

becomes unclear since the very distinction of knower and known has itself become obsolete. But is this ultimate truth or a vacuous tissue of fine words? Shelley the philosopher fails to give an answer that convinces us of his authenticity. Shelley the man and poet has reached the expansive limit of consciousness: beyond it he senses either a mystical self-annihilation in an all-absorbing, all-dissolving dream of union with the transcendent One – or else the sudden loss of the sense of reality and a reversion to fear as the limitations of our being make themselves felt again. Both patterns of response are explored in imaginative depth in Shelley's major poems.

In order to preserve poetic self-consciousness, then, Shelley's imagination consistently refuses commitment to either ultimate vision. Shelley lacks the idealistic faith of those earlier Romantics who gave themselves up unreservedly to infinite hope; at the same time he refuses to yield to the pressure of scepticism and despair of human potentialities. He maintains the keenest awareness throughout his imaginative explorations of both ultimate possibilities. This is a delicate position which has not, on the whole, been understood by Shelley's critics. Perhaps swayed by a determination to defend the philosophical seriousness of his poetry, most have tried to resolve Shelley's fundamental allegiance in one direction or the other, to scepticism or Platonism. The results have seldom been satisfactory. We must certainly be grateful to the investigators of the sceptical tradition, such as C. E. Pulos;[41] their results did much to dissipate the Victorian myth of Shelley as the ineffectual enthusiast, the angel beating his great wings in the void like some misdirected albatross out of Baudelaire.[42] But it is equally one-sided to replace the angelic Platonist, for instance, with Harold Bloom's picture of Shelley as 'the most Humean poet in the language'. Bloom contends that it is 'Hume, not Berkeley or Plato, whose view of reality informs *Prometheus Unbound* and the poems that came after it'.[43] To which the most obvious reply is that it is not Hume but Shelley whose view of reality informs *Prometheus Unbound* – or better still, it is Shelley's imagination. However useful Hume may have been to Shelley as a guide through certain realms of life and thought, the poet's imaginative response to the dark vista of scepticism is wholly individual, with a poetic power scarcely paralleled in the cool-headed writings of Hume.

As a work that approaches more nearly a recognition of the internal complexity of Shelley's consciousness, we must mention the brilliant full-scale study by Earl Wasserman.[44] He acknowledges the fascination for Shelley in intellectually opposite views, the Platonic as well as the sceptical. He traces the opposition back to Shelley's early thought, and quotes a particularly blatant example of Shelley's desire to have things, intellectually, both ways. 'I have considered it', wrote the poet in a letter, 'in every possible light & reason tells me that death is the boundary of the life of man. Yet I feel, I believe the direct contrary.'[45] On the basis of this Wasserman draws a conclusion which shapes his whole approach to the poetry. He sees Shelley as a split being, torn asunder by an inability to relinquish either the promptings of his heart or the judgements of his reason. 'Shelley's two aspirations', Wasserman writes, 'are unrelated and have different roots. . . . They are not only unrelated doctrines but also devalue each other.'[46] In his book therefore Wasserman studies what are virtually two distinct Shelleys, the one a poet of beautiful idealisms', the other of 'sad reality'.

Given this understanding, we must inevitably conclude that any effort to incorporate both voices within a unified poem is doomed to failure. Certainly that seems to be the view of Richard Cronin, who follows Wasserman at least to the extent of working within a basic opposition between 'realism' and 'fantasy' as embodied in various of Shelley's poems.[47] For Cronin, *Adonais* for example constitutes an attempt to combine Shelley's head-wisdom and heart-wisdom in a single 'two-structure' elegy. But the conflict between them is such, he writes, 'that it becomes impossible, at any rate for me, to hold the two structures together. The poem falls apart in its attempt to hold together a trust in the truths of human instinct, and a concern to register a sceptical awareness that such trust may be credulity.'[48]

In the controversy between the sceptical, Platonic and 'mixed' interpretations of Shelley, one history – as Blake said of another, still older controversy – appears to have been adopted by all parties.[49] It is the assumption that to write successful poetry, Shelley must in the end decide to follow Hume or to follow Plato, affirming his scepticism or affirming his belief. What he plainly has no right to do is to keep us suspended in the uncertainties of the middle. There is, however, a different way of approaching the matter. It is one that does less justice to the principle of the excluded middle, but also one that recognises the integrity of Shelley's poetry, which is otherwise here in danger of being lost. For it is when we move away from the level of discursive thought, to explore states of perception and feeling, that we also begin to see a sense in which the warring philosophies may not be unrelated and mutually destructive, but on some level actually complementary. In poetry they become exploratory probes, trajectories in opposing directions, within a larger and more complex reality; for, seemingly unlike most philosophers, poets tend to believe that the world of our profuse experience can never be more than imperfectly rationalised or understood. Shelley strives to enrich the experience of his conscious self in both directions, using philosophical ideas as a tool in his poetic investigations. To pursue either philosophy to its metaphysical conclusion would mean the abolition of consciousness before a transcendent absolute, whether an unknowable void or all-obliterating infinity. Self-consciousness either shrinks into nothing, or faints outward into an illimitable totality where all distinction fails. To decide in his poetry for one or the other of these absolutes would mean the destruction of the poet as an imaginative being. Individual consciousness is sustained only in the dynamic tension between them, where the boundaries of the self and the world remain to be drawn and defended by the individual mind.

There is of course an element of paradox detectable here in Shelley's attitude to self-awareness. For in one way nothing could be easier than to evade the risk of losing our conscious grip on experience as Shelley fears. That is to say, we could suppress our total response as human beings to the world-perspectives and content ourselves with a controllable world of appearances. We could suppress that terror of the void which scepticism makes us feel when we stare into the abyss of how little we know, and accept the observations of our senses, declining to enquire more deeply into the reality behind them. We could suppress that uncomfortable threat of absorption we feel when we contemplate the ultimate unity of things, and retain only an abstract faith or metaphysics. We could repress our imaginative potential, in short, and draw back from entering into any view of the world with our full humanity.

There might still be much material for art and thought, as the traditions of realism and rationalism show.[50] But for Shelley this solution is clearly impossible. His intense imagination could not bear to be confined within the commonplace regions of feeling and thought; it would have meant imaginative death.[51] And it is just here that the unique significance of Shelley's poetry emerges most clearly. For what makes Shelley's poetry of such enormous importance is that he is simultaneously a poet of self-consciousness and a visionary Romantic determined to probe beneath the surface of things. His greatest poetry is always a triumph over the threatened defeat of awareness – a rescue of self-consciousness from the impact of powerful experiences which, by their terror or by their visionary intensity, would otherwise overwhelm it: the kind of experiences of which Shelley once wrote that they 'either extinguish or are extinguished by the sufferer'. As a poet of ultimates he wishes above all to expand the scope of human experience, so as to incorporate an awareness of the polar extremes in their naked purity while yet striving to retain conscious psychic equilibrium.

It is important, therefore, to extend the two-fold critical schema of Wasserman and Cronin into a genuinely triadic one, where extremes – however tentatively – balance and self-conscious imagination becomes feasible. For the real creative tension in Shelley's poetry is not the secondary intellectual one between his idealism and his scepticism, but that primary tension between the poet of Romantic ultimates and the poet of often ironic self-awareness. It is this tension which (as we shall see) shapes the form of Shelley's longer, dialectical poems. And it is this which generates many of the subtleties and ambiguities in Shelley's tone and style. Since it is essentially a dynamic tension, it is capable of temporary resolution and stasis in a wide variety of positions: nothing has been so determinedly ignored by Shelley's critics as his amazing versatility. Sometimes Shelley's self-consciousness produces poems with the peculiar paralysis of 'Lift not the painted veil', gesturing toward alternative paths yet seeming unable to take any actual step. Sometimes, in *Julian and Maddalo* for example, no resolution is hinted at all. But in his greatest poetry Shelley achieves a unique synthesis, a fusion of visionary power and exacting awareness that approaches the clairvoyant.[52] One of those greatest poems, for me, is *Adonais*.

It is true that in the last stanzas of *Adonais* the tensions lead, as Richard Cronin suggests, to a collapse. Yet it is a collapse that has been fundamentally misrepresented. In order to understand it, we must first of all be clear that the first concern of the poem is with the living, not with the fate of the dead. Whilst lamenting the death of a fellow poet, Shelley enquires how far the human self can come to terms with the fact of death – whether our inevitable dying renders meaningless the very continuance of life in the knowledge of that end, or whether we can hope for a pattern of final significance. Cronin is perfectly correct when he observes that Shelley will not shrug away his doubts and believe in his instinct for eternal life; nor will he dismiss his hopes and resign himself to the darker prospect of his vision. But then Shelley is not, as Cronin seems half to imagine, standing with a dagger at his breast, choosing between death and life.[53] Rather, he is testing his own inner strength to face contrary visions of hope and fear, pitting his imaginative power of equilibrium against finalities between which no one can rationally arbitrate.

Sometimes in Shelley's poetry the conscious self is broken in that Promethean attempt. But at other times it is transfigured. In the last stanzas of *Adonais* the collapse we experience is not one of apathy or indecision between two opposing absolutes, but a moment of transfiguration, the poetic expansion of consciousness which is Shelley's humanised version of apocalypse:

> The massy earth and sphered skies are riven!
> I am borne darkly, fearfully, afar.[54]

He undergoes a transformation of awareness which has little to do with argument and speculation, which come to an end here. The poet offers no 'conclusion' but, in full awareness of the possibilities, without the reassurance of a committed faith but likewise free from suicidal despair, in mingled fear and hope, dares to contemplate in imagination the world beyond the painted veil. In full consciousness he trusts himself to face the fact of death and not be destroyed as a human being. His disruptive experience leads to the very edge of the describable, and ends the poem. There can be no doubt, however, that it represents a victory of self-conscious imagination beyond any submission to the absolutes of faith or despair. In the extraordinary power of the vision, Shelley finds the strength to overcome the hesitancies that prevailed in the last rhyme of the 'Painted Veil' sonnet, to conclude with the startling affirmation of that final 'are'.

2 Literary Powers

SHELLEY AND THE POETRY OF
SELF-CONSCIOUSNESS

Literary critics might have been more successful in detecting the characteristic patterns of Shelleyan imagination, if they had not concentrated so exclusively on the vexed issue of his philosophical allegiances, sceptical or Platonic. For the result is that they have written for the most part with the kind of commitment to ideas which Shelley simply did not share. Admittedly, they are at least an advance upon those critics who could find words of praise only for Shelley's personal lyrics and love-poems, those highly anthologisable short pieces of verse with seemingly little intellectual content.[1] But from the standpoint of anyone who wants to reach an understanding of Shelley's poetry as a whole, it has long been apparent that both schools of criticism signally failed to locate the poetic core of his work.

The history of criticism compels us, even upon cursory examination, to grant that the reading mind is susceptible to strange fits of short-sightedness; it proves quite unpredictably difficult to recognise a quality in an author's work if one starts with the presumption that it is not there. Yet few poets have suffered insensitive reading on the scale of Shelley, who is even now in part 'a voice not understood'. Only headlong prejudice can account for it. Nor is it any excuse to explain that a specialised form of self-conscious, witty ('Metaphysical') verse was in vogue when the foundations of modern criticism were being laid. It will not do to say that Shelley suffered because he was alien to the tastes of a T. S. Eliot or an F. R. Leavis and their seventeenth-century predilections; only a perverse determination to reject Shelley made him seem so. Otherwise it could have been noticed that, as sensitive critics like Richard Cronin are nowadays beginning to discover, some of Shelley's

26

lyrics are indeed self-consciously 'witty . . . and witty in a distinctly seventeenth-century manner'.[2] A poem like *With a Guitar, to Jane*, Cronin argues, has to be read in the artful, courtly tradition of Herrick and Turberville. And when read thus it soon ceases to resemble a supposed 'spontaneous overflow' of subjective emotion. Examples might be culled, too, from Shelley's longer works: I select one from *Prometheus Unbound*.

For purposes of comparison, let us consider first Donne's seventh Holy Sonnet, the one which begins:

> At the round earths imagin'd corners, blow
> Your trumpets, Angells, and arise, arise
> From death, you numberlesse infinities
> Of soules, and to your scattred bodies go.

The poet is gripped by the power of a traditional image, the Day of Judgement, and expresses his response in urgent, declamatory verse. And yet we feel the presence of contradictions not far beneath the surface. Rather as in the case of 'Lift not the painted veil', for instance, we find it a little disconcerting that, possessed by the vision of the Last Things, Donne is still so self-collected that he can shape his experience into the highly wrought form of a sonnet. And then the admission in the first line that the traditional 'four corners' of the earth are now known to be imaginary, drastically qualifies our faith in the tradition even while we are swept on by the force of the rhetoric – to find ourselves immediately tackling the conceptual problem of 'numberlesse infinities'. Donne's brilliant achievement in this kind of poetry has been deservedly praised. By including human doubts and reservations at the same time as celebrating the power of an imaginative vision to transport and stir us, he evades the risk of alienating his readers by a claim to justify the ways of God with an absolute outlook on the truth, as an epic treatment of religious themes like Milton's could suggest. Donne's seventh Holy Sonnet is a poetic reconciliation of human and divine. And swiftly moving, passionate verse is fused with an intense power of self-awareness, yet without compromising the genuineness of Donne's imaginative response. Imaginative energy and self-conscious precision co-exist here without contradiction. The point is precisely not, as R. G. Cox would have it, that Donne 'can stop to remember that the round world's corners are "imagin'd" '; the point is that he can remember without stopping.[3]

The passage from *Prometheus Unbound* which I have in mind is the magnificent, and highly original, finale of Act III. It too images something like a Last Day, though humanised still more than Donne's in accord with Shelley's anthropocentric view of the world. Here also we find rhetorical energy: a finely controlled crescendo of enormous power continuing up to the last syllable, yet – and here lies the originality – not leading to a fortissimo statement. The thrust of the verse keeps our expectation mounting higher and higher as though leading up to a symphonic statement of the theme, which is then lost in a 'sublimer world' beyond our apprehension. The silence into which the crescendo disappears gives us a strong experience of that 'intense inane', another of Shelley's re-echoing negations. There is unleashed a real sense of infinity – where any final assertion would only have defined limitations. The passage is actually a vision of boundless potential, though the imaginative power is now attributed not to the traditional God, but to man in a humanly recreated universe:

> The loathsome mask has fallen, the man remains
> Sceptreless, free, uncircumscribed, but man
> Equal, unclassed, tribeless, and nationless,
> Exempt from awe, worship, degree, the king
> Over himself; just, gentle, wise: but man
> Passionless? – no, yet free from guilt or pain,
> Which were, for his will made or suffered them,
> Nor yet exempt, though ruling them like slaves,
> From chance, and death, and mutability,
> The clogs of that which else might oversoar
> The loftiest star of unascended heaven,
> Pinnacled dim in the intense inane.[4]

On a first reading, we are likely to be caught up in the rapid oratory which sweeps us upward and on. The exultantly repeated 'man', the parallelisms ('but man' – 'but man'; 'no, yet' – 'Nor yet') impel us enthusiastically forward. Yet as we proceed we find that the poetry also compels our vigilance. The parallelism 'no, yet' – 'Nor yet' turns out to be misleading, we notice, since the lines actually tell us that 'chance, and death, and mutability' *do* persist into the millennium. And even at the very end the heaven of superhuman achievement is, pointedly, 'unascended', exactly as Donne's four corners of the earth are only 'imagin'd'. Just like Donne, Shelley asks of us that we are possessed by the power of an imaginative vision, and at the same time severely conscious of the inherent limitations of man's being. The paradox is greater in Shelley's case, in that the source of self-awareness is no longer the discrepancy between human and divine, but in opposing forces within man's own imagination: his aspiration toward absolute existence and the necessary contingencies of his finite nature, his acknowledgment of chance and change. Addressing us as imaginative beings, Shelley asks us to be swept off our feet by the heavenward surge of his poetry, and yet to retain our self-awareness, all in one complex mental act. In such verse he equals his own praise of Plato for 'the rare union of close and subtle logic, with the Pythian enthusiasm of poetry, melted by the splendour and harmony of his periods into one irresistible stream of musical impressions, which hurry the persuasions onward, as in a breathless career'. I have earlier used the word 'clairvoyant' to express something of the quality of that union in Shelley. In his praise of Plato Shelley goes considerably further: 'His language', he says, 'is that of an immortal spirit, rather than a man.'[5]

Despite the similarity of technique, there is no evidence that Shelley had read Donne – even though Godwin did include him on a list of recommended poets in 1812.[6] After all, the poetry of self-awareness is abundantly represented in the annals of English literature, and has perhaps modelled the very way we speak the language. The scintillations of Metaphysical wit are but one kind among many that may have contributed to nurture Shelley's sense of style, displayed in his often deceptively fluent verse. He read and admired Jonson's comedies and masques, which apply their great learning and metaphysical implications within the framework of courtly celebration.[7] We should also not neglect the importance for Shelley of Milton's shorter, 'mannerist' poems, alongside his well-known Romantic desire to rewrite the national epic *Paradise Lost*. And after meeting Lord Byron, Shelley developed his own version of that urbane, self-distancing style which Byron had derived from the eighteenth century, permitting another sort of irony – though Shelley acclimatised it to his native gentleness, refusing Byron's bitter violence.

It is another sign of Shelley's psychic integrity and the absence of trauma that he can enter sociably into so many and such different styles without losing his identity. Few poets could stake a better claim to all-round humanity on the range of their printed poetry than Shelley. He can turn from the vivid political satire of *Swellfoot the Tyrant* (with its population of pigs and chorus of parliamentary 'Boars'), or the anti-Wordsworthian literary humour of *Peter Bell the Third* (combining deep insight with devastating fun at the expense of the older poet turned pious reactionary), to the political incisiveness of *The Mask of Anarchy*, the sexual ecstasies of *Epipsychidion*, the Gothic melodrama of *The Cenci* or the Spenserian fantasies of *The Witch of Atlas*. He can switch from rolling blank verse to crystalline *terza rima*, from the sublime allegories of *Prometheus Unbound* to the most intimate, fond remembrances of days spent with a Mary, Claire or Jane; from passionate celebration of life to the most unflinching meditation on death. That Shelley came to be condemned as stereotyped, humourless, narrow, sexless and stupid by otherwise intelligent critics only a generation or so ago deserves to be ranked among those 'great mysteries' on which the popular mind seems nowadays so intent.

Shelley's humour, above all, has received scant recognition even in fairly recent times. Clearly an angel-Platonist like Shelley could never have so allowed his Romantic yearning to flag that he became susceptible to laughter! Where the evidence was awkward, even a little silent surgery could legitimately be employed to preserve the image. Yet Shelley's friends, like Shelley's poetry, testify to a lightness and verve and fast-moving humour. Specifically, his humour is of the genteel English, self-conscious type which delights in understatement and comic reserve. He is a master of the use of 'somewhat'.[8] His brilliant parody of Wordsworth's *Peter Bell* also reveals that he could judge with finesse the exact quantity of personal malice with which to flavour a general point: Nature responds to Wordsworthian advances, when Peter with eunuch-chastity lifts her skirts, with an arch smile – 'And kissed him with a sister's kiss'.[9]

Shelley's self-consciousness here is partly the satirist's art of always staying fractionally outside his subject, a wry *spectator ab extra*. But he also knew the limits of detachment, and sketched a fragment of a *Satire on Satire*. (The butt this time was Southey.) He has his broader ironies, too, beyond the purely comic, and frequently displays his sense of unacknowledged meanings and dimensions hidden from the unreflecting multitude, so that life sometimes seems to him a serio-comic triumphal procession to the graveyard. Even in his poetry of political reform, the self-conscious ironies persist so that one is made to feel the interposition of a mask or persona – the conscious choice of a 'popular' style, the assumption of the not-quite-whole-hearted voice of a determined agitator – though we have no reason to doubt the personal authenticity of Shelley's emotion.[10] It is only that it co-exists with other elements in his sensibility. Even on campaign, Shelley's consciousness retains its core of separateness.

Shelley's self-detachment is a virtue which allows us to distinguish sharply at this juncture between the poetry of self-consciousness and another literary mode which could crudely be termed the poetry of self. There is nothing in Shelley of the tendency, satirised in *Peter Bell the Third*, toward the 'egotistical sublime'.[11] What we mean by 'self-consciousness', after all, is precisely not solipsistic self-absorption like Peter Bell's, but the ability to see one's own self as if from outside, and so to that degree enter into the awareness of others. Romantic poetry is not so devoid of instances of this kind of writing as was once held, and one example which displays it in abundance is Shelley's verse *Letter to Maria Gisborne* (1820).[12]

The *Letter* has been used occasionally by critics to prove that Shelley did have a sense of humour; but really it shows much more than that. Unlike most so-called 'verse-letters', it conveys at once a real impression of shared experience. It does not selfishly detail Shelley's emotional response to Maria's absence, but delicately expresses the shared impressions and reminiscences which unite them, entering into them in loving detail. She will remember well, for a start, the untidy room where Shelley now writes his *Letter*, 'catalogised' in rueful verse at the beginning with all its fantastic bits of broken equipment and strange devices which no outsider to their intimate circle would know how to use. Maria's son Henry Reveley can generously be included, however, since he will recognise as well as she the portrait Shelley is to provide of himself amid all this familiar clutter. It is actually Henry's workshop in which Shelley is sitting, and where they planned their ambitious amateur engineering projects.

In his self-description Shelley is constantly aware of what he shares with Maria and Henry, relying on them to understand much that would seem odd or unintelligible if told to just anyone. Shelley can step outside and see that he would look, perhaps, like some weird figure from Spenser or an old romance:

> Whoever should behold me now, I wist,
> Would think I were a mighty mechanist,
> Bent with sublime Archimedean art
> To breathe a soul into the iron heart
> Of some machine portentous, or strange gin,
> Which by the force of figured spells might win
> Its way over the sea, and sport therein.

But he knows that Maria and her son will comprehend what an outsider might call his eccentricities. The whole charm of this charming poem springs from Shelley's simultaneous perception of himself from his own and Maria's point of view, and his awareness of the awkwardness and obduracy of the public language he must use to communicate with her and her son in the *Letter*.

Hence when the pains of putting the heaped-up paraphernalia into learned rhyme eventually prove too much, the point is that it does not matter, since he can say 'Henry will know / The thing I mean and laugh at me'. With his own kind of playful wit Shelley draws attention to the limits of public language, and takes delight in those limits as confirming the primacy of intimate experience. Especially delightful, because especially tortuous, is his attempt to render:

> a most inexplicable thing,
> With lead in the middle – I'm conjecturing
> How to make Henry understand.

He cannot descend on the one hand to name its prosaic name. An alternative would be to glorify it by an elaborate passage of explication – which would again be out of proportion, 'Too vast a matter for so weak a rhyme'. There is nothing for it then but mystification: he will leave it (in a suitably grand poetic phrase) a 'secret in the pregnant womb of time'.

In London, exactly as in Italy, the poem draws its subject-matter purely from shared realities – 'all / You and I know in London', as he says. Nothing else matters for the present, for this poem. The simultaneous perception of intimacy and the public setting continues in the famous pen-portraits Shelley gives of Coleridge, Godwin, Hunt, Peacock, etc. And across hundreds of miles Shelley can still refer to '*our* unhappy politics', setting aside any complaint at his exile in the pleasure of his closeness to Maria. The *Letter* even takes delight in the moon and stars for no other reason than that these same celestial lights shine down on both of them, widely separated as they are in their earthly surroundings, as if uniting them in the heavens.

The *Letter* is that rare thing: neither a poem of private symbolism nor of public persuasion, but of convincing personal relationship. It proves definitively, if proof is needed, that Shelley was not an eternal adolescent obsessed with his own private feelings, but a man who could enter into relationship with delicacy and equipoise, and with a capacity for sharing experience that was built on a mature self-assurance.

POETRY, PITY AND THE NOVEL

Despite Shelley's detachment, his many-sidedness and inner unifying strength, however, we fail to see his poetry in proper perspective unless we acknowledge the influence of two literary movements – both of them, in their way, extremes. As such they were necessarily of great and absorbing interest to a poet like Shelley who combined self-conscious imagination with an openness to ultimates of thought and emotion. These two movements are associated with the labels 'Sensibility' and 'Gothic', the literature of sentiment and the literature of fear.

The ruling imagery and tone of the literature of Sensibility is emotional and indulgent, and stands in marked contrast to the 'wit' which has characterised much of English writing in its centre channels. Equally with the horror-literature of Gothic, it examines certain limited aspects of human nature under a powerful magnifying lens. In every other respect Sensibility stands in total contrast to the fascinating Gothic mystery of fear; but both extremes are alike in their inherent tendency to obsess, to monopolise the imagination. Fear and sensibility are effective imaginative forces to the extent that they disintegrate the conscious, many-faceted self and compel it into a single form of life, charged with a single unifying energy.

In most respects Romanticism was a historical reaction against the ideals of the writers of Sensibility; Wordsworth's abusive analysis of Sensibility diction in the Preface to *Lyrical Ballads* is well known. But there were also strong elements of continuity – particularly in the work of Coleridge and Blake as well as Shelley. Indeed, it seems possible that after the manic stage of Romantic optimism had passed and its great mythical structures were crumbling in the disaster-wake of events in France, a number of the features of Sensibility were seen in a new light and took on a renewed validity. Shelley, who belongs to the first chastened generation of post-Revolutionary Romantics, was a life-long admirer of the Sensibility poets. His youthful *A Summer Evening Churchyard* is an imitation of Gray, echoing his favourite crepuscular mood of twilight solemnity, and the influence of Gray reaches far into Shelley's mature poems. Some of Shelley's most striking formulations turn out to be direct descendants from the literary fathers of Sensibility. We are told in a remarkable passage from *Adonais* for example, that:

> the one Spirit's plastic stress
> Sweeps through the dull dense world, compelling there,
> All new successions to the forms they wear;
> Torturing th' unwilling dross that checks its flight
> To its own likeness, as each mass may bear.[13]

The image is memorably Shelleyan, but looks back ultimately to Akenside's *The Pleasures of Imagination* and its representation of the work of the Creator. Though, as God, he was 'self-collected from eternal time', and all-sufficient:

Yet by immense benignity inclin'd
To spread around him that primeval joy
Which fill'd himself, he rais'd his plastic arm,
And sounded through the hollow depth of space
The strong, creative mandate.[14]

An advance in the use of the image was next made by Coleridge
in his sonnet dedicated to another Sensibility poet, the Revd
William Lisle Bowles. His poetry is described as:

Bidding a strange mysterious PLEASURE brood
Over the wavy and tumultuous mind,
As the great SPIRIT erst with plastic sweep
Mov'd on the darkness of the unform'd deep.[15]

In the passage from *Adonais*, Shelley has enriched the image
still further, restoring Coleridge's psychological simile to its
original cosmic context. Like Coleridge he may well have
connected 'plastic' energy with contemporary scientific
speculations: Richard Sulivan's *View of Nature* (1794) had
postulated 'an universal plastic power, whereby every body in
nature receives its peculiar and specific form'.[16] This would
certainly suit the twist given to the image in *Adonais*, and
demonstrates Shelley's astonishing power of combining literary,
philosophical and scientific ideas in a single poetic effect. In
further token of Shelley's reading in the poetry of Sensibility, let
us also note that in the next few lines of *Adonais* it is Chatterton
who heads the list of poets who rise from their thrones 'Far in the
Unapparent' – the poet who, according to his legend, had lived
out the fate of the characteristic hero of Sensibility, the doomed
genius.[17]

The full spiritual flowering of Sensibility, however, was not to
be confined within the domain of poetry. Some of its most
typical, or extremest, manifestations are to be found in the
medium of the 'sentimental' novel. Nowadays we tend to look
back to the novel of the eighteenth century for the origins of
'realism', having in mind its Victorian successors. But the
imaginative scope of the novel throughout the eighteenth
century was constantly expanding, and lines of evolution
separated off from the main trunk of literature in interesting

offshoots, one of which was the novel of Sensibility – in its ultimate expression, the popular 'sentimental' novel. At Eton and as a student at Oxford, Shelley was an avid reader of such voguish fiction, of which only a fraction survives in print today. To an extent unusual in a great lyric poet, therefore, we should probably reckon that his literary sensitivity was shaped by developments taking place outside poetry. We shall soon see that Gothic writing too was not primarily a poetic form, but infiltrated Shelley's mind through the famous blue-backed novels in the 'Minerva' series of popular Gothic horrors.[18] The writing of novels was among Shelley's first literary ambitions while still at school, indulged for the time by parents and printers. A little later, the disciple of Godwin was still planning to write in novel form: his characters, however, would now be expected to demonstrate the strict cause-and-effect psychology in which for a time he seems to have believed![19] Some of Shelley's prose romances will interest us shortly. Often enough, behind the broad, balanced themes of the later poet we glimpse the younger, more susceptible figure of Shelley the novelist.

The most striking quality of the literature of Sensibility, in contrast to the Augustan writing of the earlier eighteenth century, is the shift away from objectivity – above all, the extent of that shift. The Augustans would have been appalled at the breakdown of their public, rational universe in the half-century that followed the death of Pope; those born after their time, like Dr Johnson, were genuinely dismayed. In Sensibility writing by the end of the eighteenth century, subjective feeling has expanded to cover the whole canvas of the reader's attention. A narrow range of highly idealised emotions are cultivated – with a degree of ostentation that would have been profoundly shocking to the Augustans not so long before. The chief difference is that man is treated by Sensibility writers as a creature endowed by his nature with innate stores of benevolence, tenderness and pity. Their great creation, the 'man of feeling', is a kind of virtuoso in the art of experiencing his emotions, appropriately to each circumstance and with unprecedented intensity; he has the exact feeling for every occasion. Notoriously, he will often deliver himself in mid-emotion of a discourse on the infinite depths of human pathos; and when discourse comes to an end, spontaneous tears will bathe his cheeks to convey what words would only profane. Even the few acknowleged masterpieces of the sentimental school of novel-writing are today scarcely readable.

Yet in historical perspective we can still understand how thrilling Sensibility must have been. We can still sense the excitement of discovering the basic rightness of man's primary human emotions, long belittled by rationalism and rendered shameful by orthodox religion. The 'luxury of grief' and 'the sadly pleasing tear' may sound affected now: but somewhere beyond the cult-phrases we hear the voice of men who knew again the satisfaction of emotional release without the trauma of shame or the duty of suppression which Enlightenment cultural forces had long imposed. We can understand how it seemed that the Sentimentalists had sunk deep shafts of light into a knowledge of man's nature. They had opened up an infinitely rich mine of feelings to detailed contemplation. It is only that, in retrospect, we are liable to be more aware of their shortcomings than of the breakthrough which seemed so exciting to their contemporaries. We notice with disappointment that their characters are permitted to have feelings only within carefully controlled limits, and their self-expression is cautiously stylised. Man as the Sensibility novelists present him is undoubtedly a vividly experiencing, but he is also a drastically simplified being. He samples his emotions – so to speak – neat; and that analytic purity is only achieved at a certain cost, both inside and outside the strictly literary context.[20]

The cost within the literary framework may be exemplified by glancing at the English masterpiece of high sentimentality: Henry Mackenzie's *The Man of Feeling* (1771). It depicts Harley (who answers admirably to the description of the title) in numerous affecting situations, devised by the author to illustrate the propriety and moral exactitude of his feelings. We follow him in true love and in a brothel, among the nobility, among maniacs, in the company of a dear old friend, and with a testy old misanthrope, in the jostling *beau monde*, on his solitary death-bed; tearfully happy, tearfully sad: pleasingly pained with the exquisiteness of his sensations. The episodes are strung loosely together. This is inevitable because, of course, anything resembling a plot would detract from the emotional sympathies on which the reader is expected to lavish his whole attention. Any rival concern with the mechanism of events or with shifting personal relationships would necessarily deflect interest away from those delicate emotional resonances and subtle harmonic vibrations of the soul we are intended to experience. And indeed Mackenzie casts his spell – we do experience them. But the price is not merely a break with the realist tradition in the novel – it is virtually a divorce from narrative altogether. Mackenzie, moreover, is embarrassed by the implications of his art, as well as being troubled by eighteenth-century worries about verisimilitude. He therefore invents a framing fiction. The book is supposed to have been found, according to this frame narration, in a damaged state. The manuscript was ravaged by a hunting-and-shooting curate, who carried it about for use as wadding. Only fragmentary, disparate chapters are extant. In this way Mackenzie makes certain excuses for the loss of narrative possibility. In reality, that loss must be accepted as an inherent quality of sentimental writing, which is always concerned with essentially static feelings that must be isolated from change in order that they may be deepened through contemplation. The case is similar in some respects to opera, where action must end for the aria to be sung; and there, however unrealistic the demand, the situation must be suspended, must not move forward. Opera, however, is obviously not dependent on narrative in the same way that a novel inevitably is.

The technical problems of writing a novel founded on Sensibility are therefore seen to be considerable. In *The Man of Feeling* the objective, public world of action and purposive change hardly exists at all. It would interfere with the meditative purity of Harley's emotions. The world rises over the aesthetic horizon just sufficiently to touch off Harley's emotional states, then sinks once more out of view. For almost the entire duration of the novel, an intense subjectivity fills the entire screen of awareness.

Plot under these conditions, notes Sterne's 'sentimental traveller', named Yorick, collapses into 'a parcel of nonsensical contingencies'. But what to the pious adherent of Sensibility constituted a technical embarrassment, was to Sterne – the heretically ironic and slightly bawdy author of *Tristram Shandy* (1759–67) and *A Sentimental Journey* (1768) – the opportunity for a brilliant *avant-garde* liberation of narrative style. The need in Sensibility fiction for something like a justifying frame narration suggested to him the possibility of creating worlds within worlds, of inventions within inventions, nonsense within nonsense that somehow turns out in the end to be rather good sense. The Realists among novel writers had claimed that they could reproduce the true order of things in space and time; Sterne exploded that claim and portrayed his characters living largely in extravagant private worlds. Yet he also showed them liable to be rudely interrupted from time to time by inescapable 'contingencies' from outside. Conversely, the Sentimentalists had tried to detach emotion from character and situation; Sterne humorously demonstrated that this was an unattainable ideal.[21]

All this was beyond the pale to the true sentimental devotee. Even by noticing the nonsensical disjunction of the plot, Sterne has already stepped out of the charmed circle of pure Sensibility. When he plays feeling ironically against the random frustrations of circumstances, he reveals the limits of his faith in sentimental truth. He knew that sensibility in man was ultimately self-obsessed and liable to illusion. Yet he sometimes defends illusion – on initially surprising grounds. He confesses candidly:

> When my way is too rough for my feet, or too steep for my strength, I get off it, to some smooth velvet path which fancy has scattered over with rose-buds of delights; and having taken a few turns in it, come back strengthened and refreshed – When evils press sore upon me, and there is no retreat from them in this world, then I take a new course – I leave it.[22]

Thus we see that Sterne no more tries to meet the world on its own terms than does Mackenzie. Sentimental time, for example, in Sterne is never a straightforward, practical linear sequence: it darts forward and back, breaks off in uncompleted chapters, repeats itself, or sometimes fails to keep up with events altogether. Sentimental syntax can rarely hold on to its first conception and reach the period without the misadventure of a course-changing hyphen. Everything conspires to abolish our sense of a coherent world which could be the stage of constructive action. Or at least, such a world is banished to the ironic periphery for occasional reference, in order to make space for the controlled cultivation of rarified Sensibility emotion. Sterne's irony is a more convincing, effective frame of defence than Mackenzie's narrative excuses, but the 'sentiment' is there at the heart of both.

It is clear that Shelley was deeply affected by his reading of the poetry and in particular the novels of the Sensibility school. He went, too, to the European exponents of Sensibility – above all, Rousseau. He wrote glowingly to his friend Peacock of 'the divine beauty of Rousseau's imagination, as it exhibits itself in Julie'.[23] He was referring to Rousseau's *Julie, ou la Nouvelle Héloïse* (1761), which he also described to Hogg, his old student friend from Oxford, as 'the production of a mighty Genius. . . . Rousseau is indeed in my mind the greatest man the world has yet produced since Milton.'[24] And he had read Goethe's early novel of Sensibility, *The Sorrows of Young Werther* (1774), whose fame spread sensationally through Europe and which was available in two English translations before the turn of the century. Peacock in his satirical novel *Nightmare Abbey* depicts Shelley, who appears there in the character of Scythrop, in a mournful Sensibility pose, seated:

> on a fallen fragment of mossy stone, with his back resting against the ruined wall, – a thick canopy of ivy, with an owl in it, over his head, – and the Sorrows of Werter in his hand.[25]

Shelley probably also knew *Werther*'s English imitators, such as Croft's *Love and Madness* and Lloyd's *Edmund Oliver*, the latter painting distorted portraits of leading figures like Coleridge and Mary Wollstonecraft under a fictional disguise.[26] Rousseau and Goethe hover over Shelley's poetic development, the one seeming to embody the positive virtues of Sensibility writing and its approach to life, the other touching the equally important theme of the destructive power of intense imagination and feeling.

The impact of Sensibility literature can be recognised pervasively in Shelley: in the study of consciously purified emotion; in the predominance of tenderness and pity in the spectrum of inner states; in the tendency to idealise or generalise feelings rather than relate them to character and situation – all these are legacies from the tradition of Sensibility. He himself described what he regarded as his especial talent:

> In this have I long believed that my power consists: in sympathy & that part of imagination which relates to sentiment & contemplation. – I am formed, – if for any thing

not in common with the herd of mankind – to apprehend
minute & remote distinctions of feeling whether relative to
external nature, or the living beings which surround us, & to
communicate the conceptions which result from considering
either the moral or the material universe as a whole.[27]

All these Sensibility features, moreover, persist into his later
poems. The 'sentimental' style of *Epipsychidion* testifies to the
enduring hold the intellectual emotionalism of the school of
Sensibility had on the poet. Remembering Sterne's defence of
visionary escapism, it is interesting to note a similar theory in the
mature Shelley. The Youth in his fragment *Charles the First*,
being 'green in this gray world' (another Goethe allusion), is
deluded in his naïve optimism; but his thoughts are:

> like the bright procession
> Of skiey visions in a solemn dream
> From which men wake as from a Paradise,
> And draw new strength to tread the thorns of life.[28]

A 'visionary rhyme' like *The Witch of Atlas* shows that Shelley,
even late in his (admittedly brief) life, could turn from dark
realities to a play of consoling fancy. In his moral thought,
Shelley insists strongly on the practical efficacy of the
philanthropy of the 'man of feeling'. In his epic *Laon and Cythna*
(also called *The Revolt of Islam*) he strove to render vice, he tells
us, 'not the object of punishment and hatred, but kindness and
pity'.[29]

The imaginative techniques of Sensibility provided Shelley
with an aesthetic medium equivalent to his explorations in
intellectual idealism. For the discovery which lay behind
Sensibility writing may in a general way be said to be this: the
disparity between objective reality and potentially infinite
human response. Sterne, Mackenzie and the Sensibility poets all
devised methods of liberating the imagination from the
limitations of realism and rationalism, enabling it to be devoted
to that potential infinity of feeling. Emotion predominates over
objects, mood triumphs over form. Objective reality dwindles
almost to nothing, just as it does in the eye of the idealist
philosopher. From the inner perspective of infinitude,
materialism looks absurd. So for instance feels Sterne, at a

particularly moving moment in his *Sentimental Journey*, as he wipes away the tears of the beautiful Maria in a handkerchief wet with his own:

> and as I did it, I felt such undescribable emotions within me, as I am sure could not be accounted for from any combinations of matter and motion.
>
> I am positive I have a soul; nor can all the books with which materialists have pestered the world ever convince me to the contrary.[30]

The boundless nature of human desires and emotions was also for Shelley the chief evidence to his imagination of the validity of a truth beyond the 'painted veil'. It may have been with the concepts of Platonism that he tried to render that truth thinkable; it was with the style and aesthetic of Sensibility that he attempted to render it imaginable.

Admiration for the ideals of Sensibility, however, had always to contend within Shelley against his critical 'cold reasoning'. For despite the high moral cast of its preferred emotions – tenderness, pity, love – there was much that was palpably wrong with Sensibility whether as a way of life or art. An absorbed fascination with one's own feelings of benevolence, for example, does not necessarily conduce to good deeds. In fact, such meditation was time-consuming to the degree that social interaction would become virtually impossible if it were extended to the whole of life. Socially useful action had to suit itself to the 'contingent' world and could not always wait for the ripening of the 'sentimental' soul. Ann Radcliffe finds it necessary to have one of her characters warned against two aberrations: firstly, against that pride in one's own refinement 'which has been fatal to the peace of so many persons'; and secondly, against an extreme susceptibility to sentiment 'which excludes that to the calls of any practical virtue' – 'How despicable is that humanity, which can be contented to pity, where it might assuage'![31] Here we meet the practical consequences of that total concern with subjectivity we analysed earlier in art. Action becomes increasingly problematic, paralysed by inner deliberations.

An important link in the chain of reflections eventually directed by Shelley against the sufficiency of sentiment is the writing of Mary Wollstonecraft, the feminist 'hyena' and author of the *Vindication of the Rights of Woman* (1792). She also wrote two novels of a semi-autobiographical type which Shelley certainly read: *Mary* (1788) and *The Wrongs of Woman, or Maria* (posthumously published, 1798).[32] She wrote in them above all of the shortcomings of Rousseau's educational ideas – from personal experience. She thus forms our chief witness for the cost of Sensibility outside the literary framework. For if Sensibility provided little motivation for direct activity in practical terms, it also provided little defence in a rough world for a young woman breaking with convention and trying to make her own way. Page upon page of the *Vindication* turns into an attack on Rousseau and his system of morals: 'sensibility, of which self is the centre'.[33] Her novels too are an exploration of the limitations of the philosophy of sentimentality. No one can say that they are good novels; but they are the more moving as documents in that the suffering behind them is real. She finally succumbed to the pattern of the heroine in many a sentimental novel, and attempted – unsuccessfully – to take her own life. For Shelley, she was not only the mother of his second wife Mary, but already a legend. She evolved in his imagination into the romance-figure of Cythna in his 'Islamic' epic, and profoundly affected his thought.

Another influence was Southey, with whom Shelley had long conversations in Keswick in the winter of 1811–12. Southey had undergone a marked change of opinions in the mid-1790s, which he no doubt described to Shelley, as he had to William Taylor:

> Once, indeed, I had a mimosa-sensibility, but it has long been rooted out: five years ago I counteracted Rousseau by dieting upon Godwin and Epictetus . . . a book like 'Werter' gives me now unmingled pain.[34]

With personal case histories like these close at hand, Shelley began to evolve his own dialectical study of the bounds of 'sentimental' imagination. He also learnt considerably from the *avant-garde* ironic solution to literary sentimentalism represented by Sterne. In *Julian and Maddalo*, where a character of youthful idealism and refined feeling rides with a more worldly, pessimistic Count Maddalo, the young man was originally to be called Yorick – according to Shelley's draft –

after Sterne's sentimental traveller.[35] And the technique of a poem such as *The Witch of Atlas*, where an unstated dark realism lies below the surface of fantasy, might be seen as an extension of certain aspects of Sterne. In taking this direction from Sterne's work, Shelley may be seen to resemble the Romantic Ironists of Germany.

Shelley's dialectical poetry, however, evolves a pattern essentially its own. The pattern first begins to emerge clearly in *Alastor*, Shelley's earliest mature long poem, and goes on developing until the time of *The Triumph of Life*, his last uncompleted masterpiece. By means of it, at the same time as defining the dangers of Sensibility, he succeeded in rescuing many of its features and integrating them into a larger, more comprehensively human vision – his own particular brand of Romanticism.

Shelley remained fascinated by the possibilities of literary extremism, even while knowing that, if it is not to prove destructive, abstract emotion must be particularised and brought within the sphere of the conscious self. For here indeed lies the root problem of Sensibility: it failed to provide a psychological centre of gravity, or inner point of balance. Its insights remained brilliantly peripheral, and failed to root themselves in human nature as a whole. Rather than establishing equilibrium, intense Sensibility emotions lead toward instability and the dissolution of consciousness. Consider a passage like the following one from Mary Wollstonecraft's *The Wrongs of Woman*:

I rose, and shook myself; opened the window, and methought the air never smelled so sweet. The face of heaven grew fairer as I viewed it, and the clouds seemed to flit away obedient to my wishes, to give my soul room to expand. I was all soul, and (wild as it may appear) felt as if I could have dissolved in the soft balmy gale that kissed my cheek, or have glided below the horizon on the glowing, descending beams. A seraphic satisfaction animated, without agitating my spirits; and my imagination collected, in visions sublimely terrible, or soothingly beautiful, an immense variety of the endless images, which nature affords, and fancy combines, of the grand and fair. The lustre of these bright picturesque sketches faded with the setting sun.[36]

There is a deep sense of liberation – which suits the context of the plot; but this expresses itself in the progressive abolition of objectivity, with disturbing undertones. The face of heaven grows in subjective brightness, becoming an embodiment of the character's volition. Her soul expands into it, abolishing any subjective–objective distinctness. The result is an internal as well as external feeling of 'dissolution', accompanied by a 'seraphic' but suspiciously uncritical sense of complete satisfaction. The loss of objectivity also leads to ambiguity in the delirious play of images released by the experience, which are grandiose but uncertainly 'terrible' and 'soothing', the speaker does not seem overly concerned which. With the setting of the sun, consciousness approaches total dissipation and total fulfilment. On the one hand there is, or might be, an approach to a 'mystical' sense of exhilarating oneness with the world; but from another perspective there is the breakdown of awareness into an undifferentiated wash of sensation. Shelley's poetry was to explore many such ambivalent states, whose danger Mary Wollstonecraft's novel soon makes plain.

Profound but riddling commentaries on the failure of Sensibility come also from Blake. The predominant emotion in the inner life of Sensibility writers was pity, and as Blake says, 'pity divides the soul'. In pity we go out from ourselves into the soul of another person, with a resulting intensification of consciousness. But at the same time it is not self-consciousness, and the danger is that the soul will therefore forfeit its self-identity, 'In anguish dividing & dividing', without the power of reintegration.[37] It is for this reason that Blake, in *his* Romanticism, also rejects as inadequate 'the science of pity' and invokes the 'organizing', concentrating power of 'wrath'.[38] The ordering spirit in Shelley's poetry is ultimately very different from that in the poetry of Blake. Nevertheless his explorations took him along some of the same roads and alleyways of imagination.

Shelley never lost contact with the literary powers who shaped his younger mind. When he encounters, in that final, enigmatic *The Triumph of Life*, the dehumanised remains of 'what was once Rousseau', he is only retracing to its source one of the major currents that had flowed through all his life and thought. In order to understand, however, how Shelley contrived up to that point to save certain elements of Sensibility in a structure of poetic self-awareness, we need to examine the other late-eighteenth-century literary tradition which made such an enormous impact on Shelley's imagination: the Gothic.

'CONGENIAL HORRORS, HAIL!'

In Sensibility writing the idealised tendencies of tenderness and pity blot out objective awareness and heighten subjectivity to unprecedented and sometimes destructive brightness. By way of contrast, Gothic writing is preoccupied with a nightmare world-order of uncontrollable, unpredictable events where almost nothing of subjectivity can exist except that state of inner vacuum which we call terror.

A central quality of the world encountered in Gothic literature is that it is regularly experienced to be at once unintelligible and inescapably compelling. Consciousness, as embodied in the character with whom we mainly identify, is powerless, at the mercy of situations which cannot be controlled, caught up in fearful happenings which have no rational explanation. The author may provide a rationale for the seemingly irrational later in the book, it is true; but the Gothic experience springs from the terror of what cannot be understood, a world of estrangement in which we cannot grasp the significance of things. At its most effective, Gothic continues to conjure up terror in the midst of everyday scenes, making the familiar seem strange and frightening: but more often it works through the medium of a distorted 'landscape of fear' – desolate ruins, twisting corridors, foul dungeons, vertiginous towers, haunted castles. Many of the elements of Gothic had led separate lives in earlier literature. Techniques of terror had been evolved by the Jacobean dramatists; much came via Shakespeare; the 'graveyard' school of poets, Young, Blair, the Wartons, sometimes touches upon Gothic proper in its dark meditations; among novelists, Richardson and Smollett began to explore the themes of danger and suspense; ghostly presences came from folklore, superstition and foreign writers – mostly German.[39] But everything came together in a brief and remarkable tale by Horace Walpole, *The Castle of Otranto* (1764). Soon afterwards the floodgates of Gothic fiction were opened.

Popular Gothic writings, however, were not notable for their diversity. What is interesting is that even the major exponents of the genre employed what was virtually a standard range of character-types and settings. Eino Railo has well delineated the phenomenology of the 'classic' Gothic novel, and described the main types of person and landscape we meet there. The powerlessness of the central figure means that it is often a helpless young lady, imprisoned without reason or justification, or wandering through terrifying vaults and secret passages, in an agony of terror and anxiety about her pursuers, real or imaginary. Her sensitive nerves make her an ideal victim of suggestion and apprehensiveness. The 'persecuted maiden' or beautiful girl in distress is, of course, familiar from romance-stories before and since the ascendancy of the Gothic style. But as Railo points out, the extreme passivity of the Gothic heroine, her 'perpetual flight from persecutors in circumstances of great romanticism and terror', was a new development and points to something in the essential nature of the genre.[40]

A standard Gothic novel also usually contains a representative man of action. He invites identification with our active powers, which must lie dormant so long as we are sympathetically engaged with the distresses of the heroine. But for the most part of the events of the plot, his rescue attempts must necessarily be baffled and rendered ineffective. In Walpole's story he is a simple peasant, Theodore, unstained by the paralysing guilt which follows in the train of civilised refinement. In Walpole's successors, his purity and sunny nature remains largely uncompromised, but he acquires in addition a 'rococo elegance of deportment' more suited to the wooing of that gentle maiden, the heroine; by the end of the eighteenth century, he has become almost as sensitive and ineffectual as she – like Valancourt in Ann Radcliffe's *The Mysteries of Udolpho* (1794).[41]

Nevertheless, while neither hero nor heroine can exert control over the alien reality into which they are so inexplicably plunged – until the last pages of the novel – there is always a strong sense of a controlling power behind the scenes. It works, however, in an inhuman or anti-human way. It is frightening in its disregard of human feelings, which suggests that it is diabolical or stems from some 'adept' who has sold his soul, twisted his humanity out of all recognition, for the sake of unlimited power. The machinations of the villain, whether he be a devil, a 'Rosicrucian' *adeptus*, or a warped religious mind (the three classic incarnations) serve to terrorise and perplex the heroine, frustrate the hero, and give rise to the tension and expectancy of the Gothic genre. In this respect, too, the polar opposite of Sensibility writing, the Gothic novel is remarkable for the elaboration of its plot, looking forward in complexity to the modern detective story and the tale of suspense. Whenever the hero and heroine seem just out of danger, the plot takes another intricate turn and they are back in the labyrinth as lost and terrified as before. Like the reader, they must never be allowed to grasp their situation clearly, but be kept in shadows and uncertainties, while the power of the villain seems irresistible and beyond rational understanding. The novelist may moralise at the end, and chide his characters for abandoning reason and allowing the Gothic terrors to invade their souls, when all could have been naturalistically explained. But the Gothic state of mind, as we have said, is what matters imaginatively; and that depends on the appearance of an uncontrollable world, where events are shaped by a dark, inhuman power to which the only human response is terror.

Railo adds other details to his more detailed analysis, and his interpretation diverges at points from mine.[42] The pattern sketched above, however, already provides a basis for understanding the structure of Shelley's juvenile Gothic novels, *Zastrozzi* (1810) and *St Irvyne, or the Rosicrucian* (1811), neither of which deserves to be called subtle in its employment of Gothic properties. In *Zastrozzi* the helpless and appealing heroine is Julia, innocent victim of some very unlikely circumstances, loved by the young, sensitive Verezzi. The latter is unhappily tricked into marrying someone else, at what transpires to be the machinations of the wicked Zastrozzi; indeed Verezzi is manipulated throughout just as easily as Julia, and is actually carried about bodily by the villains in a state of sedation early in the plot. Driven by an inhuman desire for vengeance, Zastrozzi plans to force Verezzi to commit suicide, and eventually succeeds, before himself being hauled before the Inquisition and dying in torture with a last blasphemous yell. Interestingly, we can see Shelley edging here towards an explicitly psychological, internalised mode of fiction: not only do the names Verezzi–Zastrozzi prompt the thought that the characters are really two sides of a single mind; Shelley blurs the distinction by endowing his hero with some of the features of the villain, partly by making him the son of a ruthless scoundrel, and by partially justifying the conduct of Zastrozzi in terms of a semi-acceptable social code of revenge. We can at least glimpse a first foreshadowing of the 'pernicious casuistry' explored so profoundly in Shelley's later Gothic drama, *The Cenci*.

The fusing of characteristics from hero and villain continues in *St Irvyne*. Wolfstein and Ginotti, as D. G. Halliburton suggests, 'are the earlier two taken a step further. Wolfstein (the spiritual brother of Verezzi) becomes in the process a more culpable character. While Verezzi's only crime was to have been born the son of a scoundrel, Wolfstein is a murderer. Similarly, while Zastrozzi's crime was relatively justified (murder for vengeance), Ginotti's is far greater: he has renounced God for the gift of unending life.'[43] There is also in *St Irvyne* a heroine, much like Julia, in the shape of Wolfstein's sister Eloise. Shelley's indebtedness to traditional Gothic plots and character-types has been extensively studied – more so perhaps than the quality of his contribution to the genre really justifies; the psychological imbalances of these schoolboy productions have also been solemnly pronounced on. A much more interesting occupation, however, is to look forward through them to the increasingly complex and psychologically penetrating use of Gothic materials in Shelley's adult poetry. The psychologisation which is implicit in the mirror-picture hero and villain, for instance – and in *St Irvyne* the confusing way the characters play different social roles and have different names – gestures, however dimly, toward the fully internalised psychic drama achieved in *Prometheus Unbound*. There the arch-tyrant, the diabolical Jupiter, is also explicitly the *alter ego*, the rejected 'obverse side' of Prometheus' own mind. The heroine and indeed all the other characters in the play have also now been integrated into the single pervasive consciousness governing the whole. From a certain perspective, however, the Titan and his beloved Asia are certainly recognisable descendants of the archetypal Gothic hero and heroine. In view of what biographers tell us of Shelley's ambivalent sexuality, it is particularly intriguing to note that it is the male figure Prometheus who is now the passive victim, the prisoner in a high mountain recess like many a Gothic maiden; whilst the female projection Asia must take the active role, braving the horrors of forest, cavern and shapeless forms of darkness in order to win her lover's release![44] But under the inversion the structural similarity remains obvious. At the same time, the Gothic themes have been transfigured into universality, raised from the level of cliché-ridden plots to the plane of mythic truth.

In his perceptive study of 'the literature of terror', David Punter has advanced a sociological explanation for the emergence of some major Gothic themes, and for the genre's rise to prominence at the end of the eighteenth century.[45] Novel-writing, he argues, was a middle-class occupation; and in the late eighteenth century the middle classes were rising to positions of increased responsibility in the society of their time. On one level they were eager to rise; but rising socially also meant that they were entering a greater world whose complex functioning they had not been properly educated to understand, and of whose history they were only fragmentarily aware. Hence the widespread fascination we witness for the historical novel (with which Gothic in its mediaeval aspects sometimes overlaps), and also, he contends, with a genre expressing their fears and incomprehension of the new sphere of life into which they were being thrust – Gothic itself. The historical novel, according to Punter, filled the void of popular ignorance of the past and helped explain the world the bourgeoisie were beginning to appropriate. The Gothic novel embodied their suppressed fears of a world, already there and already operating, but operating by laws they did not comprehend or know how to control. He may well be correct in this analysis. The instance of the renegade aristocrat Shelley, on the other hand, demonstrates that, whatever their class origins, Gothic symbols had a potency that could be put to use to serve a universal and timeless vision. Terrors like those which infected the novel-writing bourgeoisie of the 1780s and 1790s after all affect everyone at some stage of life, and are probably always present in each of us at the margins of consciousness. The language of Gothic, once discovered, was not to be limited to a single time or cultural phase; in fact, it has proved its vitality by developing in many interesting ways over the last two centuries.

One of the most extraordinary directions the development took, in the work of poets like Blake and Goethe as well as in Shelley, was the imaginative use of the paraphernalia of 'Gothic' superstition to investigate the significance of the world-picture presented by – natural science.

Carlyle, writing of the character of Goethe's Mephistopheles in *Faust*, remarked on the paradox that he appears there not as the devil of ignorance, but the devil of knowledge. He winces at and despises the crude hocus-pocus of witchery, even while he makes use of it. At the vulgar revelry of the *Walpurgisnacht*, he chooses to pass incognito.[46] The 'magic' he holds out as a temptation to Faust is the gift of power over the external environment: this enables Faust, with the best of misguided intentions, to ride rough-shod over the desires of his fellow men in the pursuit of his own. Like many a large-scale town-planner, he is convinced he knows best. If he resorts to Mephistophelean violence, it is (he persuades himself) for the good of everyone as well as his own glory. Though Mephisto is costumed like a mediaeval demon, we soon recognise behind his 'magic' the kind of power over nature we should now call 'technology'; and behind the Molochian human sacrifices he extorts for speedy work on Faust's grand system of dykes, the human cost of the Industrial Revolution.

In England, Wordsworth and Blake provide the clearest documents of Romantic insight into the inimical features of the scientific world-view. 'We murder to dissect' was how Wordsworth summed it up; and Blake coined the aphorism: 'Science is the Tree of Death'.[47] Like Goethe, they realised that the effects of science in altering a relationship between man and nature which in many respects had previously continued unchanged for thousands of years were not just secondary consequences, following the introduction of technology into the running of life. Estrangement from 'nature' (in the broadest sense – including that fulfilled vision of nature which Blake calls Beulah) followed directly from the methodology of science. Bacon had noted the primary role of doubt and the importance of establishing a theory by attempted falsification, as opposed to an attitude of faith and trust. Blake retaliated by pointing out that this amounted in essence to excluding oneself from existence, adding mischievously:

> If the Sun & Moon should doubt,
> They'd immediately Go out.[48]

Descartes had reinforced Bacon's principle and completed the first foundations of objective science by drawing a line of demarcation between the thinking mind (*res cogitans*) and the domain of the calculable (*res extensa*). Those qualitative aspects of experience, apparently belonging to outer nature yet at the same time sharing the features of mental reality – qualitative value or other 'hidden' properties – were to be strictly analysed away. Nothing was permitted to be at once subjective and objective, and the whole notion of a universe suffused and held together by affinities and analogies between its parts, once a central philosophical thought, was decisively rejected. All 'occult qualities', such as earlier philosophers had conceived, were abolished from scientific thought. By its very method of isolating the measurable residuum of reality, therefore, science inevitably created a world seen as inanimate – or in human terms, 'dead'. The classical universe presents itself as alien to our subjective life of feelings, values, qualities. It is governed by 'laws' of natural necessity which our prayers and entreaties can do nothing to suspend. To liberal and religious men in the late eighteenth century this was still not a wholly accustomed world-conception, and its potential inhumanity caused a strong revulsion of feeling.

The central insight of the Romantics was that science, by creating so unaccommodating a world and presenting it as a final truth of objective knowledge, bequeathes us precisely the kind of world-view we fear most. If we accept it, we find ourselves not just in a large society which we do not totally comprehend, but in a universe which carries us along in a series of complex causes and effects we can hardly begin to fathom, impelled by an inflexible and non-human force of Necessity manifesting itself as 'natural law'. As to what the essence behind that force might be – Hume and others pronounce that we cannot know. We feel Shelley's ambivalent response as he eptomises the view:

> The greatest, equally with the smallest motions of the Universe, are subjected to the rigid necessity of inevitable laws. These laws are the unknown causes of the known effects perceivable in the Universe. Their effects are the boundaries of our knowledge, their names the expressions of our ignorance.[49]

All we can surmise about the 'unknown causes', we remember, is the 'infinite improbability' of their resembling human mind.

Rationalistic science offers us power and limited knowledge – a comprehension of external nature. In return it plays upon our deepest fears. This is the sinister dialectic of rationalism.[50] It achieves power through limiting knowledge to the sphere of the senses and the intellect; but the repressed qualitative, passionate and irrational components of experience, when ruled out of court, become all the more terrifying because they have become all the more incomprehensible. 'According to such an interpretation,' as David Punter writes, 'fear is both the root and the product of the attempt to bring all things under rational control, and rationalism will be a self-defeating system because that which cannot be thus assimilated will therefore become all the more taboo; reason will create its own enemies.' The argument he employs has a validity outside social analysis and the novel of realistic day-to-day life. It helps explain the deep reaction of Blake, Shelley and other poetic minds to the emergent cosmology of natural science, showing how scientific rationalism portrayed a world resembling in certain important respects the Gothic universe of terror we outlined earlier. Blake especially employs Gothic imagery of torture, oppression, gloomy vaults, chasms and abysses in order to render imaginable the cosmos of Newtonian science, the huge revolving 'Mills of Satan', grinding down humanity in their interminable motion and presided over by the 'God–Devil', Urizen.[51]

The argument also helps explain Shelley's changing interest in Gothic after his fateful meeting in 1812 with William Godwin, who was at once the most prominent philosopher of Necessity of the time, a potent political influence on the young poet, and in due course, after Shelley's second marriage, his father-in-law and a considerable financial burden. Mary Wollstonecraft was some fifteen years dead by the time of Shelley's second marriage, and Godwin now lived in semi-retirement and obscurity. His days of fame had been the 1790s, following the publication of the celebrated *Enquiry Concerning Political Justice* (1793), when, according to Hazlitt:

he blazed as a sun in the firmament of reputation;
no one was more talked of, more looked up to,
more sought after, and wherever liberty, truth,
justice was the theme, his name was not far off.[52]

Today the *Enquiry* reads as an indigestible and bulky amalgam of Lockean epistemology, scientific Necessitarianism, perfectibilism and philosophical anarchy.[53] Yet one can understand how Godwin's doctrine of Necessity fascinated Shelley, making the achievement of ideal society seem inevitable. Godwin started from the scientific principle of Necessity, 'generally acknowledged' to account for the workings of nature, and extended it to human mind and society. Every human act was – according to his theory – supposed to be predictable as an effect deriving from given causes. We have mentioned already that Shelley intended to illustrate this psychology in a projected novel. The result would probably have been, from a limited perspective, rather interesting – and significantly, rather Gothic.

Mind in the grip of compulsive ideas, or obsessions, is one of the themes which animate Godwin's own best novel, *Caleb Williams* – fervently admired by Shelley. *Caleb Williams* was published the year after the *Enquiry*, and its alternative title is *Things as They Are*; but it would be a mistake to suppose that it is a straightforward fictionalisation of Godwin's political ideas for propaganda diffusion among popular readers. Godwin strikes a genuinely novelistic note in his narrative inquiry into the mechanisms of mind. *Caleb Williams* is perhaps the first successful novel to exhibit a controlling view of mind as grounded in something other than character. Trains of thought move according to their own inherent laws of association, suggestion, fixation, and so on, as the early associationist psychology of Hartley had described. We recall that Hartleian ideas fascinated the young Coleridge as well as Godwin. In *Caleb Williams* the workings of mind are represented as curiously independent of the hero's inmost centre of consciousness; he watches his own mental processes detachedly, even while they draw him into situations of terror and atrocious risk. Having come to suspect his employer, Falkland, of some past crime, he spies upon him relentlessly until Falkland is unwillingly compelled to become his persecutor. Naïve though it may appear to us in retrospect to suppose that psychic processes could be easily reduced to causal sequence, it must be admitted that 'Necessity' in *Caleb Williams* does make for a compelling narrative, so that Hazlitt is no doubt substantially correct in his guess that 'no one ever began *Caleb Williams* that did not read it through'.[54] We do not possess Shelley's detailed thoughts on *Caleb Williams*; but he certainly responded to similar aspects of Godwin's later novel, *Mandeville* (1817). Shelley is gripped by the way Mandeville's 'errors arise from an immutable necessity of internal nature'; and how 'the events of the tale flow like the stream of fate, regular and irresistible, growing at once darker and swifter in their progress'.[55]

The obsessed narrator and his compulsive tale lead us once more to the core of the Gothic imagination. Examples range from Coleridge's *Ancient Mariner* to the religious fanatic of James Hogg's *Private Memoirs and Confessions of a Justified Sinner*. Hence I believe Godwin's novels are to be classed correctly – and not just for convenience – with the Gothic 'classics' of his contemporaries. The scientific cosmos had threatened man's traditional relationship to nature; to an even greater extent did the invasion of the psyche by rigid laws of 'mechanical' force seem to knock the bottom out of traditional morality. Godwin's intellect grasped at a supreme Necessity which governed human and natural actions with amoral indifference. Not many spirits were bold enough to follow him, and his ideas understandably provoked fear and anxiety. Moreover, he himself was haunted by Gothic images when he translated his vision into human fact in novels like *Caleb Williams* and *Mandeville*. Indeed it is the Gothic elements which give these books their imaginative power and distinguish them from the duller novels of social concern that were being written by men like Bage or Godwin's friend Holcroft.

The novel Godwin wrote after *Caleb Williams* moved explicitly into Gothic territory. *St Leon* (1799) employed a 'Rosicrucian' plot which indubitably influenced Shelley in *St Irvyne*. The use of the term 'Rosicrucian' perhaps demands some explanation.[56] The Rosicrucians, according to certain manifestos circulating in the seventeenth century, were a benevolent secret society devoted to the improvement of mankind and the pursuit of wisdom, the *summa scientia*. Though they were an organised Brotherhood, they did not live apart in monastic isolation; they formed an 'Invisible College', whose members were distinguished by no special dress or outward mark, but moved among the people undetected, helping them toward the goals of wisdom and harmony, and then moving on. Rosicrucians were also supposed to have discovered the secret of prolonged life. The elements of the image belonging to the Rosicrucian were soon subjected, however, to a remarkable inversion. In spite of the philanthropic aims expressed by the Rosicrucian manifesto-writers, the 'Invisible College' proved to many people extremely worrying. The notion of secret agents moving about in society undetected – perhaps even by their closest friends – and then mysteriously disappearing, agents who possessed occult knowledge of the mystery of life, was ultimately more disturbing than reassuring. In popular imagination, therefore, the Rosicrucian becomes an important figure expressing Gothic fear. He suggests a society run by secret organisations whose designs and aims are inscrutable, not understood by all; and indeed a universe in which there are mysterious powers, with whom the Rosicrucian adept of vulgar legend is soon supposed to have entered into a diabolical pact. Such, briefly, is the rationale of the Rosicrucian villains who figure so largely in the novels of Godwin and Shelley. The poet, however, as we shall see, had an interest in the thought of Rosicrucian (or near-Rosicrucian) writers like Fludd and Paracelsus which transcended this literary and legendary development.

St Leon was still more fervently admired by Shelley than *Caleb Williams*. Its aesthetic impact on his own *St Irvyne*, on the other hand, preceded the influence of Godwin's thought on his philosophy. *St Irvyne* displays very little of Godwin's social awareness at all. The Gothic exploration of Godwinism, however, had already been taken up by a novelist on the other side of the Atlantic: America's 'first professional man of letters', Charles Brockden Brown. For Brown's significance to an understanding of Shelley, we have the testimony of the poet's friend Peacock, who opined that 'nothing so blended itself with the structure of his interior mind as the creations of Brown'. He ranked four of Brown's novels, along with Goethe's *Faust* and Schiller's *Die Räuber*, among Shelley's half-dozen most favoured books. Brown's intellectual fascination with Godwinism and his imaginative working out of its sinister undertones of anxiety and fear no doubt made him particularly congenial to Shelley. Details from his reading of Brown manifest themselves in his poetry, from *Laon and Cythna* to the famous lyric *To Constantia, Singing* and beyond.[57] The continuing presence of influences from Brown also makes it clear that those critics must be wrong who see a shift away from interest in the Gothic after Shelley's encounter with Godwin in 1812.[58] It is rather that thereafter Shelley was less dazzled by the stage properties of Gothic, and more concerned with using Gothic techniques in aid of deeper inquiry. His Gothic quest is internalised rather than abandoned. He now uses the symbolic language of fear and apparition to delve into the reaches of the mind, to the dark, semi-conscious sensations which accompany social and intellectual life.

Already in *St Irvyne* Shelley had explored the invasion of the soul by psychic compulsions. When Eloise, for example, tries not to think about the 'mysterious stranger', the immediate effect it has upon her is that a 'painful recurrence of almost mechanical force' impresses itself on her 'disturbed intellect'.[59] We stand here at the opposite pole to the self-determined subjectivity of the novel of Sensibility. Terror denotes the shrinking of subjectivity from the threat of external invasion and annihilation, from the force of unassimilable aspects of reality. The result, however, is in one respect parallel: an intensification as well as an endangering of consciousness. Shelley remained fascinated by the heightened consciousness of fear for the rest of his life; in contrast to those who see Shelley's interest in the Gothic declining in his later years, Richard Holmes has brought out the poet's constant interest in 'the abnormal state of acute perception, the potential force of terror hovering at the margins of thought'.[60] But Shelley was also aware that this path led to states of the 'disturbed mind', obsession and paranoia – even when it posed as a way of rationalism and science. His thoughts were to receive their fullest embodiment in the sombre meditation of *Mont Blanc* (1816). There Shelley registers the ultimate ambiguity of the Godwinian vision of Necessity, its intellectual plausibility to the sceptical enquirer into the hidden causes of nature, its Gothic terror to the seeking imagination. Like the stylistic methods of Sensibility, Gothic furnished Shelley with a means of delving beyond the 'painted veil' of sense-reality; the results in each case, however, proved very different. Shelley remained profoundly uncommitted – unless to the truth of imagination as a whole. No more than the psychic–sensual indulgence of Sensibility could the visionary terror of Gothic furnish him with a finally satisfying conception of the imagination's world.

Neither the soul-shuddering images of Gothic nor the luxurious emotions of Sensibility ever succeeded in monopolising Shelley's creativity. Increasingly, he made use of both in a higher synthesis, a Romanticism which could relate the energies of human vision *in extremis* back to a common centre. We can see this in one of the last efforts Shelley made to write a prose romance: *The Assassins* (1814). But first we must mention the work of Ann Radcliffe, a novelist who affected the evolution of English Romanticism profoundly, and who presented Shelley with a preliminary fusion of the elements of Gothic and Sensibility. Like Shelley, she was interested not only in intensity of consciousness, but in inner harmony and (though not in Shelley's political sense) in constructive social life – both of them things outside the range of Gothic or Sensibility as such.

THE CLOSED MIND AND THE OPEN SOCIETY

The nurture of the emotions in the literature and life-style of Sensibility arose historically in reaction against the scientific rationalism of the Enlightenment, its worship of fixities and of the analytic powers of the mind. Gothic fear, on the other hand, represents the dark penumbra of rationalism itself. From a wider point of view, therefore, the two movements must appear correlatives, twin sides of a single reality, opposite poles of one imaginative whole.

It may be helpful to refer back to the opposite types of perceptual experience described at the outset of the first chapter. For it is again on the level of experience that the essential complementarity of the two poles emerges most strongly. We recall the state of self-immersed contemplation, and its contrary state of full involvement with the surrounding world. Yet on the plane of experience it is clear that it is when we are most inwardly sunk in thought that our awareness of the world makes it appear most external. And we are never more fully involved in the outer world than in those activities, like absorbed reading, when we cease to be aware of its otherness. The imaginative and intellectual ventures in which these boundary regions of perceptual life are implicated must, therefore, in so far as they strive toward a synoptic vision of life, acknowledge each other as indeed 'twin Destinies'. The first sketch of such a synoptic view was made by a novelist whom we have already mentioned. In Ann Radcliffe's most successful novels *The Mysteries of Udolpho* (1794) and *The Italian* (1797) the questions of the right use of reason, and the dangers of yielding to excessive emotionalism or excessive fear, are elaborately examined through the medium of the large-scale romance.

The Mysteries of Udolpho was Radcliffe's first great success, and it is still in many ways her most interesting production. It is usually classed as a Gothic romance, but the reader in search of horrors has to wait for them – for several hundred pages! The first, idyllic part of the book is written in the pure spirit of Sensibility, full of glowing landscapes touched with the sublime, exquisite sighs and tender reflections. St Aubert and his daughter Emily discourse at leisure on 'taste' and 'sentiment', which form the basis of life as well as art. 'Virtue and taste', explains St Aubert, 'are nearly the same, for virtue is little more than active taste, and the most delicate affections of each combine in real love.' Active taste is epitomised in 'tenderness, simplicity and truth'.[61] This triunity of virtues has already stepped bodily into the novel in the shape of Valancourt, Emily's devoted lover, who serenades her repeatedly to prove his taste as a lutanist in addition to his (less obvious) more practical abilities. His care proves disconcertingly ineffectual, and when St Aubert dies, Emily is abducted by the villainous Montoni.

Sensibility is now put to the test outside the idyllic pastoral world of the first section of the book. Montoni, whose purposes are never clearly revealed but only hinted at towards the end of the novel, transports Emily to the dilapidated Gothic castle of Udolpho, where she is systematically terrorised. It soon becomes clear that Emily's education in sensitivity and the 'luxuries of *ennui*' has afforded her little firm grip on the actual, and now lays her open to unreal fears. The devaluation of reason permits the cultivation of refined feeling – but also the enthronement of superstition and terror. Montoni can exploit Emily's susceptibility for his own (unknown) ends; her sentimentalism is actually what enables him to manipulate her, and to play upon her irrationality to impress her with a sense of his illimitable, 'supernatural' power. Weakness invites violence.

Sensibility also raises unreal expectations of a 'romantic' kind, and these fantasies Radcliffe's feeling for actuality constantly delights in puncturing. Above all, Emily's expectation of being rescued by Valancourt simply never comes to fulfilment – though they are eventually reunited. Such sentimental expectations are dangerous, Radcliffe implies, and when disappointed can lead to a morbid withdrawal from the social world, causing a whole life to be wasted in self-obsessed meditation or guilt. Illusion invites both exploitation, and devastating correction from the nature of 'things as they are'. Radcliffe's Promethean villains also tend to be men who were once of deep and perhaps refined feeling, in whom the normal currents of affection have turned awry through guilt or pride. We have already the quoted St Aubert's warning that pity must be made to live up to moral action on the one hand, and that sensibility must not become pride in one's own refinement on the other. A Montoni is thus in a sense nothing but the inverse reflex of an Emily: both are incarnations of sensibility, one pure and susceptible, the other warped and egotistic.

But if the expectations of excessive 'romantic' feeling are exposed as unreal, so are the terrors of supernaturalism. By the end of *Udolpho*, every mystery has been explained away – through contrivance, coincidence or delusion. And the prevailing voice at the end of the novel, when the excitement is over, does not come from some 'sublimer world' but proclaims a 'triumph of good sense'. The pendulum-swings of rapture and despair which have characterised the love of Emily and Valancourt settle down into 'a tempered and rational affection'. A barbed remark from old Theresa, Emily's sensible servant-woman, pointedly suggests that anything else is an extravagance only the idle rich can afford. When Emily and Valancourt are close to separating forever over a point of decorum, she exclaims: 'to see how gentlefolks can afford to throw away their happiness! Now, if you were poor people, there would be none of this.'[62]

Radcliffe's later novel *The Italian* contains many of the features familiar from *Udolpho*. The standard of writing, however, is consistently higher: the profusion of incidents is trimmed within a shorter compass; and the whole prefaced by an admirably brisk and effective introductory scene. Yet it soon emerges that *The Italian* is a less radical literary experiment than its predecessor, and more obviously committed to defining the proper confines of an attitude of realism. Exquisite emotion and fear of the supernatural are now set against a strong comic voice – the devoted but down-to-earth Paulo. Ellena and Schedoni may be better realised as personalities than Emily and Montoni, their equivalents in *Udolpho* – but this in return detracts from their elemental power, individualising and particularising the psychological forces mirrored archetypally in their less clearly focused predecessors. Sometimes Radcliffe becomes almost the forerunner of Jane Austen in the mocking, ironic reduction of her characters' grand illusions to plain matter-of-fact. From *The Italian* to the straightforward parody of *Northanger Abbey* is a relatively – and surprisingly – short step. In the end Radcliffe's mind seems to have closed against the dimensions of experience she set out in *Udolpho* and its predecessors to explore. She finally recommends the attitude that it is better not to gaze into heaven and hell. Without Shelley's equivocation, she urges us not to lift the painted veil. Beyond lie irrational terror and illusion.

It has been said that Radcliffe invented the man that Lord Byron tried to be; she influenced Coleridge and Keats, Charles Maturin and 'monk' Lewis. We can also recognise in her romances a forerunner of the dialectic which runs through Shelley's work. *Zastrozzi* and *St Irvyne* are of course strongly imbued with images and names taken directly from Radcliffe. *St Irvyne* might be seen as a first clumsy attempt to integrate a Sensibility novel (the episodes of Eloise and Nempere) into a Gothic tale.[63] The pattern in Shelley's poetry emerges in full clarity in 1815 in *Alastor*: but it is prefigured in *The Assassins*, composed but left uncompleted the year before. Here many of the influences we have discussed come together. Vivid sensibility makes the landscape a mirror of heightened emotion; 'Rosicrucian' themes begin to emerge before the fragment leaves off; the social preoccupations of the new pupil of Godwin are married to the dialectics of Radcliffean romance.

The Assassins is one of Shelley's least discussed works – oddly, since as Richard Holmes points out it stands in the mainstream of his thought on the issues of freedom, love and violence.[64] Historically, the Assassins were an Ismaili sect whom Shelley had encountered in Sales de Lisle's novel *Le Vieux de la Montaigne* (1799), the book from which he borrows the incident of a man dropping out of the sky. But Shelley's Assassins are his own invention, having little to do with the Islamic fanatics of the eleventh century. The legend Shelley devised was evidently intended to have been his retelling of the story in Johnson's *Rasselas* of a community inhabiting a 'Happy Valley', untainted by the decadence of European society. Shelley moves the scene to the Lebanon instead of Abyssinia – and there are significant differences in his portrait of ideal social life. More strikingly still, there are differences when an inhabitant of the 'Happy Valley' returns to the outside world.

A small group of speculatively minded Christians are described escaping from the fall of Jerusalem after the Jewish Revolt. Perhaps Shelley was recalling the semi-legendary flight of Jewish Christians to Pella. They are already free from the 'gross delusions of antiquated superstition', and their views 'considerably resembled those of the sect afterwards known by the name of Gnostics' – which Shelley takes to mean (again unhistorically) that they 'esteemed the human understanding to be the paramount rule of human conduct'; this sounds considerably more like Shelley himself than like any Gnostic that we know of. Liberated in the course of succeeding centuries from almost every remaining trace of oppressive superstition, the Assassins realise Shelley's ideal of radical democracy, occupying their remote valley of Bethzatanai in a condition of Godwinian freedom from 'positive institution'. 'Love, friendship and philanthropy, would now be the characteristic disposers of their industry. It is for his mistress or his friend that the labourer consecrates his toil; others are mindful, but he is forgetful, of himself.'[65]

More subversive than his picture of communal life, however, are the results of his experiment in sending one of his Assassins back into the great world of 'the corrupt and slavish multitude'. Dr Johnson's Rasselas soon wearied of strenuous existence outside the 'Happy Valley', and returned resignedly to its confines. But the Assassin, firm in his Shelleyan conviction that 'man is eminently man' when he has awe for nothing but the infinity of the universe, is made of sterner stuff. He would not be able to help noticing the arbitrary powers abused by kings, which powers would seem to him 'dreamy nothings' and the kings themselves 'phantasms of misery and mischief, that hold their deathlike state on glittering thrones'. He would become in short an implacable enemy of the state. The 'Rosicrucian' motif now undergoes a sort of re-reversal back to positive status:

> Against their predilections and distastes an Assassin, accidentally the inhabitant of a civilised community, would wage unremitting hostility from principle. He would find himself compelled to adopt means which they would abhor, for the sake of an object which they could not conceive that he should propose to himself. Secure and self-enshrined in the magnificence and pre-eminence of his conceptions, spotless as the light of heaven, he would be the victim among men of calumny and persecution. Incapable of distinguishing his motives, they would rank him among the vilest and most atrocious criminals.[66]

The passage has disquieting implications of terrorism, half raised into light, which were to be repudiated by the poet of *Prometheus Unbound*. There is no reason to think that Shelley would have approved personal violence in the struggle for freedom; even so Godwin, had he ever been allowed to see *The Assassins*, would certainly have noticed a distinct parting of the ways on Shelley's part from his own tactic of reason and the triumph of argument. The reformer-poet had been treated too much like an Assassin or a Rosicrucian by English society already in 1814 not to throw his full weight behind the image of the misconstrued idealist, whatever extreme measures might be hinted.

The imaginative potency of Shelley's description of an ideal community in *The Assassins*, however, is more generally sustained by means of a technique learnt purely from Radcliffe – the symbolic use of the environment to suggest enduring dimensions of experience. The landscape of Shelley's 'Lebanon' derives geographically almost totally from Radcliffe's Apennines and Alps in *Udolpho* and *The Italian*, reinforced only from Shelley's travels in France and Switzerland at the time of writing. We are a long way from a Wordsworthian vision of 'natural objects'. Rather, in the tradition of Sensibility, nature is scanned for emblems of subjective feeling. Moreover, human monuments of past high civilisation have been absorbed into nature in ruined Bethzatanai, so that the very rocks are sculpted with 'the lore of ancient wisdom' in 'mystic characters' which speak 'volumes of mysterious import, and obscure significance'. As a result, says Shelley, 'in the season of its utmost prosperity and magnificence, art might not aspire to vie with nature in the valley of Bethzatanai'.[67]

By this means of employing landscape as an extension of cultural forces, Shelley succeeds in symbolically depicting an open society. It is open in the first instance to a Radcliffean appreciation of the picturesque vistas of cloud and stream their mountainous situation provides:

> Far below, the silver clouds rolled their bright volumes in many beautiful shapes, and fed the eternal springs, that, spanning the dark chasms like a thousand radiant rainbows, leaped into the quiet vale, then, lingering in many a dark glade among the groves of cypress and of palm, lost themselves in the lake. The immensity of these precipitous mountains with their starry pyramids of snow, excluded the sun, which overtopped not, even in its meridian, their overhanging rocks. But a more heavenly and serener light was reflected from their icy mirrors, which, piercing through the many-tinted clouds, produced lights and colours of inexhaustible variety. The herbage was perpetually verdant, and clothed the darkest recesses of the caverns and the woods.[68]

The scene might have been rendered by Emily St Aubert in her journal. Shelley's Assassins, however, are open to more intense sensations than Ann Radcliffe's limited imagination may have been able to envisage. For 'the immediate effect of such a scene, suddenly presented to the contemplation of mortal eyes', and not repressed by the weight of 'custom' in the 'abhorred world', is quite startling:

> They ceased to acknowledge, or deigned not to advert to, the distinctions with which the majority of base and vulgar minds control the longings and struggles of the soul towards its place of rest. A new and sacred fire was kindled in their hearts and sparkled in their eyes. The epidemic transport communicated itself though every heart with the rapidity of a blast from heaven. They were already disembodied spirits; they were already the inhabitants of paradise. To live, to breathe, to

move, was itself a sensation of immeasurable transport. Every new contemplation of the condition of his nature brought to the happy enthusiast an added measure of delight, and impelled every organ, where mind is united with external things, a keener and more exquisite perception of all that they contain of lovely and divine. To love, to be beloved, suddenly became an insatiable famine of his nature, which the wide circle of the universe, comprehending beings of such inexhaustible variety and stupendous magnitude of excellence appeared too narrow and confined to satiate.[69]

There are presentiments of the *Skylark* ode here, as well as of *Alastor*. But one thing is clear: where Radcliffe closed her mind and finally drew back, Shelley follows through the energies of imagination to the meridian height of their intensity. Sensibility breaks through into vision.

Yet Shelley does not ignore the perils charted in Radcliffe's dialectic of romance. Nature in Bethzatanai can veer round from glowing serenity to 'strange scenes of chaotic confusion and harrowing sublimity'; the mountains 'surrounding and shutting in the vale' can suddenly become Gothic crags and icy precipices, haunted by spectral shapes:

> Blue vapours assumed strange lineaments under the rocks and among the ruins, lingering like ghosts with slow and solemn step. Nearer the icy region, autumn and spring held an alternate reign. The sere leaves fell and choked the sluggish brooks; the chilling fogs hung diamonds on every spray; and in the dark cold evening the howling winds made melancholy music in the trees. Far above, shone the bright throne of winter, clear, cold, and dazzling. . . . The cataracts, arrested in their course, seemed, with their transparent columns, to support the dark-browed rocks. Sometimes the icy whirlwind scooped the powdery snow aloft, to mingle with the hissing meteors, and scatter spangles through the rare and rayless atmosphere.[70]

The anticipations now of Shelley's sombre *Mont Blanc* show that the Assassins of his imagined ideal community also live vitally open to nature's terrors and might of freezing destruction. Thus are they prevented from declining into subjective dreamers or impractical mystics in perpetual reverie.

Wherever social life extends, it makes of nature a transparent medium of spiritual perception; but around society, 'surrounding and shutting in the vale', is the fearful and unknown whose power must also be acknowledged. 'They that direct the changes of this mortal scene breathe the decrees of their dominion from a throne of darkness and of tempest' is another message comprised in Shelley's brief fragment of romance.[71] The blessed vale itself must be won – in context both literally and metaphorically – from the 'empire' of the wolf and tiger, and the ruins of Bethzatanai resound to the brute cries and screams of bird and beast of prey.

Before breaking off composition of *The Assassins*, Shelley took care to establish the harmonious centre of life after the huge perspectives of landscape in the opening chapters. When the never-to-be-completed story finally begins to be related in Chapters III and IV, we are shown scenes of individual care and family affection. Like Radcliffe, Shelley sees society between opposing forces, which must be played off against one another in order to achieve the balance of normal life. He too weighs fear against illusion, so as to evade the dangers of extremism. But Shelley also paints the picture of a society open to ecstasy and terror, with an equilibrium that is not achieved at the cost of closing the mind to ultimate vision. In Radcliffe's *The Italian* we feel that after all the door to a wider understanding of life is falling shut; in *The Assassins* it is swinging open.

3   Occult Qualities

Is it that in some brighter sphere
We part from friends we meet with here?
Or do we see the Future pass
Over the Present's dusky glass?
Or what is that that makes us seem
To patch up fragments of a dream,
Part of which comes true, and part
Beats and trembles in the heart?
(Shelley, fragment composed 1819)

Shelley's scientific interests have been studied, with extremely valuable results, by several interpreters of his life and thought. After some fifty years, the pioneering work of Carl Grabo still deserves to be read; and his approach has been taken up and modified by others since, most notably perhaps by Desmond King-Hele. They have collectively shown the presence of an archipelago of scientific references scattered through the ocean of Shelley's poetry, and amply demonstrated the importance of the poet's readings in that scientific versifier and evolutionist Erasmus Darwin, in Humphry Davy, in Herschel and many more, for anyone who wishes fully to take in the breadth of Shelley's mind.[1] Thanks to their efforts many Shelley readers now know, for example, that the meteorology of *The Cloud* is accurate and knowledgeable; or that the volcano passages in *Prometheus Unbound* reflect detailed study on Shelley's part in contemporary seismological theory.[2] Yet the manner in which Shelley deploys his scientific information and so integrates it into the substance of his poetry has been on the whole the theme of fewer investigations. Shelley uses his knowledge of science in such an extraordinary manner – certainly one which would have surprised many of those great scientific authorities just listed – that some discussion surely seems called for.

We must therefore return to Shelley's examination of the extreme states of consciousness, which we have just been discussing more from the standpoint of their literary

67

background. For it is once more there that we shall find the link between the literary and the intellectual facets of Shelley's imagination.

We have seen that the two literary movements which flowered in the late eighteenth century, Gothic and Sensibility, were extremist movements. As such they led to discoveries in the heights and depths of the human psyche, and in the extremes of style. Both provided the imagination with conditions under which an unprecedented intensification of awareness became possible – at a certain price. And both ultimately tended, when pursued in their full intensity, to break down the equilibrium of the self through their one-sided energies, so that the intensification of consciousness might finally lead to a breakdown of consciousness altogether. In Sensibility, the imagination drowns in the excess of its own delights; in Gothic terror, the intensity of fear squeezes subjective life to nothing through an invasion of outer darkness.

In the 'synoptic' Gothic–Sensibility romances of Ann Radcliffe, the constant approach to the limits of consciousness is striking: so much so, that it can sometimes seem as if an Emily or an Ellena, when she is not swooning away in refined Sensibility raptures, must invariably be somewhere fainting in terror – being granted by the author very little normal life in-between. These tendencies were obviously open to parody. But from a more serious point of view, they could be taken by a poet such as Shelley to indicate a particular, radical quality of the imagination; namely, that at the height of its activity imagination may link our minds directly with those hidden depths of our being which cannot be brought into direct consciousness. One of the most significant sections in Shelley's *Speculations on Metaphysics* is that containing his observations on the way an image, or idea, may show what he calls 'an intimate and unaccountable connexion . . . with the obscure parts of my own nature'.[3]

Beyond the point of that observation, however, investigation appeared to be blocked by the nature of consciousness itself. The potent poetic image seems to touch the depths of our slumbering inner nature, but further efforts to raise the forces of the depths into the light of consciousness all culminate in failure, intellectual and imaginative. Scepticism attempts to deal with the issue by consigning the realm beyond the observable to the abyss of unknowing – yet leaves the human sense of vacuity unassuaged. Idealism offers an apparently total realisation-in-consciousness – but thereby loses touch with its own foundations and ends in solipsism or uncertainty. Sensibility emotion likewise closes itself off from contact with the disturbing depths of human nature in its need to preserve clarity and purity of feeling; and visionary Gothic fear expresses an obsession with the excluded. Along all these paths, consciousness either fades out beyond a certain point – or, if we try to sustain it, becomes involved in a destructive dialectic of self-dissolution or terror. And yet for Shelley to reject these avenues of exploration would mean to close the gates of perception – to seal up the imagination within the confines of the painted veil.

Reaching out imaginatively in one direction and then in the other, Shelley locates no firm outside foundation, and many of his poems are the records of voyages of destruction. But his poetry does also record another experience, which at times could free the imagination from its seemingly insoluble dilemma. Remaining spiritually open to ultimate possibilities of ecstasy and terror, like the Assassins in his fragmentary romance, Shelley found that under such conditions his perception could on occasion be overshadowed by a power from the unconscious depths. It was not to be perceived directly, remaining an 'occult' – though palpable and of transfiguring force; nor could its presence be compelled. He came to think that the mystery of its overshadowing was intimately connected with what he called 'beauty' and what he called 'love'. But strange to say, it was also inescapably linked with his excited response to the discoveries of natural science, so that the distinguishing characteristic of his poetic science may be said to be its constant association with the sense of hidden reality. To put it a different way, all science tended to become for Shelley 'occult science'.[4]

OCCULTISM, MAGIC AND MAGNETS OF THE MIND

Shelley's fascination with occultism and magic, an essential ingredient of his interest in science quite apart from his love of everything 'Gothic', goes back to his childhood, and was perhaps even part of a family trend. Grabo has speculated that

Shelley's grandfather, 'old Sir Bysshe . . . may have collected
. . . books on alchemy, magic, Rosicrucianism', etc.[5] If so, it was
in the family library that the infant Shelley began his esoteric
researches, with which soon after he intrigued and terrorised his
younger sisters. Roger Ingpen says that the boy Shelley 'passed
much of his leisure in the study of the occult sciences, natural
philosophy, and chemistry; his pocket money was spent on
books "relative to these pursuits, on chemical apparatus and
materials," and many of the books treated of magic and
witchcraft'.[6] Looking back on this time, Shelley was to write:
'While yet a boy I sought for ghosts', describing his boyish
'Hopes of high talk with the departed dead'.[7] His sister
Elizabeth remembered many mysterious tales Shelley used to
tell, from their very earliest days, and recalled one or two
inexplicable incidents.[8]

Later, whilst an undergraduate at Oxford, Shelley continued
his studies of a scientific, especially chemical–alchemical nature.
His friend Hogg has left a description of Shelley's rooms in
University College worthy of a stage-design for the first scene of
Faust, the poet brooding timelessly amidst a confusion of retorts
and other instruments:

> as if the young chemist, in order to analyse the mystery of
> creation, had endeavoured first to reconstruct the primeval
> chaos. The tables, and especially the carpet, were already
> stained with large spots of various hues, which frequently
> proclaimed the agency of fire. An electrical machine, an
> air-pump, the galvanic trough, a solar microscope, and large
> glass jars and receivers, were conspicuous amidst the mass of
> matter. . . . There were bottles of soda water, sugar, pieces of
> lemon, and the traces of an effervescent beverage. Two piles
> of books supported the tongs, and these upheld a small glass
> retort above an argand lamp. I had not been seated many
> minutes before the liquor in the vessel boiled over, adding
> fresh stains to the table, and rising in fumes with a most
> disagreeable odour. Shelley snatched the glass quickly, and
> dashing it in pieces among the ashes under the grate,
> increased the unpleasant and penetrating effluvium.[9]

His reading included the reputable authorities in eighteenth-
century chemistry; but it also embraced the writings of
Paracelsus and Basil Valentine, and perhaps those of English

alchemical adepts such as Ripley. By this time, the young Shelley needed to satisfy his intellect as well as his fascinations, and his attitude to the material miracles of alchemy was sceptical. He explained carefully to Godwin that all these 'ancient books of Chemistry and Magic were perused with an enthusiasm of wonder, almost amounting to belief' – almost, but not quite.[10] His reaction to the pretensions of alchemical magic was probably much the same as that of De Quincey, who also dabbled in Rosicrucian and magical literature – for instance in his response to what the latter denounced as the 'insolent vaunt of Paracelsus, that he would restore the original rose or violet out of the ashes settling from its combustion'. Nevertheless in the *Defence of Poetry* Shelley made of that vaunt a memorable image for the foredoomed but richly rewarding exercise of translation.[11]

Upon examination it turns out that poetry and alchemy have frequently lived as close neighbours. Like earlier experimenters, Shelley must certainly have noticed how the chemical processes in his retort – subtle, startling, violent or imperceptibly slow by turns – were suggestive of ideas and analogies for the workings of the human heart. Indeed, Charles Nicholl points out, there had always been a side to alchemy according to which the 'alchemist's probing, purifying, transforming operations became a kind of mirror for psychic discoveries and changes'.[12] His meditations on the astonishingly complex physical occurrences inside the Hermetic egg, or glass vessel, were a way of contacting those 'obscure parts' of the mind, as was Shelley's interest in the power of alchemical and other symbols. The alchemical transmutation of the psyche depended, not on understanding the chemistry of the Work, but on the play of images and inner forces released within the adept during his long vigil at the *athanor* where the incubation took place. Shakespeare and Ben Jonson had drawn upon its imaginative resources long before Shelley, though they had not both treated it with equal solemnity; Donne and Vaughan had revelled in its potentialities for far-flung metaphor and hidden interconnections. A contemporary European parallel to Shelley again suggests itself in Goethe, whose strange *Novelle Elective Affinities* brought the chemistry of interacting characters strictly up to date in terms of the latest scientific theories; but the background in his case was alchemical too.[13]

A knowledge of the alchemical dimension in Shelley's images can sharpen our detailed response to his poems. Take for example his description of the Devil in *Peter Bell the Third*:

> A leaden-witted thief – just huddled
> Out of the dross and scum of nature;
> A toad-like lump of limb and feature,
> With mind, and heart, and fancy muddled.
>
> He was that heavy, dull, cold thing,
> The spirit of evil well may be.[14]

We discover a new exactitude when we observe that Shelley is speaking alchemically. The 'heavy, dull, cold' Devil with his leaden wits is then in fact clearly compounded of the basest metal, lead: the furthest away from gold on the scale of refinement. (Though it is no surprise when, two stanzas later, the Devil imagines proudly that 'his gold's might' has set the minds of the learned aflame!) Clarification emerges, too, from the realisation that the toad in alchemy often stands for the crude *materia prima* – quite literally 'the dross and scum of nature'. If we are to believe the commentary on Sir George Ripley's *Vision*, the Toad in the first stages of the Work 'ingenders so venomous a Nature, that truly in the whole World there is not a ranker Poyson, or stink, according as Philosophers witness'. Very appropriately, therefore, Shelley relegates this evil substance to his smog-ridden Hell. Furthermore, in the Devil's three-fold confusion of mind, heart and imagination we can readily detect an allusion to the three alchemical principles in man, symbolically called Salt, Sulphur and Mercury of the Philosophers, which the alchemical *opus* can separate out from the dregs of the *prima materia* in the adept's regeneration from the chaos of the soul. Shelley's spirit of evil is recognisably the alchemical principle of dullness and weight which has to be overcome in the process of the Work – put, in this playful poem, to a playful use. But elsewhere, alchemical themes and Paracelsian conceptions figure more seriously in Shelley's poetry.

The wonderful description of the flowers in the garden around the Sensitive Plant, for instance, seems to me to owe very little to Shelley's notes from Davy's *Elements of Agricultural*

Chemistry,[15] for all that work's emphasis on the mutuality and interdependence of forces (chemical, electrical, gravitational) in the environment:

> The flowers (as an infant's awakening eyes
> Smile on its mother, whose singing sweet
> Can first lull, and at last must awaken it),
>
> When Heaven's blithe winds had unfolded them,
> As mine-lamps enkindle a hidden gem,
> Shone smiling to Heaven, and every one
> Shared joy in the light of the gentle sun;
>
> For each one was interpenetrated
> With the light and the odour its neighbour shed,
> Like young lovers whom youth and love make dear
> Wrapped and filled by their mutual atmosphere.[16]

Not only do the mine-lamps suggest that Paracelsus was not far from Shelley's mind, but there is a strong suggestion of a passage from his treatise *De origine morborum invisibilium*. Paracelsus describes there the 'Mumia' or principle of vitality, significantly called 'the flower of man': significantly because *The Sensitive Plant* as a whole rests on the analogy between human life and the flowers. Paracelsus also mentions a variety of flowers: pinks, lilies, chelidonium; all are sustained by the 'Mumia' so long as they are attached by stem, roots, etc. to the nutrient earth. The 'Mumia' itself is invisible, whether in man or in other living organisms. In man, it can be affected by the imagination and extend its influence to other beings, reminding us strongly of the mutually interpenetrating flowers:

> As the odour of a lily passes from the flower into the surrounding air, so the vital force contained in the invisible body passes into the visible form, and beyond it.

Conversely, Paracelsus is concerned to explain the phenomena of sickness and death in similar terms. The 'Mumia' departs from organic, living forms – unseen by earthly senses – and decay soon sets in. But the 'Mumia' itself does not suffer:

The life that made them live is not dead, but it is departed from the dead form; and if it could be restituted, the form could be made to live again.[17]

Life and death exist from the limited perspective of our ordinary senses, surely a conclusion suggestive of *The Sensitive Plant* once more:

> That garden sweet, that lady fair,
> And all sweet shapes and odours there,
> In truth have never passed away:
> 'Tis we, 'tis ours, are changed; not they.[18]

Shelley's phrasing, however, is at once more strictly Platonic and, simultaneously, touched with a profound scepticism about Paracelsus' optimistic prospect of recovering what has passed – restoring the violet from the crucible.

We shall encounter more cases of Shelley making use of alchemical and Paracelsian occult ideas. These examples must suffice for the present, since we have also to consider a different source of Shelleyan magic. After leaving Oxford, Shelley continued to mingle with occultly inclined company: the circle of friends around Thomas Love Peacock seems to have been strongly imbued with occult interests, in which Shelley no doubt frequently took a leading role. But the real occult 'authority' in the circle was a man named John Frank Newton, the author of an extraordinary and learned defence of vegetable regimen entitled *The Return to Nature* (1811), and a keen student of zodiacal and mythological–oriental antiquities. Shelley mentions him already in the *Notes* to *Queen Mab*; and he is the original of Mr Toobad, the mystical Manichaean millenarian in Peacock's satirical *Nightmare Abbey*.[19] A man of wide reading and uncritical conclusions, he was nevertheless a sufficiently powerful character to fire the imagination of both Peacock and Shelley with his glimpses of a primal mythological truth. He must have been an invaluable guide through the maze of occult literature, old and new, for those who wanted to read it; and there is some evidence that, probably under his auspices, a particularly important contribution to ritual magic and occult theory in England made its influence felt in the Peacock–Shelley circle. I refer to Francis Barrett's compendious work *The Magus* (1801) (see Figure 1).

THE

MAGUS,

OR

CELESTIAL INTELLIGENCER;

BEING

A COMPLETE SYSTEM OF

OCCULT PHILOSOPHY.

————◦◦———

IN THREE BOOKS:

Containing the Antient and Modern Practice of the Cabaliftic Art, Natural and Celeftial Magic, &c.: fhewing the wonderful Effects that may be performed by a Knowledge of the

Celestial Influences, the occult Properties of Metals, Herbs, and Stones,

AND THE

APPLICATION OF ACTIVE TO PASSIVE PRINCIPLES.

EXHIBITING

THE SCIENCES OF NATURAL MAGIC;

Alchymy, or Hermetic Philosophy;

ALSO

THE NATURE CREATION, AND FALL OF MAN;

His natural and fupernatural Gifts; the magical Power inherent in the Soul, &c:; with a great Variety of rare Experiments in Natural Magic:

THE CONSTELLATORY PRACTICE, or TALISMANIC MAGIC;

The Nature of the Elements, Stars, Planets, Signs, &c.: the Conftruction and Compofition of all Sorts of Magic Seals, Images, Rings, Glaffes, &c.;

The Virtue and Efficacy of Numbers, Characters, and Figures, of good and evil Spirits.

MAGNETISM,

AND CABALISTICAL OR CEREMONIAL MAGIC;

In which the fecret Myfteries of the Cabala are explained; the Operations of good and evil Spirits; all Kinds of Cabaliftic Figures, Tables, Seals, and Names, with their Ufe, &c.

THE TIMES, BONDS, OFFICES, AND CONJURATION OF SPIRITS.

TO WHICH IS ADDED

Biographia Antiqua, or the Lives of the most eminent Philosophers, Magi, &c.

The Whole illustrated with a great Variety of

CURIOUS ENGRAVINGS, MAGICAL AND CABALISTICAL FIGURES, &c.

————◦◦———

BY FRANCIS BARRETT, F.R.C.

Profeffor of Chemistry, natural and occult Philosophy, the Cabala. &c. &c.

———————————

LONDON:

PRINTED FOR LACKINGTON, ALLEN, AND CO., TEMPLE OF THE MUSES,

FINSBURY SQUARE.

1801.

FIGURE 1 *Title-page from Francis Barrett, 'The Magus' (1801)*

Barrett's title-page declares the book to contain 'A Complete System of Occult Philosophy', subdivided to include 'the Sciences of Natural Magic', 'Alchymy', 'Magnetism' and 'Cabalistical or Ceremonial Magic'; and its author to be Francis Barrett, F(rater) R(oseae) C(rucis). He had small groups of disciples, it appears, in London, possibly in Cambridge and elsewhere; and it was probably Barrett's stream of Rosicrucianism which a little later inspired the occult novels of Bulwer-Lytton.[20] Systematic, however, Barrett cannot be said to be: rather than a system of occult philosophy, his book is an anthology (without detailed acknowledgments) of the classic magical texts of the mediaeval and Renaissance *adepti*, drawing heavily on the so-called *Fourth Book of Occult Philosophy* attributed (wilfully) to Agrippa of Nettesheim, the *Heptameron* attributed to Peter de Abano and the *Book of Secrets* of Abbot Trithemius. Many lesser and more obscure texts were also used in its compilation, from pseudo-Democritus to Saint Martin, and many that I do not pretend to recognise. Shelley may have found some of its material familiar already since it was employed by Gothic writers, as Timothy d'Arch Smith points out, as a useful quarry for 'authentic' mediaeval touches in their fiction.[21] At any rate, there are several signs of its influence, indirectly or directly, upon him.

For one thing, Barrett like Shelley and Newton recommends a vegetarian diet. And the benefits attributable to vegetarian subsistence go beyond waking life:

> When therefore we are sound in body, not disturbed in mind, our intellect not dulled by meats and drinks . . . but chastely going to bed, fall asleep; then our pure and divine soul, being free from all the evils above recited, and separated from all hurtful thoughts, and now freed by dreaming, is endowed with this divine spirit as an instrument, and doth receive those beams and representations which are darted down, as it were, and shine forth from the Divine Mind into itself; and, as it were in a deifying glass, it does more certain, more clear and efficaciously behold all things than by the vulgar inquiry of the intellect, and by the discourse of reason.[22]

Shelley put the whole idea more compactly:

Some say that gleams of a remoter world
Visit the soul in sleep, – that death is slumber,
And that its shapes the busy thoughts outnumber
Of those who wake and live.[23]

This is different from the more common conception of the soul
rising into higher spheres, the possibility considered by Southey,
for example, in *Joan of Arc*:

Or that the soul, escaped its fleshly clog,
Flies free, and soars amid the invisible world.[24]

The less usual conception we find in Shelley's *Mont Blanc*
corresponds exactly to the description given in Barrett, where
the soul receives those 'beams . . . which are darted down . . .
and shine forth' from the divine world, Shelley's gleams from a
transcendent reality. There is a correspondence, too, in the
shared idea that the visions of the soul surpass the 'busy
thoughts' of the waking, the 'vulgar inquiry of the intellect' –
though Shelley is less strong in his hint that the world of
slumbrous 'shapes' is more real than waking actuality.

Barrett may also fill in something of the background to the
title of Shelley's *Alastor*. Many nineteenth-century critics – who
presumably had the benefit of a classical education – took this to
be a variant of Alastair and the name of the hero of the poem.
Peacock, however, claiming in his *Memoirs of Shelley* to have
originated the title, reveals that the *alastor* is a *recherché* piece of
classical demonology, the name applied to a spirit of evil. The
theme itself was certainly familiar: Shelley had used it in his
juvenile 'Ghasta; or, The Avenging Demon!!!' from *Original
Poetry by Victor and Cazire*. But how had the *alastor* come to the
attention of Peacock and his circle? The answer may be that it
figures in Barrett's *The Magus*.[25]

There are many other potential points of contact between
Barrett and the detailed image-making of Shelley's poetry. Let
us only add that there is much in Barrett on the subject of the
magical projection of images, those *eidola* which fascinated
Shelley throughout his life; there is much of Persian (Magian!)
mythology, which like vegetarianism was of prime interest both
to Shelley and John Frank Newton; and more on the perennial
occult subject of toads.[26]

But Barrett's encyclopaedic book may also serve to bring before us the deeper question about Shelley's occult involvement. Granting, from these examples, and those of other researchers, that the poet is frequently to be found remembering, or half-remembering, or unconsciously echoing the notions of a Paracelsus, an Agrippa or a Francis Barrett – what are we to conclude? Was it all a childhood obsession (like the sailing of paper boats) which Shelley never outgrew?

We have already suggested that it was something more; but what was it which so convinced Shelley that he could find in the recesses of occult literature some key to the mysterious depths of life? The answer would seem mainly to lie in the fact that the great occult authorities, whatever else they may have been, were keen students of the power of imagination.

From a certain perspective, indeed, Paracelsus deserves to be regarded as the first modern investigator of the imagination. The older, traditional Christian estimate had not been such as to inspire interest ('We have followed too much the imagination of our own hearts,' many Christians still recite today). But for Paracelsus the imagination was the sun in the little universe of man. It was, more audaciously, effectually the presence of the Holy Spirit within him. From his medical experience, Paracelsus had noted the influential role of imagination in getting well – and also of the pathological imagination as a source of sickness. It was perhaps from Paracelsus directly that Blake evolved his Romantic doctrine of the Imagination as the essential man.[27] And through the murky medium of occultism and German metaphysics Paracelsus exerted a vast subterranean influence upon Romantic ideas generally. Barrett's *The Magus* is full of passages stressing the importance of 'strong imagination' for the would-be adept. No outward ceremony or magical incantation can prevail on its own, 'neither is it brought into act, unless it be roused up by the imagination, inflamed and agitated by a most fervent and violent desire'. Or again, a vivid pictorial imagination is regarded as a first step toward supernormal capacities of vision – in other words, clairvoyance.[28]

Moreover, we should beware of denigrating occult thought or of identifying it entirely with the Gothic penumbra, the shadow of irrational fear around the scientific universe. The rationalistic cosmology of the Enlightenment had darkened that penumbra by acknowledging only the clearly defined and delimited; but at the outset of the nineteenth century, a retrospective view of the previous century's scientific world-picture was beginning to suggest that there might be more mystery in things. The clockwork cosmos governed by mechanism and the crude knock of atom against atom was starting to give way in the scientific consciousness to a universe of 'energies'. The hidden connections between phenomena were once more the subject of attention, and described in terms of invisible forces like electricity and magnetism. The better part of occult thought took on a new relevance in this period of increasing open-mindedness, suggesting an alternative to the 'corpuscularian philosophy' of material particles that could assume considerable intellectual plausibility. After all, its claims did not now look so far-fetched. Man could examine the far reaches of the cosmos through powerful telescopes, and observe the minutiae of nature through the microscope. Why might not other – 'clairvoyant' – extensions of vision be conceivable? In technology, advances had at last brought the benefits as well as the social problems of industrialisation to a wide public. Such things as air-travel (until recently a fantasy) were a demonstrable possibility in the balloon air-ships which intrigued many other minds besides that of Shelley.[29] With the researches of Galvani, moreover, scientists seemed on the verge of uncovering the principle of life itself. Already in the mid-eighteenth century John Wesley had been convinced that electricity was the 'soul of the universe'. If power from the lightning could on the one hand be tapped by a kite and put to technologically effective use; if electricity was also the force generated by certain fish, who used it to shock and stun their prey; if Galvani had shown that it is actually electricity which produces movements in the limbs – then what might not man be able to achieve by a right concentration of his natural body-electricity, or some closely related force?[30] In this climate of thought, the occultists' aspirations and methods need by no means appear absurd.

The occultists, furthermore, were taking new pains to adopt a little of the approach and language of science. Barrett presented himself as sceptical but unprejudiced, for example, in his estimate of what the great adepts of occultism had been able to perform, 'leaning neither to the side of those who doubt every thing, nor to them whose credulity takes in every report to be circumstantially true'. (The description applies at least as aptly to Shelley.) He reassures his readers that he does not demand blind faith, 'our purpose being to clear the understanding of errors, and not to enforce any thing but what appears to be substantiated by nature, truth, and experiment'. His express aim was impartially 'to investigate the natural magic of the soul'.[31]

In such an atmosphere, Shelley could open his Preface to *Frankenstein, or The Modern Prometheus* with the remark that the experiment it described was in principle 'not of impossible occurrence' – though the unfolding of the theme, he admitted, was essentially fictional.[32] Victor Frankenstein's commingling of modern and occult science, obviously based by Mary upon Shelley himself, was probably not untypical of many of the more daring and speculative minds in those years of scientific adventure. The instance of Coleridge, whom Shelley admired and distrusted, comes immediately to mind. But as his life progressed, Shelley continued to meet and to be influenced by many individuals with similar inclinations.

Godwin was infected by the enthusiasm, and not very many years after the rationalistic pronouncements of the *Enquiry Concerning Political Justice* was to be found devising Gothic novels and studying Hermes Trismegistus; even Mary Wollstonecraft had read her Swedenborg – though perhaps more out of curiosity concerning what Blake was to term his 'Sexual Religion' than from any obscurer motive.[33] Shelley, of course, did not know Blake's work: but on one level Blake's 'prophetic books' are a testimony to the importance of occult ideas on a much wider scale in popular revolutionary circles, following a tradition of radical thought going back to Gnostic and semi-Gnostic groups like the Ranters at the time of the Civil War.[34] The tyrant, after all, is a worshipper of the outer surface of things, ruling by sheer external power. Those who look for some hope of a restored social order of equity and humanity must inevitably look to those invisible, psychological and spiritual aspects of man over which the oppressor has less power. At any rate, occult interests were firmly established in the inner circle of radicals around Shelley by the time he bodily transposed it, in 1818, from England to Italy. Both Mary and Claire seem to have made more-than-casual astrological studies a part of their way of life – Mary using astrological concepts to explain, for example, the train of unlucky events which overtook them every spring in that unhappy land.[35] However, the next and last great upsurge in Shelley's interest was brought about when his cousin Medwin, as Medwin himself relates in his somewhat lopsided *Life of Shelley*, introduced the ménage in 1821 to the wonderful practices of Mesmerism.

'Shelly had never previously heard of Mesmerism', writes Medwin. 'I shewed him a treatise I composed, embodying most of the facts recorded by its adepts, and he was particularly struck by a passage in Tacitus, no credulous historian, who seriously related two cases (witnessed he says by many living) in Egypt, that might stagger the most sceptical.'[36] Despite Medwin's characteristically self-important claim to have introduced Shelley to animal magnetism, the poet must certainly have known something already of its phenomena. At the very least, he had read Mary Wollstonecraft's diatribe on astrologers, magnetisers and spiritists in the latter part of the *Vindication* – scathing as her remarks there may be.[37] And he must have read in the older occult literature of the magic based on 'magnetic' affinities; the ideas once more reach back to Paracelsus, were diffused by Boehme and his disciples including, in England, William Law, and discussed by all manner of 'Rosicrucians' from Robert Fludd down to Francis Barrett. It may on the other hand be true that Shelley was still unaware of the controversial new 'scientific' status accorded to animal magnetism following the campaigns of Mesmer and his pupils.

It is still hard to evaluate Mesmer objectively today.[38] Fundamentally, the 'animal magnetism' he described represented the power of the soul (*anima*) to act upon the body so as to produce or relieve symptoms. In a general sense, therefore, Mesmer's cures anticipate the development of modern theories and therapies like psychoanalysis. Like these modern developments, Mesmerism challenges the older notion of Enlightenment thinkers such as Locke that ideas are in essence powerless images in consciousness, passive reflections of the perceived world, suggesting that at some level ideas may directly affect organic process. There is, historically, a clear line of descent: research on animal magnetism lay behind the work of Freud's mentor, Charcot – and indeed, Freud himself seems to have been familiar with much 'occult' thought.[39] Typical of Mesmer's theories, however, is his stress on the agency of an ethereal 'fluid' medium of the mind's influence, analogous if not identical with the elemental ether which, according to contemporary ideas, carried the invisible material force of the magnet.[40]

Shelley had had repeated intuitions that the human form might be the focal point of organising energies, perceptible or half-perceptible in states of heightened sensitivity. A recurrent image is the luminescence around the adored body of incarnate female beauty, burning through the material vesture which seems to hide it and extending, like an electrical field or the force of a magnet, into the surrounding space. Mesmer finally gave him an exact vocabulary with which to render it, of which he took advantage in writing of his vision of Emilia Viviani and her surrounding aura (or 'glory'):

> The glory of her being, issuing thence,
> Stains the dead, blank, cold air with a warm shade
> Of unentangled intermixture, made
> By Love, of light and motion: one intense
> Diffusion, one serene Omnipresence,
> Whose flowing outlines mingle in their flowing,
> Around her cheeks and utmost fingers glowing
> With the unintermitted blood, which there
> Quivers, (as in a fleece of snow-like air
> The crimson pulse of living morning quiver,)
> Continuously prolonged, and ending never,
> Till they are lost, and in that Beauty furled
> Which penetrates and clasps and fills the world;
> Scarce visible for extreme loveliness.[41]

Such a luminary of Shelley's world could also explicitly be said to 'dart / Magnetic might into its central heart', thus acting as a power linking the individual as one pole with the far reaches of the universe as the other, uniting the focal centre of energy with the half-apprehended harmonies of the unfathomable world reaching into infinity. Further, this 'intense diffusion' of magnetic energy through the all-pervading ether could easily be connected on to the ideas of physical science. Erasmus Darwin expounded in prose and verse his belief in 'ethereal fluids of magnetism, electricity, etc.', and interestingly, the great eighteenth-century scientist Emanuel Swedenborg (before turning visionary) had written extensively on the magnetic fluid, and the vortical or whirlpool movements which explained at once the phenomena of magnetism, gravitation and the orbits of the heavenly bodies, in his *Principia* – subtitled *A Philosophical Explanation of the Elementary World*.[42]

In *Prometheus Unbound* Shelley had already compared the gravitational attraction between earth and moon simultaneously to sexual love and magnetic force.

> *Moon*: I, thy crystal paramour
> Borne beside thee by a power
> Like the polar Paradise,
> Magnet-like of lovers' eyes.

What interested Shelley, Desmond King-Hele points out, was evidently the idea of an underlying unitary power behind all the invisible energies of nature – psychological, magnetic, cosmic.[43] Again in the *Epipsychidion*, the all-interpenetrating power so strongly felt around Emilia and Shelley's other loves becomes an occult dimension holding together human and cosmic life, the phenomena of meteorology and astronomy and the human heart. These are perhaps among the finest instances of Shelley's poetic use of science to suggest a universe very different from the orthodox scientific world-view, a restored universe of human values and hidden analogies, occult interconnections. Thus Shelley attempted, with fascinating results, to integrate the new science into the sense of cosmic harmony that had prevailed in more traditional models of the universe.

The idea of an etheric, fluid world of forces interfused with the physical, of course, antedates Mesmer by centuries. And Shelley, as we have seen, had already been thinking along similar lines before the 'mesmeric revelation' of 1821, having been influenced perhaps by earlier occult sources. But Mesmer is important in that he drew attention to a particular aspect – namely, the therapeutic. It was his discovery that by touch or by a fixed gaze he could throw his patients into spasms, put them into trance states, or anaesthesia, and that under these conditions a kind of healing could take place of a certain range of symptoms. The sceptical academic investigators of Mesmer's work narrowly – though very effectively – missed the point when they objected that it was all the result of 'imagination'.[44] What should have been a spur to examine the powers of the mind became an easy excuse for dismissal. Animal magnetism interested Coleridge, as it interested Shelley, on the contrary, precisely by its suggestion that at the primary level the mind or imagination might not be the inert mirroring of outer reality that Locke had supposed, but an active force, possibly connected with man's sense of organic living warmth.[45] Shelley told Medwin what he thought were the consequences of Mesmerism. It implied, he said, 'that a separation from the mind and body took place – the one being most active and the other an inert mass of matter'.

Hence Mesmerism came to occupy a place alongside Shelley's broad 'Platonism' in opposition to the sceptical, materialist tendency in his thinking (though we cannot rely too much on the details of Medwin's report). Its phenomena suggested that there might be experimental means, as the occultists claimed, of investigating the active power hidden in the philosophers' concept of causation – what Shelley called 'the unknown causes of the known effects perceivable in the Universe', declared by the sceptics to be necessarily unknowable. If, however, in states where ordinary consciousness was suspended, the mind could exert direct healing control over the body, and possess clairvoyant, or even psychokinetic abilities as described by magnetisers, then the notion of a world of ideal forces underlying the physical universe beyond the 'painted veil' of normal perception gained immensely in plausibility. The riddle of the unconscious forces in the depths of the soul and the problem of the limits of knowledge converged in the concept of an occult, primary level of mind and existence. The problem of building a bridge from such a 'primary' level of reality, on the other hand, to the passive ideas and images of ordinary consciousness remained an obstinate and acute one.

Shelley's practical experience with Mesmerism served to emphasise the difficulty. After Medwin and Mary Shelley had experimented with magnetising him, the primary consciousness suddenly showed a disquieting inclination to take over. Shelley reverted to his old boyhood habit of sleep-walking – and sometimes got himself into dangerous positions, though fortunately the upstairs windows were barred.[46] A lady magnetiser was also employed, and the poet's fascination with the relationship of psychic healer to patient, coupled with his own unease about his health, produced the occasional poem *The Magnetic Lady to her Patient*, centred on the theme of the patient's strange power of self-diagnosis when in the magnetised condition. The painful surgical operation Shelley thought he might require, however – lithotomy, the removal of stones from the bladder – would prove fatal. As ever, deep fears lie close beneath the charmed surface of his poetry.

Magnetism had been employed as an analogy for the workings of the unconscious mind before Mesmer: by occultists and by Shelley. Especially remarkable is a passage from the English Behmenist, William Law, where he discusses (or declines to discuss) the issue of free will. A magnet, he contends, moves strictly according to the laws of magnetism. But if it could be interrogated on its movements, it would probably regard itself as self-moved and autonomous, just as man does. And in actuality, he adds, the same does hold true for the motive powers of the soul:

> For all is *magnetism*, all is *sentiment*, *instinct*, and *attraction*, and the freedom of the will has the government of it. There is nothing in the universe but magnetism, and the impediments of it. . . . This is the *life*, the *force*, the *power*, the *nature* of everything, and hence every thing has all that is really good or evil in it; reason stands only as a busybody, an idle spectator of all this, and has only imaginary power over it.[47]

This is an extreme interpretation. It might have appealed to Blake, who had equally little reverence for reason, that idle busybody of a spectator. He shared the vision of man motivated from the elemental depths, moved by those Giants of the abyss 'who are our Energy' and 'who formed this world into its sensual existence'. But Shelley, like Coleridge, sees more value in the conscious deliberations of reason. For them thought may become more than the irritating busybody on the sidelines.

When in Act II of *Prometheus Unbound* Asia and Panthea are conveyed to Demogorgon's subterranean throne by an invisible force – 'as steel obeys the spirit of the stone' – they are certainly being transported by a power which Shelley thought of as manifesting itself both in the natural universe and in the depths of the unconscious psyche.[48] But the transportive power does not itself solve any of the ultimate issues. When they arrive before the ebony darkness of Demogorgon's cave, all the important questions still remain to be asked.

SPECULATIONS ON METAPHYSICS

' "Ay, metaphysics", he said, in a solemn tone, and with a mysterious air, "that is a noble study indeed! If it were possible to make any discoveries there, they would be more valuable than anything the chemists have done, or could do; they would disclose the analysis of mind, and not of mere matter!" '[49]

And so we come to consider Shelley's own pronouncements on the investigation of the mind, embodied in his recorded conversations and prose fragments of speculative thought. The evidence bears out much that we have said about the characteristic mixture in Shelley's mind of passion and reserve, commitment and doubt. 'That which the most consummate intelligences that have adorned this mortal scene inherit as their birthright,' Shelley urges, 'let us acquire (for it is within our grasp) by caution, by strict scepticism concerning all assertions, all expressions; by scrupulous and strong attention to the mysteries of our own nature'.[50]

The fragments collected by Mary Shelley under the rubric *Speculations on Metaphysics* show the poet's constant fascination with psychic phenomena. From his poetry we have seen that the tradition of magic and occultism seemed to him, at least on some occasions, to have opened a rent in the 'painted veil' of mundane perception – though an opening which created problems for the understanding. But just as he therefore refused simple commitment to the inscrutable power of the unconscious depths in the manner of Blake or William Law, so Shelley also strikingly refuses to regard the phenomena of mind as grist to the mill of a constructive metaphysical system like that of Plato or Hegel. He has some sharp phrases for those who 'gave Logic the name of Metaphysics' in that way, substituting for real research 'a concatenation of syllogisms'.[51]

Here we must unfortunately fly in the face of the evidence of Medwin, who asserts in connection with the passage on Shelley and animal magnetism that the poet regarded magnetic phenomena as support for a proof of the soul's immortality. It is impossible to say whether Medwin's memory is at fault, or whether he succumbed to wishful thinking; but Shelley's resistance to this type of argument, so strenuous in every part of his letters and other writings, must be sufficient to cast the gravest doubt upon Medwin's reliability. Shelley was very careful to define his own conception of the science, and would clearly have liked to dissociate it from earlier notions by employing a different title. But: 'Metaphysics is a word which has been so long applied to denote an inquiry into the phenomena of mind, that it would justly be considered presumptuous to employ another.'[52] We should not allow the word to blind us, however, to the novelty and modernity of Shelley's empirical, introspective approach.

The difference between his idea of 'an inquiry into the phenomena of mind' and traditional metaphysics can perhaps best be brought out by examining a conversation with Byron and 'Monk' Lewis which Shelley mentions in his journal of events for the European tour of 1816. The subject of the conversation was that of ghosts: but the issue is not so much whether or not Shelley believed in ghosts (since he plainly regarded them as facts of experience, however they were to be explained) as the kind of implication Shelley was prepared to concede to occult phenomena.

> We talk of Ghosts. Neither Lord Byron nor M. G. L. seem to believe in them; and they both agree, in the very face of reason, that none could believe in ghosts without believing in God. I do not think that all the persons who profess to discredit these visitations, really discredit them; or, if they do in the daylight, are not admonished by the approach of loneliness and midnight, to think more respectfully of the world of shadows.[53]

The belief in, and fear of ghosts, Shelley notices, is deeply ingrained in human feeling. Yet the argument advanced by Byron or Lewis seemed to him a position held 'in the very face of reason'. For all that, it was a well-established mode of reasoning and reveals that at least one in that learned company had been studying the Cambridge Platonists. For it reproduces almost *verbatim* the passage in which Ralph Cudworth defended belief in ghosts as a Christian doctrine. The grounds of his argument were:

> if there be once any visible ghosts or spirits acknowledged as things permanent, it will not be easy for any to give a reason why there might not be one supreme ghost also, presiding over them all and the whole world.[54]

Perfectly true, so far as the argument goes. But as an aid to Christian belief, the argument only works when we think in terms of rival commitments: it presupposes the historical existence and plausibility of a complete Christian system of thought already there as an alternative to scepticism. An indubitable spirit-manifestation might have considerable force, under such circumstances, in persuading the undecided and irresolute to commit themselves to the religious world-view rather than the secular. Shelley, however, did not think in terms of alternative monolithic philosophies in that way. Hence for him the argument loses its force.

Shelley distrusted speculative systems, seeing them to be logic writ large and projected into cosmology with no constraints or guarantees of continuing validity. He distrusted idealism when it went beyond possible experience to affirm absolutes. He distrusted ultimate scepticism too, of course – partly on the grounds of ghosts, 'metaphysical' phenomena and the deeply ingrained human sense of the supernatural. What engages him in his constant fascination with occult and magical ideas is not the possibility of constructing a theology, but the very reverse: the possibility of penetrating beyond the 'painted veil' in a concretely imaginative, experimental way, without presuming upon some absolute truth and yet at the same time freeing oneself from the paralysis of pure scepticism. A metaphysical system of thought usurps the role of the self in its cognitive quest by demanding a total allegiance; scepticism usurps by denying the possibility of higher knowledge *tout court*. Shelley's proposed 'inquiry into the phenomena of mind' is an attempt (comparable in fundamental attitude to much we have mentioned in his poetry) to peer into the depths of life directly, face to face, without abnegating the conscious self in its encounter and confrontation with the world. In investigating Shelley's occult interests and concept of 'metaphysics' we are thus returned once more to the central concerns of his work, and may therefore begin to appreciate what he meant in saying that its results might prove more valuable than anything that could be done in the physical sciences, when he spoke in such solemn and enthusiastic terms on the subject to Hogg.

Richard Holmes has suggested that Shelley's metaphysics is an anticipation of something like modern depth-psychology.[55] This is true, but inadequate to characterise what Shelley intended; really it resembles a wider field that would take in also what we nowadays call psychical research, and it also poses questions about human identity which are still today in the domain of philosophy. Here it is worth examining in some detail what Shelley says in the *Speculations on Metaphysics*, for the light it will later cast on the workings of his imagination. Though only sketchily, he offers bold perspectives for a view of mind and human creativity.

Shelley's own awareness of the hidden depths within the psyche and the compelling forces of the unconscious led him to reject the older philosophical notion of the self as 'thinking substance' (*res cogitans*). Moreover, the sceptical Hume had shown that the perception of self as a substantial presence simply did not occur in a wide range of typical, everyday experience. Hume's conclusion had been that our experience of the ordered world is less the experience of a substantial self than a 'habit of mind', based upon the constant recurrence of certain 'ideas'.[56] But Shelley's response, though indebted to Hume, is rather different. He also challenges the dualism of mind versus world (we have already seen how Mesmerism prompted him to do so too, in another way), but without Hume's reductive intent. Instead of assuming to begin with a mind confronting the universe, and then trying to argue one side of the dichotomy away, Shelley looks at the whole in terms of process, dynamically. He does not regard the diversity and multiplicity of experiences, perceptions of objects and events, as standing over against a unitary substantial self, having somehow to be reduced to it or requiring the self in its turn to be analysed away: he sees how the variety of experience is the raw material from which individuality shapes itself. If we start by examining experience, he notes, and try to isolate 'mind' as such within it, we shall end with a negation or an empty abstraction. But if we look at experience dynamically, we may be enabled to see how events and perceptions are organised and incorporated into an individuality.

Shelley tackles the problem directly in a passage from the *Speculations on Metaphysics*. He registers the difficulty of the interminable variety of raw experience, but adds immediately that this is necessary both for a knowledge of the world of things around us and for the existence of individual consciousness. For: 'These diversities are events and objects, and are essential, considered relatively to human identity, for the existence of the human mind. . . . Mind cannot be considered pure.'[57]

Shelley does not believe that man can be guaranteed his existence or that he can adequately affirm his identity merely on the basis of a concept (such as 'imperishable soul', 'thinking substance', etc.). Likewise he is aware that the self is not a percept accompanying all other percepts throughout our experience, the notion which had been exploded by Hume. Man's mind and identity cannot be considered 'pure', i.e. apart from his empirical experience, at all. Man achieves his identity, separating himself out from the world-process, through organising and connecting his experience and thought, making judgments, accepting and rejecting ideas, actively defining the limits of his being. In one and the same process he establishes objectivity in his knowledge of outer reality, and fashions what Shelley calls 'that connexion in the train of our successive ideas, which we term our identity'.

Man's self-awareness is therefore a less-than-straightforward affair. Man, in Shelley's view, finds his identity in the connecting of his experience, in his continuing personal history as an activity of self-definition. But the roots of that activity lie below the level of consciousness, as Shelley notes in a Wordsworthian passage of the *Speculations*. Of the roots of his being, therefore, man cannot be directly conscious through perception or conceptual thought. Hence all that Shelley can directly say on the matter is: 'We are intuitively conscious of our own existence, and of that connexion in the train of our successive ideas, which we term our identity.'[58] In the results of the activity (the 'connexion' of ideas and perceptions) we discover what 'we term our identity', but of the foundations of the activity on which it rests we have ultimately only an intuitive, undifferentiated awareness. It was in the hope of exploring further the hidden depths where that activity originates that Shelley turned to the occultists and the phenomena of magic, as a possible link between the profundities at the source of our being and the world of conscious experience. If Shelley possessed a continued hope of man's immortality or super-earthly destiny, it did not lie in a philosophical, Platonic 'proof' of the soul's imperishable nature, but in something resembling Goethe's intuition (which he confided to Eckermann) of the primacy of activity. 'To me,' Goethe commented, 'the eternal existence of my soul is confirmed from my concept of activity; if I work on incessantly till my death, nature is bound to give me another form of existence when the present one can no longer sustain my spirit.'[59] It is no accident, in view of his dynamic philosophy of the self, that Shelley not only remained open to the possibility of man's immortality but that he often dallied with the idea of reincarnation. Plainly he too felt that activity must somehow embody itself in ever new natural forms when the present ones have worn out, and that the self must go on to expand its range of connections when it has outgrown the scope of its present life.

But here Shelley refuses any dogmatic conclusions. In his poetry, he registers the appeal of images and intellectual doctrines, exploring rather than affirming, entertaining ideas rather than committedly asserting them. In his philosophical *Speculations*, we have the merest beginning of a developmental view of mind and knowledge; and we may doubt whether the conceptual materials then lay to hand to continue it, or whether Shelley could have forged the intellectual instruments he would have needed to continue it himself. What is important for us, however, is the information Shelley's philosophical approach gives us about his own underlying experience of the self: the sense of identity as an achievement, a victory wrested from the flux and variety of empirical experience, the establishing of coherence and connection. Obviously such a mode of self-awareness feels very different from a consciousness assured of the substantial presence of a 'thinking thing' (*res cogitans*). In this respect, Shelley is part of a larger cultural shift toward a new experience of the self which extends far beyond our scope of discussion – but which certainly has a great deal to do with the rise of Romanticism. Within English Romanticism, Shelley offers a unique clarity in the articulation and poetic realisation of self-awareness in its tension with the energies of imaginative experience.[60]

Against the background of Shelley's dynamic sense of the self we can place the patterns of thought and imagination whose background we have discussed in earlier chapters of this book. The conscious self, as we have seen, is never a 'given' for Shelley's experience, but is defined in the balance of forces which threaten to overwhelm and 'extinguish' it. The self is constantly rescued from the brink of extinction; but we can now also appreciate how Shelley regards the risk, the urge to further expansion of consciousness, the openness to yet more variety of experience, as essential to the process. 'Mind cannot be considered pure' – identity itself emerges from the struggle against mental dissolution. The answer can therefore never be a static consolidation of the mind's resources, an acceptance of the world on this side of the 'painted veil', and the injunction not to lift the veil must always be partially disobeyed. In this way we can understand, too, the tendency of intense mental states in Shelley's imagining to move toward an existence of their own, straining against the controlling self at the centre of awareness. The mind in Shelley's view must constantly permit imaginative intensities to undermine its unity, in order to regain that unity once more in a continuous process – rather as walking upright depends upon a controlled abandoning of static balance in order to regain a momentary equilibrium after each step forward.

The tendency of Shelley's experiences to attain to a kind of separate existence, a daemonic half-life of their own, has in fact been frequently noticed. From being a boy, Shelley enjoyed yielding himself up to self-dramatisations and daemonic energies, impersonating fiends and monsters for the delight and terror of his friends. Later he justified his sense of spiritual presences through Plato's notion of the innumerable daemons, regarded as intermediaries between the divine and mortal worlds in *The Banquet* which Shelley translated and loved. These were not just ideas to Shelley, but sometimes strong experiences. His notebooks are full of drawings showing mountains, lakes, streams, skies – and often enough they are populated by curious, sub-human beings, evidently elemental creatures which Shelley imagined, or saw, living there (see Figure 2). Neville Rogers is surely correct in explaining the famous incident at Tan-yr-allt in February 1813, when Shelley was attacked in the night by a mysterious assailant, as an encounter between the poet and one of the 'monsters of his

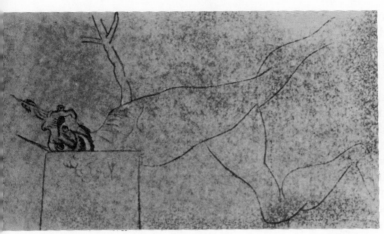

FIGURE 3 *The Tan-yr-allt assailant:*
sketch by Shelley

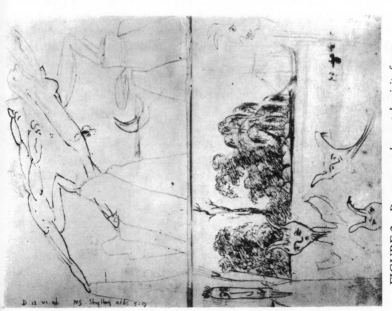

FIGURE 2 *Daemons, elemental spirits from*
Shelley's notebooks

thought' (see Figure 3). In an overwrought mood, one of Shelley's imaginations took on for a time a frighteningly independent reality; he even fired a gun at it, and was able to sketch its hideous appearance on a wood screen.[61] After the death of Claire Clairmont's daughter by Byron, Allegra, for example, he was walking by the sea with Edward Williams in the moonlight along the Gulf of Spezia, when he suddenly went rigid and stared into the surf. Apparently he saw a naked child rising out of the sea, its hands clasped, and could only keep saying 'There it is again! – there!', as if he expected Williams to see the apparition too. Williams attributed the incident to an overactive imagination, 'a sort of natural magic'.[62]

Basing himself on a passage in *The Triumph of Life*, Richard Holmes concurs with Medwin in regarding Shelley's 'world of ghosts and spirits' as 'projections' of his own personality, 'parts of himself left behind, or in the name of his old sceptical master Lucretius, "idols", self-created delusions, and none the less real for that'.[63] But we must remember that these are extreme cases, bordering upon the pathological state where the 'connexion' of personal history and identity is lost, and the mind is attacked by its own creations. Under more normal conditions, Shelley's sense of the daemonic led less to a feeling of the dissolution of identity in a cloud of phantoms than to a dramatic image of the self: the idea that the mind might be a theatre where contending and interacting psychic forces play out their struggle, and from the balance of whose powers man's own identity asserts itself in a victory of dynamic equilibrium. In this way, Shelley moves toward a picture which could reconcile his appreciation of the powerful, compelling forces of the unconscious (shown in 'magnetism', etc.) and of the need to preserve the reasoning moral faculties of the higher mind.

Similar conceptions were not unknown already in the eighteenth century. Andrew Baxter's *Enquiry into the Nature of the Human Soul* (1737) had speculated boldly on the nature of dreams, in which he observed that man's creative powers are unleashed to a greater extent than in everyday life. Since, however, the soul is 'asleep' throughout, and its inherent rationality no longer prevails, Baxter proposes that the dreams are caused by other beings acting through man's sensory organisation. As daemonic beings, they might be good spirits or bad. John Beer has shown that Baxter's ideas were of interest to both Coleridge and Southey, as well as anticipating Swedenborg.[64] But Baxter represents a 'safer' philosophy of mind than Shelley, for all his awareness of the potential force and terror of the imagination. His central aim, as Beer points out, is to preserve the soul inviolate as a theological *ens rationale*, defending it vigorously against any imputation of irrationality, rather than opening up a dynamic view of the dreaming imagination. Nevertheless it is interesting to see the direction of thought taken by a writer on the soul who was still read in the Romantic period. Such thought was to be taken much further by Blake – even more strongly influenced by occult ideas than Shelley – when he saw man as an interplay of 'Giant' forces below the level of consciousness, the Four Zoas or Eternals who are in every man, and who figure as 'Visionary forms dramatic' in the tremendous imaginings of the 'prophetic books'. At the other extreme to Baxter, Blake loses almost all interest in the conscious, rational soul; his attention is fastened on the play of energies beneath the surface. Between them, adopting what is arguably the more coherent and balanced view, comes Shelley's conception of the mind and its daemonic forces. Joined with what the poet learned from alchemy, magic, science and magnetism, Shelleyan daemonology is an important constituent in the mixture which was to create the psychic theatre of *Prometheus Unbound*.

From the perspective of Shelley's science of Metaphysics, or 'inquiry into the phenomena of mind', we can at any rate begin to appreciate why it was that the polar extremes of experience, where consciousness breaks down or loses coherence, were of such importance in Shelley's concept of the imagination's world. And we can perhaps also begin to understand how it was that for Shelley scepticism and idealism, intense Sensibility emotion and Gothic fear, were not simply opposing literary and philosophical traditions. The 'twin Destinies' of imaginative search were not for him contrary systems, but manifold states of being and complexes of feeling with a life that seemed at least half their own, – so that Shelley was often inclined to treat them less like rival philosphies of life than like living beings themselves: those daemons and other 'monsters of my thought' he saw and sketched in his notebooks.

PLANETARY MUSIC

The intellectual descendants of Hume still provide many of the philosophical assumptions of literary criticism today. From the 'empirical' approach of the New Criticism to its latter-day successors and refinements, critical approaches follow recognisably in the general direction pointed out by Hume. Even the newest, much-trumpeted techniques of 'deconstruction' etc. can be seen to resemble Hume's sceptical analysis of the self. The advocates of deconstruction undertake to expose the illusory presence of a governing, intentional mind – in the name of the autonomy of imagination, its ability to register cultural and psychological forces which no individual mind can claim to control. In this situation, Shelley's dynamic view of self-consciousness and his profound acknowledgment of the uncontrollable energies of imagination, while at the same time finding room for the deliberative moral self, still asks for urgent consideration and his findings seem as relevant now as they seemed hard to comprehend a century and a half ago.

Shelley found one particular image with which to sum up his sense of the relation, both continuous and broken, between the concealed dimensions of human experience and the limited sphere of conscious control: 'planetary music'. That harmony of vast cosmic spaces is often heard in the music of Shelley's poetry. But it is also the music of man's individual soul, an idea often employed by Sensibility writers, and inherited by Shelley from them as well as from Platonic speculators on the *harmonia mundi* and its echo in the microcosm, man.[65] In the *Epipsychidion* it appears as a music from beyond the normal faculties of consciousness, like the unutterable sweetness of speech of Emilia Viviani:

> And from her lips, as from a hyacinth full
> Of honey-dew, a liquid murmur drops
> Killing the sense with passion; sweet as stops
> Of planetary music heard in trance.

And as the lightnings of her eyes are like the reflections dancing at the top of a well too deep to be sounded, this music too comes from regions 'too deep / For the brief fathom-line of thought or sense'.[66] Hence, Shelley wrote elsewhere, the poet is like 'a nightingale, who sits in darkness and sings to cheer his own solitude with sweet sounds; his auditors are as men entranced by the melody of an unseen musician, who feel that they are moved and softened, yet know not whence or why'.[67]

Yet Shelley does not suggest that we abolish the self, or rule it a delusion. The planetary music indeed would overwhelm our puny nature if heard in its cosmic splendour; but the poet is an individual man among men, and can accommodate it only to his limited capacity, even though his images have a resonance beyond his private understanding. A place is found for the conscious self, albeit an unstable and precarious one, one shot through with the Shelleyan paradox of revelation and concealment:

> The beauty of the internal nature cannot be so far concealed by its accidental vesture, but that the spirit of its form shall communicate itself to the very disguise, and indicate the shape it hides from the manner in which it is worn. A majestic form and graceful motions will express themselves through the most barbarous and tasteless costume. Few poets of the highest class have chosen to exhibit the beauty of their conceptions in its naked truth and splendour; and it is doubtful whether the alloy of costume, habit, &c., be not necessary to temper this planetary music for mortal ears.[68]

Shelley's literary, philosophical, scientific and psychical studies provide a background to his thought which will serve as an invaluable guide in the chapters to come, where we turn to the detailed interpretation of some of his major verse. The coordinates we have established – above all, the tension and dialectic between the polar extremes of awareness – will allow us to see individual poems within the setting of Shelley's complex acknowledgment of alternative realities. That in turn should remind us that each poem is to be read as an exploration, an effort in shared experience, often as the posing of a wider question, rather than as a monument to Shelley's philosophical ideas. For though Shelley may justly be called a dialectical poet, he is of a fundamentally different cast of mind from, say, W. B. Yeats. In the instance of Yeats, points out Denis Donoghue, there is an oscillation from one view to its contrary from one creative period to the next. 'Sometimes one side of a question will hold Yeats's affection for years, but sooner or later conflict begins again.'[69] With Shelley, on the other hand, one is always aware of the whole constellation of forces and rival directions of thought. Although a poem may take as its theme only one aspect of Shelley's mind, a work hardly ever seems to amount even to a temporary 'statement of faith'; in a poem written next day, or the next week, one often finds Shelley thinking in the contrary way with equal poetic force and imaginative conviction. Rarely, in fact, do his greater poems fail to call attention at some point to their own possible ironic reversal and limitations. In Shelley's imaginative development there are indeed 'twin Destinies', not 'phases of the moon'.

Our interpretation of Shelley's work will not therefore follow a strictly chronological framework – though we shall try to respect the differences between the earlier and the later poet. We shall take, to begin with, poems such as *Mont Blanc*, the *Skylark* ode, *Alastor* and the *Hymn to Intellectual Beauty*, the poems in which the rapidly evolving poet first managed to define in important respects the scope and style of his poetry in the formative years between 1815 and 1820. The phase culminates, and transcends itself, in the composition of *Prometheus Unbound*. At this stage of his career Shelley is, in Blake's term, a 'Mental Traveller', an explorer of states of mind and perception through the cycles of existence. Sometimes he seems to himself to be a wanderer in dreary night; sometimes to have lost his way under the hill and to be dreaming strange dreams; sometimes to be hastening toward the light on the horizon.

> He wanders, like a day-appearing dream,
>   Through the dim wildernesses of the mind;
> Through desert woods and tracts, which seem
>   Like ocean, homeless, boundless, unconfined.

Sometimes he is accompanied on his travels by human or supernatural companions; oftener he is a solitary pilgrim, with only the revolving stars to light his way.

To keep pace with Shelley, however, and to comprehend the continuously shifting vistas which pass before our eyes on the mental voyage, we must be prepared to look beyond the perspectives of literature, science and even of philosophy. We must plot our course against the huge backdrop of the great myths of good and evil which have given meaning and value to human life over the millennia of religious history. Though Shelley modestly backed down from a projected 'great work, embodying the discoveries of all ages, & harmonising the contending creeds by which mankind have been ruled',[70] we must be prepared to encounter gods and daemons from Greece, India and Iran; to hurl defiance at the tyrannic Demiurge, God of repressive Law; to wrestle with angels, and enter the delusive paradise of Lucifer. Shelley offers a new resolution of these mythic forces, and with it a new vision of what it means to be human.

4 On the Devil and Devils

In Shelley's mature poetry the contrary tendencies of mind become mythical presences, complex 'daemonic' forces which the poet works to relate to man's conscious centre of being and his moral preoccupations.

Plato's daemons were a race occupying a position in the hierarchy of things midway between gods and men. Shelley's daemons, however, stand rather intermediate between mind and world, and convey his sense of the mind as an active agent. Whereas Locke regarded knowledge as passive reception, Shelley's poetry portrays the mind in the process of transformation, modifying existing forms and presuppositions to accommodate the freshness of the new, learning wisdom through constant adaptation – not just knowledge through compilation. The psychic powers who weave the veil of appearances and web of thought which mediates reality to our mind are continually at work, little though we may be aware of them. Shelley sees the delicacy of the balance that enables us to cope with the impinging world around us and maintain a healthy self-awareness. A predominance of one power can soon make us lose grip on objective fact, and the mind can build itself into an unreal inner world; a tip the other way can leave us helpless before a threatening, inhuman landscape. It is part of Shelley's importance that he thus recognises the moral dimension in all knowing. To create imaginative forms for these precariously balanced forces on the margins of human consciousness, Shelley made use of – and reinterpreted for his own purposes – some of the mythological visions of East and West. The orthodox scheme of God and the Devil proved too simple to describe the workings of psychic energies which sometimes threatened the inherent balance of the mind.

100

THE AHRIMANIC PHILOSOPHY

> A match between Scythrop and Mr Toobad's daughter would be a very desirable occurrence. She was finishing her education in a German convent, but Mr Toobad described her as being fully impressed with the truth of his Ahrimanic philosophy, and being altogether as gloomy and antithalian a young lady as Mr Glowry himself could desire for the future mistress of Nightmare Abbey. (Thomas Love Peacock, *Nightmare Abbey*)

Ahriman, the evil daemon of the Zoroastrians, is agonised or negative Thought. He is the source of all falsity, deceit, doubt, destruction and spiritual darkness. According to the sacred books of the ancient religion of Iran, although the material world was not Ahriman's creation it did come into being because of his primordial act of aggression. It is the domain where the powers of light, summed up in Ohrmazd, are temporarily defeated – until the last days of the universe. For though Ahriman as the spirit of darkness is co-eternal with the divine light, he will finally be overcome.[1]

This tremendous imagination has been one of the most powerful and persistent myths in religious history, from the Iranian prophet Zarathustra (or Zoroaster) who first proclaimed it centuries ago up to the present day with our uncompromising awareness of evil. In Manichaeism, its dualism entered into Christianity to constitute a heretical challenge to the teaching of God the Creator – the most dangerous rival system orthodoxy had to face. The successors of the original Manichaeans in the Middle Ages, the Bogomils and Cathars were ruthlessly persecuted until they were stamped out by the champions of orthodox Christianity, though their doctrines and some of their literature still survive. Driven underground, the tradition of dualism continued to appeal to scattered groups of religious enthusiasts and visionaries, until in due course it exercised its sway over the imaginations of some of the modern Romantic poets, above all Shelley. Wordsworth, Blake, Byron, Southey and Peacock were also touched by its power – but none so profoundly or importantly as Shelley.[2]

Our epigraph from Peacock's *Nightmare Abbey* rightly suggests that Shelley found the myth of Ahriman, not in the handbooks of comparative mythology but in an already living contemporary form. We have already met the personalities behind Peacock's characters: Scythrop, Mr Glowry's wayward son, is Shelley himself. Mr Toobad is John Frank Newton, the authoritative occultist of the Peacock–Shelley circle at Marlow. It was the latter who expounded a new form of the Ahrimanic myth, in such a way as to capture the imagination of Peacock (always stimulated by scholarly antiquities) who even began to sketch out an ambitious, never-to-be-completed epic called *Ahrimanes.*[3] It was probably through Peacock that Shelley too became firmly engrossed in the study of 'the Manichaean philosophy' and the conception of the sinister Ahriman. Newton saw in the prevalent materialistic thought and culture of his own age the ruling presence of the Ahrimanic spirit. He saw it in the rationalism of the post-Enlightenment sciences which denied the divine in nature; in the psychology which denied human freedom and creativity and submitted man to a dark Necessity, ascribing 'to this Principle of Evil a compulsive power over our wills, and that so very absolute and strong, that it is not only out of our own disposal whether we will commit wickedness or not, but such as even God himself is not able to control or overpower';[4] he saw it in views of history which denied or neglected the importance of the Mysteries and secret societies;[5] and in a cuisine which had abandoned vegetarianism for the fallen delights of a carnivorous diet, taking man out of his innocent harmony with nature. It was Newton's vegetarian ideas which first brought him to Shelley's attention. But it was his wide and sometimes eccentric range of knowledge which ultimately had the greater effect on Shelley's poetry.

Newton's conviction had it that the core of the ancient Mysteries (secret rites celebrated in antiquity at Eleusis and elsewhere) was astrological. The Zodiac was the key to the harmony between man and the cosmos, and the guardians of ancient knowledge had long preserved the details of its meaning and construction, keeping the mysteries it contained secret from the profane and veiling them in arcane symbols and rites. A complete cosmology and history of the world was to be found by those who contemplated the twelve zodiacal signs aright. The Greeks, and classical astrologers generally, were only echoing much more ancient conceptions deriving from the East – Egypt, India – and so stretching back to the beginnings of recorded history. The particular Zodiac discovered at Dendera (see Figure 4), on which Newton based his ideas, we now know to represent a late stage of mythic and astrological syncretism; but in the mind of John Frank Newton, and many orientalists of the day, it justified the conception of a primordial astrological

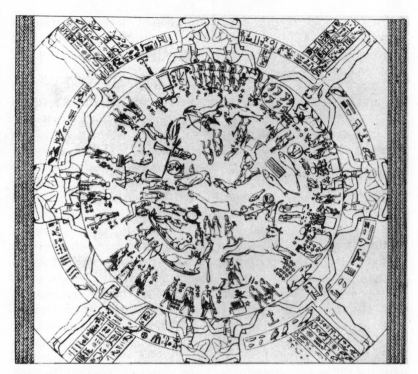

FIGURE 4   *The Zodiac of Dendera – 'wild images / Of more than man,
where marble daemons watch / The Zodiac's brazen mystery': from
Dominique Denon, 'Voyage dans la Basse et la Haute Egypte' (1802)*

wisdom at the foundation of religion.[6] Newton was certainly
familiar with the work of prominent oriental scholars like Sir
William Jones, Faber, Maurice, Moor, Wilkins and others,
including French authorities like Dupuis, whom Newton does
not actually mention but whom it has been shown he owes a
good deal. A division of the signs of the Zodiac into four
quarters, each ruled by a different god, gave him a four-fold set
of correspondences binding together Indian, Iranian, Egyptian
and Greek mythology – an influential combination which
proved useful to Shelley in the cosmology of *Prometheus
Unbound*. Already in *Alastor* he pictured the ruined temple of
Dendera, with its:

> Stupendous columns, and wild images
> Of more than man, where marble daemons watch
> The Zodiac's brazen mystery, and dead men
> Hang their mute thoughts on the mute walls around.[7]

The traditional inscrutability of ancient Egyptian wisdom always kept a hold over Shelley's imagination. But the real excitement was generated by the Iranian connection in Newton's ideas.

Interest in Iranian antiquities was partly a phenomenon of the late eighteenth century, resulting from a number of discoveries and a certain amount of progress being made in the understanding of ancient Persian languages, bringing the religious ideas of Zoroastrianism into the focus of contemporary debate. The undecipherable inscriptions on old Iranian kingly monuments had been discussed in Europe since 1602, when the Spanish–Portuguese ambassador to the Persian court remarked with Shelleyan irony that their language was completely unknown, the characters being 'neither Persian, Arabic, Armenian nor Hebrew, the languages now in use in the district; so that everything contributes to erase from memory that which the ambitious king so desired to render eternal'. No progress had been made a century later in decoding the inscriptions, so that Thomas Hyde (an important early student of Iranian religion) concluded that they were made up by someone at random, combining wedge-form into as many permutations as he could. Almost inadvertently he thus originated the modern name of the script: cuneiform (Latin *cuneus* = wedge). In 1765 Carsten Niebuhr brought back copies of numerous inscriptions and published them in a French and in a German colume, proving that they were indeed writing – but very little else. Efforts at decipherment continued to be made, however, by such men as the Baron de Sacy, Frederik Münter and others whose names may well have been known in the Peacock– Shelley–Newton circle.[8] At any rate, it is noteworthy that Shelley's heroine in *Laon and Cythna* seems to be aware of the latest philological discoveries:

> And on the sand would I make signs to range
>   These woofs, as they were woven, of my thought;
> Clear, elemental shapes, whose smallest change
>   A subtler language within language wrought:
>   The key of truths which once were dimly taught
> In old Crotona.[9]

For cuneiform had finally been read successfully in 1802 by the German scholar Grotefend. Evidently Cythna regards it, with

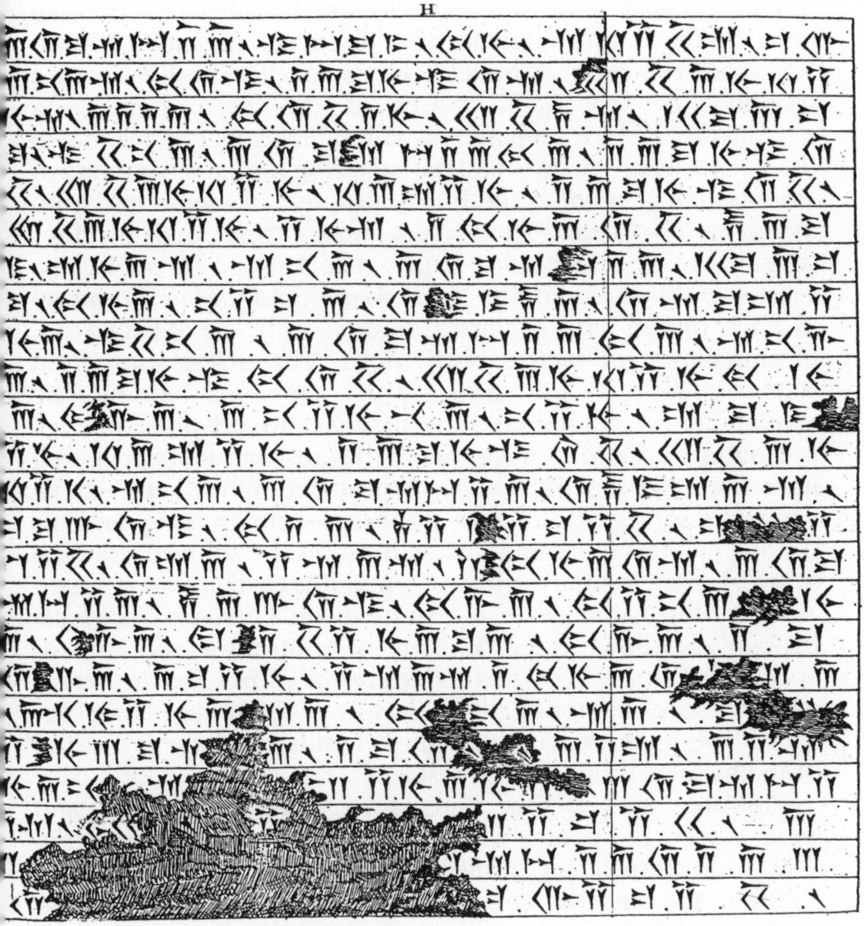

FIGURE 5 *Cuneiform inscription: – 'Clear, elemental shapes, whose smallest change / A subtler language within language wrought': from Carsten Niebuhr, 'Voyage en Arabie' (1776).*

its multiple combinations of 'clear, elemental shapes' as the original language of thought, and the older respect for the primitive quality of hieroglyphics had been definitively ousted. The cryptic reference to the sage of Crotona reminds us that, according to some traditions, Pythagoras was himself a disciple of Zoroaster.[10]

The crucial step forward in fathoming the ancient script had been made as the outcome of a discovery of another kind. Abraham-Hyacinthe Anquetil du Perron had in 1754 seen a fragment of the sacred books of the Zoroastrians – a circumstance which set him on a path of investigation leading to the Far East, where he found the surviving Indian community of Zoroastrians known as the Parsis and, by fair means and foul, managed to extract from them manuscripts and precious religious texts. Du Perron returned to Europe to publish an extensive translation of the *Zend-Avesta, ouvrage de Zoroastre* in 1771, on the basis of Parsi traditions as to the meaning and pronunciation of their sacred books. The information from classical authors was now vastly supplemented by the availability of whole texts of hymns and religious poems, attributed to Zoroaster himself.[11] Interest in and speculation upon the religion of old Iran boomed accordingly. Stuart Curran has cited some fifty titles of books in which Shelley and his friends might have found information on the subject – though some of them are fairly obscure – and it is certain that Peacock and Newton were aware of Anquetil du Perron's discovery. Probably Shelley was too. Iranian enthusiasm was widespread, and even Robert Forsyth's *Principles of Moral Science* (from one of whose chapter-heads Shelley drew the phrase 'a passion for reforming the world') was partly cast in the form of a vision of the ancient Iranian sage Hystaspes!

Voltaire had said that Zoroaster's writings preceded, and were indeed the source of the Bible and the religions of the West; his reductive approach was followed by Dupuis and Volney, the latter's *Les Ruines* certainly being known to Shelley.[12] To the mythological syncretists, on the other hand, the *Avesta* was not so much a means of exploding the 'revealed religion' of the Bible as of regaining an original wisdom. In this they were following in an earlier tradition of interpreting the ancient myths which had flourished in the Renaissance, grafting onto it the new scientific discoveries of the philologists. For to Ficino and Pico della Mirandola and their successors, Zoroaster had been one of the *prisci theologi*, one of the divinely inspired thinkers, that is to say, in a line descending from primordial times down to Plato. Ficino, who was influenced by the Byzantine scholar Gemistus Pletho, sometimes put Zoroaster first on the list before the renowned Hermes Trismegistus himself; on other occasions he supposed that poetic theology began simultaneously with Zoroaster among the Persians and with Hermes among the Egyptians. Henceforward, Zoroaster was an integral part of the revived Hermetic–magical tradition, and it is worth pointing out that the figure who appears in the work of Shelley and John Frank Newton is by no means purely the ancient Zarathustra, author of the *Avesta* dating back a millennium before the time of Christ, but 'the magus Zoroaster' – the magician and *priscus theologus* seen through the spectacles of the post-Renaissance Neoplatonic revival.[13]

There is no doubt that Newton was acquainted with the more solid work of Anquetil du Perron, Dupuis, etc. But he was equally happy citing the Neoplatonists or the work of de Gebelin – now remembered as the founder of the 'occult' interpretation of the Tarot cards.[14] Moreover, the figure of 'The Magus' had recently been given a new lease of life in Francis Barrett's handbook of that name. The Magi were originally a priestly Iranian caste or tribe, already famous in antiquity for their fire-worship and mysterious practices. Later the term came to be used more disparagingly. In the New Testament we have both the good Magi who came to the nativity, known to them by star-wisdom, and the wicked adept Simon Magus who covets the miracle-working powers of the apostles. Again it was the Renaissance Hermetists and Neoplatonists who restored the idea of the Magus to its religious dignity: the idea of the man who could control or manipulate the elemental powers of *magia naturalis*, 'the natural magic of the soul'. The great, revered original Magus Zoroaster played an important role in re-establishing the authority and dignity of that idea.

Barrett's magical textbook contains a 'particular and interesting account' of 'Zoroaster, the son of Oromasius'.[15] He was the first Magus – and thus the prototype of what Barrett's reader wants to become. With his usual undecisiveness, Barrett presents the several incompatible images of Zoroaster, citing both modern researchers such as Thomas Stanley's *History of Oriental Philosophy* and a scattering of classical sources. But he manages to include a remarkably brief and forceful resumé of the myth of Ahriman:

That a war arose betwixt the army of light and that of darkness, which at last ended in an accommodation, of which the angels were mediators, and the conditions were that the inferior world should be wholly left to the government of Arimanius for the space of 7000 years, after which it should be restored to light.[16]

Here we have the core of the idea so important to Mr Toobad, Peacock's parody of John Frank Newton:

He maintained that the supreme dominion of the world was, for wise purposes, given over for a while to the Evil Principle; and that this precise period of time, commonly called the enlightened age, was the point of his plenitude of power. He used to add that by and by he would be cast down, and a high and happy order of things succeed; but he never omitted the saving clause, 'Not in our time'; which last words were always echoed in doleful response by the sympathetic Mr Glowry.[17]

We notice that it is the darker aspects of the Zoroastrian vision which seem to have been taken up by the Marlow circle. By ineluctable Necessity the world-as-it-is has been given over to Ahriman, the Evil Principle. In Peacock's *Ahrimanes*, the mortal lovers Darassah and Kelasris struggle helplessly against that all-ruling Necessity, temporarily weighted in favour of the Evil Principle, and the plan of the poem makes it clear that no one has any chance of altering the nature of things. Hence, although we are promised the coming of the saviour Mithras at some point in the future, in imaginative terms Necessity and Ahriman have become virtually identical. The lovers' only course in Peacock's earlier outline of *Ahrimanes* is total retreat from harsh reality into the South Sea paradise of Oromaze and his genii; and in the second, more ambitious version, Peacock dissolves the moral struggle into a tissue of illusions, where it turns out that Darassah in her heart of hearts is thoroughly in the grip of the Evil Power and Kelasris is actually an Oromazian divinity in mortal disguise, so that the outcome of events is ultimately fixed by the root-nature of the characters.[18] Perhaps one reason why Peacock never finished *Ahrimanes* was that he discovered epic action to be impossible within the Necessitarian universe he had created.

The association of Ahriman with Necessity is one which also helps us to understand Shelley's use of the myth. He escapes the paralysis of Peacock's imagination in the face of unalterable Necessity, however, by internalising the 'two spirits' into psychological powers, as in the following passage from his late essay *On the Devil and Devils*:

> The Manichaean philosophy respecting the origin and government of the world, if not true, is at least an hypothesis conformable to the experience of actual facts. To suppose that the world was created and is superintended by two spirits of a balanced power and opposite dispositions, is mainly a personification of the struggle we experience within ourselves, and which we perceive in the operations of external things as they affect us, between good and evil. The supposition that the good spirit is, or hereafter will be, superior, is a personification of the principle of hope . . . without which, present evil would be intolerable.[19]

For Shelley, the contest of Light and Darkness, Ohrmazd and Ahriman, is less an objective feature of the world than a myth which may serve to articulate man's response to the world. Ahriman is an imagination that will be mythically relevant to our inner response when we view the world under the terms of an intransigent Necessity; for the world is such an unsatisfactory place that, if we thought it unreformable, the 'present evil' of our state would indeed be intolerable. Ohrmazd is likewise mythically relevant to the attitude of hope which must in some measure offset our recognition of the 'Necessity of hate and ill' if our life is to be acceptably human. Of course, Shelley does not believe that the mind (or the world) can be analysed 'pure'; he is not therefore interpreting the Iranian dualistic myth merely subjectively. His interpretation rather concentrates on the point of interaction where man encounters the world, in action and understanding – and, from the converse side, on external things 'as they affect us'. He thereby achieves a greater metaphysical depth, penetrating to the 'daemonic' level of imaginative realisation, while Peacock is still manipulating ideas and allegories. And far from besetting moral action with a withering paralysis, Shelley makes the myth turn upon man's achievement of a balance of forces that leaves him free to act, or even spurs him to do so with hope. Nevertheless, darkness and evil are not to be ignored.

A further dimension of the daemonic imagination of 'Ahriman' perhaps became clear to Shelley through another work which claimed an Iranian ancestry. In *The Magus*, Francis Barrett refers to various literary traditions which mention the books attributed to the great Iranian prophet; some of them, he adds, 'were printed, together with the versis of the Sybils at Amsterdam, in the year 1689, according to Opsopaeus's edition, Oracula Magica Zoroastris, cum Scholiis Plethonis & Pselli'.[20] He means the *Chaldaean Oracles of Zoroaster* which, so far from being early products of Persian literature comparable to the *Gathas*, originated in the hot-house Gnostic–Neoplatonic atmosphere of late antique culture, into which any Iranian elements have been thoroughly absorbed. Here again we have to do, not with the ancient reformer of Aryan religion, but with the 'Magus Zoroaster', the product of a long mystical–philosophical tradition.[21] The Byzantine commentaries of Psellus and Pletho had accepted the authority and antiquity of the *Oracles*, which had persuaded Ficino to do likewise, so that these strange documents had become an accepted part of the picture of Zoroastrian wisdom – and magic.[22] Whether Shelley believed them authentic it is impossible to say; but there are resemblances in idea and expression which hint that he may have known them. And they may have been instrumental in clarifying for his imagination the link between Ahriman, Necessity and the state of fear.

'On beholding thyself, fear!' – says one of the *Chaldaean Oracles*.[23] The imagery of the fragments also constantly stresses the fear and anxiety undergone by the Mental Traveller in his progress toward cosmic and spiritual knowledge. There are the fathomless voids and abysses, the dark and winding passageways, the fitful bursts of energy from the 'Intellectual Whirlwinds' as from the 'fountainous craters' of volcanoes. In common with the Gnostic, Hermetic and magical literature with which it is contemporaneous, the *Chaldaean Oracles* conveys a sense of the cosmic system as a vast prison-house in which man is trapped and subjected to the sway of an alien compulsion. 'O! how the World hath inflexible Intellectual Rulers', reads another oracle in the collection.[24] The sense of oppression is much the same whether the alien power is considered to be the force of astrological Necessity (*anangke* or *heimarmene*) or the cyclical determinism of Stoic thought, a world repeating itself endlessly, cause following cause in inevitable sequence. For man to become aware of himself in such an oppressive universe is in truth a fearful undertaking; but the Gnostic, the alchemist, the magus, attempt it because they believe that their spiritual discipline will allow them to rise above the sphere of Fatality. That is also a claim, made for the sect of Theurgists who used them, put forward by the *Chaldaean Oracles*.[25]

The world-estrangement of Gnostics and Neoplatonists in the first centuries of the Christian era, whence the *Oracles* come, was not based fundamentally on a Swiftian disgust at the messiness and animality of human bodily functions, as has sometimes been said. It was much more a reaction to the materialist world-view with its cosmos of Necessity, demonstrated by the orbits of the stars (one must remember that astrology was a part of 'science' in those days), and its human implications. The cosmic vertigo expressed in the recurring 'voids' and 'abysses' testifies to the inner emptiness experienced when people contemplated that vision. What we find in world-estranged Gnosticism and magic is not so much revulsion at man's corporeality in a physical universe, as a *horror vacui* – a terror of the void that is felt when nothing but man's natural being is recognised and given its place.[26] That terror can be shirked in many ways; but it must be faced by anyone who would, in the words of the *Oracles*, 'explore the River of the Soul'. And it brings each explorer, in crossing the inner vacuum, into the domain of the Ahrimanic: the power of Negation, the denial of the hope of human self-realisation in an inexorable universe. Shelley must have recognised in the *Chaldaean Oracles* many of his own imaginative experiences as he struggled to come to terms with the world of sceptical and materialist thought, when he considered the possibility that at the foundation of things there might only lie a brute force, unknowable in its own nature but infinitely unlikely to resemble human mind. So the *Oracles* warn of:

> a faithless Depth, and Hades wrapped in clouds, delighting in unintelligible images, precipitous, winding, a black ever-rolling Abyss . . . and therein is established the Throne of an evil and fatal force.[27]

It is hard to resist speculating that readers in the Peacock–Shelley–Newton circle would unhesitatingly have identified the seat of power in this dark 'oracle of Zoroaster' as the Throne of Ahriman.

Stuart Curran has shown that Shelley might have been aware of authentically Iranian – if slightly unorthodox – traditions which would have confirmed the link between scepticism and the evil daemon. Some Zoroastrians taught that the Surpeme God was meditating, when he doubted his power and design: immediately from his doubt Ahriman came into being.[28] But whether or not he knew the Iranian story, Shelley most probably was aware of 'sceptical' connections from his classical reading and education. These connections centre, curiously enough, around the fifth-century-BC philosopher Democritus of Abdera, the founder of atomism and one of the earliest sceptics in Greek intellectual history. We know that he was a figure of some importance to Shelley, in part of course for his sceptical inclinations. But he was also the subject of some interesting and controversial discussion in the well-known classical writers Pliny, Aulus Gellius and Diogenes Laertius, which seems to reveal a paradoxical second side to his character.

The sceptical orientation of the familiar Democritus is well illustrated in some of his surviving aphorisms:

> Man must know that he is far removed from things as they really are.
> And it will be clear that it is extremely hard to know how everything is in truth.
> As things are we perceive nothing that is certain, but only what alters according to our organisation and to the onrushing or counteracting patterns.

And there is the famous summation: 'Truth is sunk in an abyss'.[29] Obviously this was a man who, like Shelley, had looked down the dark abyss of how little we know, and grown dizzy. At first sight, moreover, Democritean scepticism appears to be the product of emergent Greek rationalism. The figure of Democritus in late classical times, however, was the focus of legend and rumour; and nothing that was said of him must have seemed more striking to Shelley than the numerous statements to the effect that this Greek relativist and sceptic had learned his wisdom from the Magi of Persia.

Pliny, in his immense encyclopaedia of natural and pseudo-natural knowledge, mentions many of the wonder-working properties of plants and adds: 'They were first brought to the notice of our part of the world by Pythagoras and Democritus, who followed as their authority the Magi.'[30] The connection is consistently maintained. Democritus is revered as 'this famous scientist, the keenest student next to Pythagoras of the Magi'; Pythagoras had written on magical plant-potions and 'Democritus also composed a similar work. Both of them visited the Magi of Persia, Arabia, Ethiopia and Egypt.'[31] Diogenes Laertius also relates Democritus' travels in the East and regards him as a pupil of the Magi and Chaldaeans, and the tradition was accepted by Clement of Alexandria. We hear of magical or alchemical books written by Democritus – some of them are quoted in Pliny and in the *Noctes Atticae* of Aulus Gellius.[32] He is said to have written the alchemical treatise *Cheirokmeta*, and the comprehensive *Physica and Mystica* dealing with the occult forces of nature and the soul. According to Synesius, Democritus learnt his alchemy from the Iranian sage Ostanes; and there survives a passage from the *Physica* recounting how the philosopher raised the dead Magus in order to learn from him the final, uncommunicated secrets of combination. The Master would only say, however, that the books were in the Temple. Having searched in vain, and continuing his researches until the great work was achieved, Democritus later happened to be in the Temple at a festival, when suddenly of its own accord a pillar split open and there were the books of Ostanes, confirming in every detail the work Democritus had completed. In addition, they contained the celebrated alchemical formula of the unity and dynamism of substance:

> Nature delights in nature.
> Nature conquers nature.
> Nature dominates nature.

What is here attributed to Ostanes in an Iranianised tradition, of course, was elsewhere given the authority of Hermes Trismegistus, Apollonius of Tyana and many others.[33]

The raising of the shade of Ostanes in the *Physica* recalls other stories about Democritus which link him strongly with tombs. Pliny says that Democritus entered the tomb of the magician Dardanus to obtain his works. He says that there are some who would deny the philosopher's connection with magic and the truth of such tomb-raiding tales, 'but it is all to no purpose, for it is certain that Democritus especially instilled into men's minds the sweets of magic'.[34] Diogenes Laertius offers an explanation of Democritus' obsession with tombs by remarking that he went to graves and solitary places in order to carry out experiments with *eidola*, mental projections. Either he wanted to have a clear field of projection, undisturbed by crowds of people whose minds were also a source of *eidola*, or he may have been in search of particular emanations, it is not clear which.[35] But we see that Democritus combined many of Shelley's prime concerns in his remarkable and wide-ranging mind: a powerful scepticism, interest in magic and telepathic projections, etc. Though a basic materialist, observes Jack Lindsay, Democritus

> was extremely interested in strange phenomena, in occult forces, which he believed had a physical or scientific explanation if enough was known about them. Probably indeed it was this mixture of attitudes that drew the alchemists to him – an ardent quest for definite explanations, and an open mind towards forces of sympathy and antipathy, attraction and repulsion, which acted at a distance and could not yet be explained: together with an omnivorous curiosity and persistence of research.[36]

Precisely the same qualities must have engaged Shelley, with the addition that he would also have been drawn to Democritus' alchemical works; and, above all, to his knowledge of the wisdom of the Magi.

With the benefit of modern scholarship we nowadays have little difficulty in noticing the composite nature of the philosopher–alchemist–Magus Democritus. Most of the alchemical books under his name, for example, appear actually to derive from one Bolos of Mendes. It was he who united the traditions of Egyptian alchemy with the exotic ideas circulating under the authority of the Persian Magus Ostanes (whether or not the historical Democritus really travelled in the East); and according to Columella it was he who wrote the *Cheirokmeta*.[37] Yet historical authenticity is not the important point for our study of Shelley. From the viewpoint of the mythological studies being carried out in Marlow, Shelley's classical knowledge can only have added yet another brick to the wall of evidence. From every side the arrows pointed toward the teachings of Zoroaster and his disciples, such as Ostanes. That 'abyss' which had to be plumbed in the search for truth, the great gap between what we know and unknown reality, described by Democritus, was also the Ahrimanic void of Zoroaster's *Chaldaean Oracles*. The new philological discoveries confirmed Ahriman as the spirit of Doubt and proved the immense antiquity of the Iranian sages. The prophecies of the reign of Ahriman, moreover, had been fulfilled in the age of rationalism and technology, the vision of a world governed by immutable Necessity, a vision at once magnificent and profoundly terrifying, and the grip of Empire over the world which even the French Revolution had failed to loosen.

Many of these thoughts were in Shelley's head when he left England on his first European expedition to visit the Alps. And they came together for the first time in a definitive poem when he stood in contemplation, in the year 1816, before the huge ice and rock mass of the greatest peak in Europe – Mont Blanc.

LANDSCAPES OF FEAR: *MONT BLANC*

Critics of the calibre of Earl Wasserman and Harold Bloom have presented *Mont Blanc* as the greatest poem of Shelley's intellectual scepticism. And that it is.[38] But it is also much more: for the fears and doubts it expresses are by no means limited to those probing intellects who have immersed themselves in philosophical thought. Yi-fu Tuan, in his recent book, has studied the pattern of 'landscapes of fear' in many cultures and many times, emphasising the constant presence of fear at the periphery of consciousness and the numerous ways that have been devised to deal with it. For a landscape, as we have already seen, is not just a given complex of perceptions; it is a mental construction upon such a complex, which can therefore readily be made to stand for the attitudes or feelings of an individual or a society. And fear is particularly rich in landscapes ranging from terror to anxiety, alarm to unease.

Indeed it seems possible that everything we do is shadowed by half-defined fears and anxieties, so that our existence is only made bearable through the defences we erect. 'The minimum requirement for security is to establish a boundary', writes Yi-fu Tuan, 'which may be material or conceptual and ritually enforced. Boundaries are everywhere, obviously so in landscapes of fences, fields, and buildings, but equally there in the worlds of primitive peoples.'[39] The genesis of fear is almost coeval with the origins of human society, arising out of man's definition of himself and his ordered world against the natural environment. Certain very rudimentary human groups examined by anthropologists do suggest that 'fearless' societies can exist – and that in places which we, in the secure technological West, would regard as dangerous locations: the tropical rain-forest, desert and scrub. But even the most rudimentary forms of village life bring with them a throng of fears and their correlative taboos. Evil spirits rapidly congregate in the world-conceptions of primitive cultivators, prompting the following remarks from Yi-fu Tuan:

> Villagers everywhere create a humanised landscape out of an original wilderness, knowing that they can maintain their creation only through sweat and constant vigilance. Despite a surface appearance of calm, village life can be full of uncertainty and stress, exacerbated (perhaps) by a sense of transgression against nature. Under such circumstances, the imagination is quick to populate space with lurking evil spirits.[40]

The urge to consolidate the humanised landscape from village into city, following a familiar dialectical pattern, both provides increased safeguards against the terrors of alien nature and also intensifies the opposition, making wild nature seem all the more inimical to the design of human life. Asserting his otherness to nature, man creates a landscape of fear – and perhaps of guilt.

Some such process of self-definition as anthropologists see in the emergence of culture inevitably occurs also in the life of each individual. And Shelley has a suggestive passage in the essay *On Life* which shows his grasp of its significance. 'Let us recollect our sensations as children,' he wrote:

> What a distinct and intense apprehension had we of the world and of ourselves! Many of the circumstances of social life were then important to us which are now no longer so. But that is

not the point of comparison on which I mean to insist. We less habitually distinguished all that we saw and felt, from ourselves. They seemed, as it were, to constitute one mass. . . . As men grow up this power commonly decays, and they become mechanical and habitual agents. Thus feelings and then reasonings are the combined result of a multitude of entangled thoughts and of a series of what are called impressions, planted by reiteration.[41]

R. G. Woodman had elicited the important features of Shelley's thought in this passage. 'When the prototype emerges in the creation of its object, that object tends with time to break loose from its source and take on an autonomous existence. When this happens the universe of created objects is conceived as something separate from the mind of the perceiver. . . . Shelley identifies this mode of perception with reason.'[42] The original apprehension of unity, Shelley adds, can be recovered at a higher level by the 'Intellectual Philosophy' he advocates.

Thus Shelley presents the process of man's self-definition in reaching maturity as also being the process by which he comes to perceive the world as external, alien. We grow up, and in so doing learn to distinguish what we see and feel from ourselves. The underlying principle is that of emergent reason, our faculty of making distinctions and of grasping connections between analytically separate entities. Hence the end-product is a world of outwardness on the one hand, and the mind decayed to a 'habitual and mechanical agent' on the other. Another product of the process, as we have seen, is the genesis of fear. But we can also turn the argument about: the fear which is a corollary of self-definition, we can say, is something that must be faced by everyone who wishes to grow up. If we are unwilling to live with the fear that is an integral part of maturity, we condemn ourselves to infantile dependency – the source of the infant's security. If however we confront the fears, there is at least the chance that we can win through to the higher-level 'unity' offered by Shelley's vision.

Yi-fu Tuan points out that when the boundaries collapse, the result is mental illness. The schizophrenic suffers from the absence of the reassuring coordinates established by the consensus of adult society. Ordinary things seem strange, or appear to cover hidden depths of terror.

Such is not the world of the normal child and adult, and yet it does have something in common with the world of exceptionally gifted people. They ask strange questions. What we take for granted they find queer; what we accept as stable and closed they perceive as changing and open. Unlike schizophrenic patients, however, geniuses welcome – or at least, are highly tolerant of – uncertainty. The circle is breached, but they believe it can be healed at a higher level of generalisation.[43]

Shelley's dynamic conception of the conscious self means that his genius above all flourishes upon uncertainty, upon the risk of the hitherto unknown. He is prepared to face not only the common fears of ordinary men and women growing up in the unstable world, but also the dark regions of those who leave in some degree the assured world of social reality, of those who risk madness and disorientation. This means that he is enabled to experience with an extraordinary intensity – but he faces a correspondingly intensified landscape of fear.

In *Mont Blanc*, the intellectual themes of Shelley's scepticism become great poetry in expressing the deep fears which have been felt by humanity over ages of spiritual history. Those fears have also been expressed in mythologies and legends, such as shaped Shelley's awareness. John V. Murphy points out that Shelley draws upon the imagery and resonance of Gothic writing, with its archetypally terrifying 'haunted castle': 'it is not inappropriate to consider, from the narrator's viewpoint, the mountain and its ravine as a tremendous castle that mirrors the mind's uncertainties and wonderings'.[44] That is certainly true. But now in Shelley's poem the Gothic terror is deepened through the complex themes which accompany it – the themes of scepticism, Necessity, self-consciousness, etc. In the creative womb of Shelley's imagination all these ideas came together into a manifold entity, into something of a 'daemonic' force and concreteness. Having witnessed the destructive power of the glaciers which creep ineluctably down the ravine of the Arve, annihilating anything which stands in their path, Shelley wrote in a long and fascinating letter to Peacock:

These glaciers flow perpetually into the valley, ravaging in their slow but irresistible progress the pastures and forests which surround them, and performing a work of desolation in ages which a river of lava might accomplish in an hour, but far more irretrieveably. . . . The verge of the glacier, like that of Bossons, presents the most vivid image of desolation that it is possible to conceive. No one dares to approach it . . . there is something inexpressibly dreadful in the aspect of a few branchless trunks which nearest to the ice-rifts still stand in the uprooted soil. The meadows perish overwhelmed with sand and stones.

Perhaps Peacock would know the daemonic power which they suggest to Shelley's imagination:

Do you who assert the supremacy of Ahriman imagine him throned among these desolating snows, among the palaces of death and frost sculptured in their terrible magnificence by the unsparing hand of necessity, and that he casts around him as the first essays of his final usurpation avalanches, torrents, rocks and thunders, and above all, those deadly glaciers at once the proofs and symbols of his reign.[45]

Whatever Peacock may have pictured, that was certainly the vision embodied in Shelley's poem.

The poem of *Mont Blanc* is an interior monologue, the representation of a mind in the activity of contemplating a natural scene of great power and beauty, and the thoughts which arise about it. We do it wrong to regard it as a 'statement': rather it attempts to articulate the exploration of a sequence of ideas and their relationship to the objective world from which they take their point of departure. The poem has a dramatic structure which reveals the mind's response to those thoughts, involving Shelley's deepest emotions as well as his sceptical, intellectual capacities. And the whole moves toward the apprehension of a 'daemonic' power which is neither purely inward nor external, a hidden reality – albeit of an extraordinarily negative kind.

Mont Blanc rightly begins, therefore, with reflections of the poet's mind, already influenced by the scene before him but translating its sights into general metaphors of mind:

The everlasting universe of things
Flows through the mind, and rolls its rapid waves,
Now dark – now glittering – now reflecting gloom.

It is only at the end of the first section of the poem that we are allowed to focus sharply on 'a vast river' which 'Over its rocks ceaselessly bursts and raves'; at the outset the river is half-defined, its physicality lost in the poet's concern with mental process. That concern naturally leads him to reflect that the kaleidoscopic world of experience subsists in a perceiving mind, and that human consciousness itself is therefore a tributary stream to the vast flux of perceived objects. He continues his description of the universe of experience as:

> Now lending splendour, where from secret springs
> The source of human thought its tribute brings
> Of waters, – with a sound but half its own,
> Such as a feeble brook will oft assume
> In the wild woods, among the mountains lone,
> ·Where waterfalls around it leap for ever,
> Where woods and winds contend, and a vast river
> Over its rocks ceaselessly burst and raves.

The perceiving mind is not closed in on itself, solipsistically; but it receives impressions from the great world surrounding it, just as the sound of a 'feeble brook' in the Alps is augmented by the sounds of wind and waterfall and the great glacial river in its vicinity. Although we seem to ourselves individual beings, our experience is but half our own. The movement of thought here is embodied in the poem's shift, via the simile of the 'feeble brook' to a realisation of the physical landscape.

The second section of the poem confronts that landscape directly: 'Thus thou, Ravine of Arve.' It celebrates the marvellous variety of natural phenomena in that 'many-coloured, many voiced vale', which on the basis of the first section may be interpreted as the type of the whole objective world. Shelley is awed by its magnificence – the 'old and solemn harmony' of the pines swayed by the wind, its mists and shadows, the shimmering of its

> earthly rainbows stretched across the sweep
> Of the aethereal waterfall, whose veil
> Robes some unsculptured image.

He evokes all the splendour of natural manifestation, all that delights our senses of sight and sound, even smell (the odours of the mountain forest), all that impresses us with the tremendous resources of phenomenal reality – the rivers, tempests and echoing caverns of the ravine. Here Shelley approaches nearest to the popular estimate of the Romantic nature-poet. Gradually however, his awareness having diffused itself through all the panorama of the natural scene, his consciousness turns back upon his own observing self:

> My own, my human mind, which passively
> Now renders and receives fast influencings,
> Holding an unremitting interchange
> With the clear universe of things around.

This is the account of the mind's passivity given by Hume and Locke, whose arguments had persuaded Shelley that 'Mind cannot create, it can only perceive'.[46] And Shelley makes it plain that there is nothing in his celebration of natural glory to compel us beyond the description of mind given by Ahrimanic philosophy. The mind enters into relationship with the 'clear universe of things' and passively reproduces their impressions in human consciousness. In accepting the empiricists' description as adequate to his experience of contemplating nature, however, Shelley discovers in the mind's inability to transcend pure passivity a boundary of knowledge. He finds himself powerless to gaze into the ultimate source of things or phenomena. He cannot grasp the empowering 'causes'. Power – or what he calls later in the poem 'the secret Strength of things / Which governs thought' – enters human mind 'in likeness' of the irresistible force of the Arve glacier as it descends from the remote mountain's 'secret throne', inaccessible beyond its ice-gulfs; just as at the other pole the 'feeble brook' of individual mind brought its tribute from 'secret springs'. As to what that actualising Power may be in itself, or where it originates, the poet has no knowledge.

So far, though, the poem has treated the poet's response as if this were wholly confined to reflecting the clear images of natural objects. Yet Shelley's musings in fact tend not to rest content with given reality, but to rise above the 'darkness' of the external world, withdrawing by stages into the inner cavern which is the deeper haunt of poetry. Confronted with the natural scene, Shelley instinctively seeks within himself an answering reality in the desires of the heart. Any such search, however, is hopeless within the terms established by the poem, and the poet's breast despairingly recalls its shades and phantoms. Only then does Shelley find himself suddenly confronting again the unassimilable vision of the dark ravine in an unexpected climax – 'thou art there!'

> One legion of wild thoughts, whose wandering wings
> Now float above thy darkness, and now rest
> Where that or thou art no unbidden guest,
> In the still cave of the witch Poesy,
> Seeking among the shadows that pass by
> Ghosts of all things that are, some shade of three,
> Some phantom, some faint image; till the breast
> From which they fled recalls them, thou art there!

Unable to find any adequate embodiment for the poetic energies within him, the poet's urge toward self-realisation turns outward again, tearing through the bounds of knowledge set to it earlier and straining after a reality more complete than that of the physical world.

> I look on high;
> Has some unknown omnipotence unfurled
> The veil of life and death? or do I lie
> In dream, and does the mightier world of sleep
> Spread far around and inaccessibly
> Its circles?

Having torn aside the veil of phenomenal reality, the poet is unable to assert any positive vision; even the nature of the experience is in doubt.

Shelley begins the third section of the poem by considering the possibilities – a mystic revelation, from beyond life and death; a dream-vision, illusory and empty; or perhaps, as the occultists say, containing gleams of a transcendent truth, more rich and complex than waking reality. But these suggestions remain unconfirmed. They are conjectures thrown into the emptiness which opens up beyond the veil of familiar experience, the void into which human consciousness threatens to disappear altogether, like the 'homeless' clouds dissipated by the winds against the mountain steeps. The transcendent Power remains unknown, imaged in the unscalable Mont Blanc whose awesome summit now finally breaks into view through the clouds almost exactly half-way through the poem which bears its name:

> Far, far above, piercing the infinite sky,
> Mont Blanc appears, – still, snowy, and serene.

All questions and speculations as to its nature or origins are unanswerable: 'None can reply – all seems eternal now'. The intellect grasps Power in its manifestation as the causal chain of Necessity, the law which governs thought and all things under the dome of heaven. The inhuman and amoral Strength of things Shelley intuits in the rock and ice of Mont Blanc towers above the transience of particular events and occurrences in remote serenity; but in the human heart these images inspire terror rather than tranquillity.

Truly it is a vision to teach 'awful doubt', or in Shelley's mysterious phrases:

> faith so mild,
> So solemn, so serene, that man may be,
> But for such faith, with nature reconciled.

Faith in the all-sufficiency of nature comes as close to reducing man to the grandeur and insensibility of the physical universe as it can while remaining faith, and so an act of mind asserting man's separateness from nature. One step further, and man would be plunged into that suspension or consciousness (perhaps hinted at in Wordsworth's 'A slumber did my spirit seal') when sensory impressions temporarily cease:

> the strange sleep
> Which when the voices of the desert fail
> Wraps all in its own deep eternity.

Man as a being of passive perception can know nothing beyond the range of his senses except that blank suspension. And yet his very reflections upon the world he perceives drive him beyond it into the darkness. Like the plants awakening in spring he longs to leap up with a bound from the 'detested trance' of such a winter of the spirit, the freezing vision of the inaccessibly other-than-human. The terrifying otherness of the world confronts Shelley in this lanscape of fear, the Ahrimanic power which inhabits Mont Blanc.

Mont Blanc thus moves towards an apprehension of the Ahrimanic void behind the sense-world, an apprehension that comes to us when, as Shelley wrote elsewhere, 'we find within our own thoughts the chasm of an insufficient void'. That yawning vacuity is all that we can humanly experience of the Power in the mountain and the ever augmenting masses of ice. Man flies in dread from the vicinity of its creeping glaciers, the unfathomable rifts which cut across his path, its desert peopled only by storms, savage birds of prey and wolves, its hideously scarred and riven formations of rock. In the fourth section Shelley expands the vision of negation still further into an anti-world of destructive might:

> there, many a precipice,
> Frost and the Sun in scorn of mortal power
> Have piled: dome, pyramid, and pinnacle,
> A city of death, distinct with many a tower
> And wall impregnable of beaming ice.
> Yet not a city, but a flood of ruin
> Is there, that from the boundaries of the sky
> Rolls its perpetual stream; vast pines are strewing
> Its destined path, or in the mangled soil
> Branchless and shattered stand; the rocks, drawn down
> From yon remotest waste, have overthrown
> The limits of the dead and living world,
> Never to be reclaimed.

Having lifted the veil of sensory knowledge, Shelley finds no ultimate reality, but a mere Power which is the negation of all human experience. In human terms it is pure alienation – solitude and vacancy. In the last section Shelley evokes the mystery of the hidden source of Power, of vast physical energy without external manifestation, immense potentiality unrealised, still set apart 'in its tranquillity' from human awareness: snow piling in the darkness of moonless nights, winds howling unheard, the distant 'voiceless' lightning's force innocently expended. With this disturbing dislocation of our normal perception, Shelley makes us feel with frightening intensity both physical vastness and the terror of the vacuum, the void confronting the human spirit when it stands before the natural forces of creation and destruction.

Behind the empirical mode of thought, and its vision of nature experienced as external to man, Shelley found the Ahrimanic void. And yet for all his vision's negativity, he does not suffer total annihilation. Even at the end of the poem he survives as an articulate consciousness, and he draws from his experience a wisdom – though it is one 'so mild, so solemn, so serene' that it verges upon what he shortly afterwards termed 'the wisdom of a high despair'.

The 'naked countenance of earth' on which he has looked, he says, and 'even these primaeval mountains / Teach the adverting mind'. He returned to a thought half-formulated in the earlier fragment *The Assassins*: the notion that the fear and doubt of the unknown, which exists always at the margins of consciousness and of social life, may be a power necessary to their continuing vitality and renewal. Without that periphery of terror, consciousness might decline into self-absorbed, narcissistic satisfaction. Society, if it refused to face that surrounding fear, might retreat into a system of internal tyranny, the tyrant playing upon the people's basic need for security. Indeed, Shelley saw in much that passed for religion and politics a strong confirmation of these very tendencies. To become a Mental Traveller, therefore, and revisit the sources of primordial fear had its value for one strong, sensitive and wise enough to survive the experience. The Ahrimanic terror which could frighten men into passive obedience and refuge in tyranny could also, when faced and understood, become a force for change toward social and spiritual maturity:

> Thou has a voice, great Mountain, to repeal
> Large codes of fraud and woe; not understood
> By all, but which the wise, and great and good
> Interpret, or make felt, or deeply feel.

Shelley's philosophy here does not depend upon the metaphysical idea of Necessity leading to inevitable progress, a concept extraneous to the poem which some critics have brought in.[47] It puts the value of the response to the dark 'landscape of fear' firmly with man himself. For this reason, the poem does not end on a note of philosophical assertion. It ends by posing the question of the significance of the Ahrimanic void to the total working of human imagination. That question occupied Shelley all through his later career.

SHELLEY, GOD AND THE SUBLIME

Present-day travellers in the Alps can still find, in the course of their walks, small plates of metal nailed to the rock at the site of an especially spectacular vista. They bear inscriptions from the Bible, frequently from Psalm 111: 'Great are the works of the Lord'.

These small but edifying reminders and pointers for the wayfaring Christian to the divine Creator may also serve to bring into focus certain questions about the 'atheist' Shelley's ode to Mont Blanc and the Power inhabiting it. For *Mont Blanc* should be set against the tradition of literary visits to the Alps made for the express purpose of celebrating the 'sublime' aspects of the created world, of which Coleridge's *Hymn before Sun-rise in the Vale of Chamouni* (1802) is a magnificient result. Coleridge's *hymn* was based upon a German poem by Friederike Brun (whom he mentions in the title-heading); but it also had precedents in English, such as T. S. Whalley's *Mont Blanc: An Irregular Lyric Poem* (1788); and many travellers have left their impressions and prayers in diaries and correspondence. Yet Earl Wasserman is, I think, wrong in wanting to believe that Shelley's experience in Chamonix was a religious one, and that in *Mont Blanc* our 'enmity with nothingness is put at ease by a visionary knowledge of the absolute Power behind all worldly action, or, in more appropriately religious terms, of a transcendent and absolute divine Cause that gives meaning to our limited existence in an instable and illusory world'.[48]

Coleridge, in the *Hymn before Sun-rise*, sees the bald rock-mass of Mont Blanc, he sees 'The Arve and Arveiron at thy base / Rave ceaselessly', he sees the darkness 'substantial, black', and like Shelley passes in contemplation from the perceptible to an intenser reality beyond. That reality is voiced by the mountain and the cataracts and the ice-falls:

> And they too have a voice, yon piles of snow,
> And in their perilous fall shall thunder, GOD![49]

Yet Coleridge knew that the mountains spoke thus only to one who knew how to interpret their language, who already knew by faith of the moral goodness of the Creator as well his power and wisdom. 'A Barbarian,' wrote Coleridge in *The Friend*:

> so instructed in the power and intelligence of the Infinite Being as to be left wholly ignorant of his moral attributes, would have acquired none but erroneous notions even of the former. At the very best, he would gain only a theory to satisfy his curiosity with; but more probably, would deduce the belief of a Moloch or a Baal. (For an idea of an irresistible invisible Being naturally produces terror in the mind of uninstructed and unprotected man, and with terror there will be associated whatever had been accustomed to excite it, as anger, vengeance, &c; as is proved by the Mythology of all barbarous nations.)[50]

Coleridge saw in addition that the case was not devoid of more modern application. The Deists who reasoned their way from the material universe up to a First Cause, identified with God, seemed to him to require a certain dishonesty if their claim to support religious belief were to be accepted. In fact, a thinker like Bolingbroke (the mind behind the poetry of Pope's *Essay on Man*) 'removed Love, Justice, and Choice, from Power and Intelligence, and yet pretended to have left unimpaired the conviction of a Deity. He might as consistently have paralysed the optic nerve, and then excused himself by affirming, that he had, however, not touched the eye.'[51]

Now whatever may be said about *Mont Blanc* it is, like all Shelley's mature poetry, ruthlessly honest. And it was written, as we have seen, 'under the immediate impression of deep and powerful feelings excited by the objects which it attempts to describe', without a religious belief in the Creator-God of Judaic tradition. Shelley starts, a child of the modern age, from the natural world which impresses itself upon his mind, and moves from there to an apprehension of the hidden actualising Power: the 'secret Strength' of natural reality from one point of view, and the principle grasped by the intellect as causal Necessity from another. But he will not arbitrarily choose to believe, like the disingenuous Deists, that his vision affirms the traditional conception of God. In his agnosticism Shelley does not undertake to deny the existence or the possibility of such a being. Yet certainly in Mont Blanc he has no intuitions of a morally beneficent Deity. He has a vision of Power and Intelligence; but where the believers in God the Creator project the human qualities of 'Love, Justice, and Choice' he feels only the darkness of the unknowable. Hence he comes closer in certain ways, being what Coleridge terms an 'uninstructed and unprotected man' to the Ahrimanic mythology of 'barbarous nations' in his naked intuition of an inhuman Power.

Perhaps the significance of Shelley's extraordinary revaluation of traditional ideas in *Mont Blanc* can be illustrated more clearly if we examine the various elements against the historical value-changes expressed in the great myths underlying the conflict of visions. For we have here more than a clash of philosophies; whole world-views with their attendant moral and cultural dimensions are engaged in a complex process of imaginative redefinition.

Those early Iranians (in common with many ancient and oriental peoples) did not experience the world primarily as something objectively separate from life and spirit. In sunlight and growth they felt spiritual presences; and in cultivating the land they felt themselves to be sharing, as men, in the work of Ohrmazd and the forces of light. Sometimes, however, the world rudely asserted its otherness and intractability – in the failure of crops, storms and other natural disasters, or more generally in its need to be worked upon, transformed laboriously, before it became a medium for the spiritual forces of life and growth. From man's encounter with the alien intractability of his environment, the fears and doubts which it stirred, they crystallised the myth of Ahriman, whose forces of darkness and recalcitrance have infected the pure light-universe of Ohrmazd and his spirits. Things have therefore lost their primal transparency and vital interconnection; under Ahriman's influence they have fragmented, and become opaque to light and spirituality.[52]

A very different *Weltanschauung* confronts us when we turn to the Judaic tradition of the Old Testament. The separateness, inertness and opacity of things which seemed to the ancient mythologists of Iran the very presence of the evil daemon, was for Judaism the natural condition of things, to be accepted as a matter of course. Indeed, the Jews had long been forbidden by their divine Law to see – let alone worship! – the presence of divinity in any part of the material universe.[53] The world was to be accepted in its factuality, as devoid of informing spirit and Deity. After our study of 'landscapes of fear', perhaps we can understand why to those outside Judaism that world-view seemed potentially terrifying. Even Greek philosophy for the most part regarded the cosmos as divine, a great animal pervaded by a spirit or God. Those who take the trouble to read the *Refutation which Destroys All Doubt*, a work by the Zoroastrian writer Mardan al-Farruk, can still feel the religious horror a worshipper of Ohrmazd felt when he read the opening chapter of Genesis, where Yahweh fashions a world from the elements of a dark, chaotic ocean. Perhaps we can understand, too, why he could only identify the Jewish Creator-God with – Ahriman.[54]

Mardan al-Farruk's perspective, however, proves to be too narrow. Just as he cannot understand, being a pious Zoroastrian, the Judaic acceptance of an inert material universe, so also he cannot understand the Judaic doctrine which for thousands of years effectively neutralised the Ahrimanic terror of that universe – the doctrine of creation. The vast and frightening aspects of nature, mountains, wildernesses, storms, only increase man's awe and reverence for the grandeur of the God who is acknowledged as their Creator. The universe may be purely material, mere product; but it is the product none the less of an unutterably sublime creative activity of God at the beginning of things. The immensities of cosmic space glimpsed in the night sky still send a shudder along the spine; but those very immensities also tell of the glory of the God who has made the stars his footstool. Wild beasts on the periphery of human settlement are still fearful realities; but even Leviathan and Behemoth are divinely created, 'the first of the ways of God'. So long as the biblical teaching of the creation retains its power over men's minds, the terror of the Ahrimanic is swallowed up, subsumed in the glory and sublimity of God the Creator. The doctrine of creation must thus rank among the greatest imaginative achievements in the history of civilisation, permitting man to hold at bay his fears and anxieties, and to live for the first time in a radically demythologised universe.

The literary tradition of sublimity lying behind the *Hymn before Sun-rise*, it is true, traces its origins in theory to the work of a Greek, conventionally identified with Longinus, and his famous treatise *On the Sublime*.[55] However, in reality Longinus for long made little headway against the head-current of mimetic and pragmatic ideas in writing and art. In modern times, as M. H. Abrams has pointed out, the full effect of Longinian critical thought made itself felt in English literature only through the conjunction with religious tradition deriving from the Hebrew Bible.[56] Indeed, most unusually for any Greek writer, the first-century-AD classical rhetorician himself cites the creative *fiat* from the first chapter of Genesis as an instance of sublimity, paving the way for an effective synthesis. The early-eighteenth-century critic John Dennis drew attention to this, and the religious (pagan) character of many of Longinus' examples; and the full breakthrough came in the mid-century with Bishop Lowth's delivery of his *Lectures on the Sacred Poetry of the Hebrews* (published 1753), a comprehensive literary examination of the Old Testament which was to be of considerable importance for the rise of Romantic thought. Few of the classical literary concepts (of mimesis, plot, character, etc.) seemed to fit the Psalms or the Prophets. Hence Lowth's 'dominant concern is with language and style – especially with the "sublimity" in which Hebrew poetry has no peer – and with the source of these elements in the conceptions and passions of the sacred writers'.[57]

The Longinian approach, when once conjoined to the poetic tradition of the Bible, helped create a new creative tradition in style and genre, issuing after due time in Coleridge's *Hymn before Sun-rise* and its analogues: a tradition in which awesome, or overwhelming, or terrifying sensations were evoked and resolved within the poetic framework into a sense of 'sublime' grandeur. Mountains, seas or other 'horrid' landscapes were frequent subjects. It is notable that Ann Radcliffe makes extensive use of 'sublimity' to relieve the unresolved horrors of Gothicism in her voluminous and many-sided romances.

For 'sublimity' overcomes the disintegration of consciousness in the terror of the Ahrimanic by means of a powerful unifying power in the soul, strong enough to assert the unity of the psyche in the face of a world of alienation. Yet it is at the same time a factor in the human soul-life which evades rather than concentrates self-awareness. The influential theorist of the movement Edmund Burke, in his *Philosophical Enquiry into the Origin of the Sublime and the Beautiful* (1756), explains:

> The passion caused by the great and sublime in nature, when those causes operate most powerfully, is Astonishment; and astonishment is that state of the soul, in which all its motions are suspended, with some degree of horror. In this case the mind is so entirely filled with its object, that it cannot entertain any other.[58]

Self-consciousness, together with the powers of reasoning, judgement and so on, is swallowed up in the overwhelming impression of sublime amazement. The mind's powers are entirely concentrated upon the object, leaving virtually no resources of self-definition, which are 'suspended' in the encounter with a degree of terror essential to the experience of the 'sublime'. The result is at once a sense of boundlessness and of powerful unity, qualities in which the Judaic tradition locates the nature of the Divine. Through the awestruck worship of the Creator of what was vast and fearful as well as organised and 'beautiful' in nature, man could live within a vision of the world where the terror of Ahrimanic estrangement was effectively distanced. At the same time, this involved a necessary limitation in the degree of attainable self-consciousness – albeit this was already greater than in the primitive oriental sense of complete spiritual plenitude from which Judaic culture marked so significant a departure.

The sublime doctrine of creation extended its influence over many centuries, affecting scientific thought and literary experience through to the beginnings of modern science in the eighteenth and nineteenth centuries. Then its hold started to slacken; in the first line of *Mont Blanc* Shelley declares a breach with the tradition *in toto*: 'The everlasting universe of things'. Here at once it is plain there is no Creator, but a self-existent and eternal cosmos. Questions about ultimate origins are later shown to be meaningless in terms of the poem's cosmology, which no longer points the way to a Coleridgean, Judaeo-Christian God. But once the hold of the doctrine of creation is loosened – then the terrifying figure of Ahriman must again be faced by the individual consciousness of the poet, who can no longer share the burden of fear with an infinite and benevolent Father. And that, it seems to me, is precisely what we see happening in *Mont Blanc*.

Shelley demonstrates in his heretical ode to the secret Strength inhabiting Mont Blanc the renewed relevance of the Ahrimanic mythology in the age of modern science, the fears and pressures of man in the scientific cosmos. Again the intensity of self-awareness is purchased at the price of such fears, and we try to ignore them at our peril. In *Mont Blanc* Shelley faces them, and manages still to believe at least in the possibility of a fully human life within sight of their dark circumference. But he rends wide apart the genre of the mountain-ode which sustained Coleridge in the *Hymn before Sun-rise*. In his hotel in the Alps he boldly signed himself 'P. B. Shelley, atheist'.[59]

It would be a gross simplification to say that Shelley found no further need for God. We cannot say with Richard Holmes that Shelley received in Chamonix a revelation, the content of which was that there is no God.[60] The evidence is that the later Shelley remained open to the idea of some Being who might furnish the ultimate reality behind Power and Mind alike; it is only that he ceased to need him as the great Craftsman who fashioned all things, of whom he had not the slightest inkling when he stood before the largest mountain in Europe.[61] He saw there only a freezing vision of Ahrimanic power.

According to Zoroastrian theology, Ahriman was co-eternal with the spirit of light, a fact of the universe from the beginning. Yet he was consistently refused the title of a god, accorded to Ohrmazd. We should likewise be extremely wary of accepting Earl Wasserman's religious estimation of Shelley's experience in *Mont Blanc*. We know today even better than Shelley, since we live in a more technological and mechanised world, how easy it is to worship the spirit of Power, and how dangerous such worship can be. *Mont Blanc* is a poem about the dangers as well as the potentialities of confronting the Ahrimanic void, and brings Shelley to the brink of despair. It is not a poem which offers any easy optimisms. It shifts an enormous weight of responsibility into the hands of those 'wise, and great, and good' who understand the mountain's ambiguous message. God the Creator was a jealous God, who effectively took the work of creation out of man's sphere; soon after the Bible creation-history, we recall, comes the cautionary tale of man's ill-fated exertions at the Tower of Babel. The modern universe offers a hugely expanded scope for man's creativity. Shelley in *Mont Blanc* meditates on the necessity, alongside man's newly gained freedom, of a profound responsibility, and an increase in real, not indulgent, self-awareness.

LUCIFER, OR THE FADING STAR

> It is an isle 'twixt Heaven, Air, Earth, and Sea,
> Cradled, and hung in clear tranquillity;
> Bright as that wandering Eden Lucifer,
> Washed by the soft blue Oceans of young air.
> (Shelley, *Epipsychidion*)

It is one of the many paradoxes in ethical and religious history that the sublime activity of material creation which the Jews attributed to their God should have appeared, in the eyes of a pious Zoroastrian, sheerly Ahrimanic. And it is a measure of the gulf separating Judaism from other ancient oriental religions that it knows nothing of a wicked cosmic daemon, but that it originated instead a completely new myth of the origin and nature of evil. The Austrian philosopher Rudolf Steiner has well distinguished between those religious and poetic myths on the one hand which recognise a source of error in the Ahrimanic alienation, and those which acknowledge an equally delusive but opposite power, a tempter to inner pride, on the other. For the former type, the dualism of ancient Iran furnishes the most complete model; for the contrary power – whether or not recognised as a tempter – the image whose potency was felt long before Isaiah invoked it ironically in a famous rhetorical passage of prophecy, was the morning-star or Lucifer, the 'planet of infinite desire'. 'All that arises in the course of history,' says Steiner,

> in the guise of wonderful programmes, marvellously beautiful ideas, by which it is always believed that somehow or other a return can be made to the Golden Age – all this has its origin in the Luciferic tendencies which flow into man. Everything by which he tries to loosen his connection with reality, to soar above his actual circumstances – all this points to the Luciferic.[62]

It was the special contribution of Semitic myth, set out in the Old Testament and later embodied in the disposition of Christianity, to portray Lucifer as the tempter who offers man God-like knowledge for the satisfaction of his own yearnings. 'For God doth know', says the serpent in *Genesis* to Eve by the forbidden Tree, 'that in the day ye eat thereof, then your eyes shall be opened, and ye shall be as gods, knowing good and evil.'[63]

'I cannot discover why he is called Lucifer,' complained Shelley, 'except from a misinterpreted passage in Isaiah, where that poet exults over the fall of an Assyrian king, the oppressor of his country.' The celebrated 'Hellel ben Shahar' ('Day-star son of Dawning') passage remains in many respects a puzzle to scholars today, despite an increased awareness of the mythological background. What is certain is that Isaiah did not invent the image. Many had thrilled to its power before him, nor did the light-bearing star lose any of its fascination in the centuries after he introduced it into orthodox Judaeo-Christian tradition.[64] Despite his puzzlement, Shelley responded to its lure with some of his most breath-taking verse, as when in *Epipsychidion* he holds out to Emily the prospect of a sheltered isle, a place of dream-fulfilment, of total realisation of the self, the land of heart's desire. It is touched by the beauties of heaven and of earth, of air and of water; there all is clear and tranquil and weightless, and the burden of the mystery is lifted; an island:

> Bright as that wandering Eden Lucifer,
> Washed by the soft blue Oceans of young air.

It is as lustrous, and almost as lonely, as the morning-star in the brightening blue of the sky. The few 'pastoral people native there' relieve without disturbing the essential solitude of the place, and its fullness of sensation, satiating but not clouding the sense, leaves no room for hidden wants:

> And all the place is peopled with sweet airs;
> The light clear element which the isle wears
> Is heavy with the scent of lemon-flowers,
> Which floats like mist laden with unseen showers,
> And falls upon the eyelids like faint sleep;
> And from the moss violets and jonquils peep,
> And dart their arrowy odour through the brain
> Till you might faint with that delicious pain.
> And every motion, odour, beam, and tone,
> With that deep music is in unison:
> Which is the soul within the soul – they seem
> Like echoes of an antenatal dream.[65]

It is a Shakespearean magic island: but without a Caliban, and without the disruptive drama of tempest. We are returned to the second type of Shelley's 'contrary landscapes', which opens out into the infinity of the soul and its boundless, dream-filled spaces. And we approach once more the realm of 'planetary music', blending the world of empirical awareness into the hidden heights and depths, the seen into the unseen, the world of waking into that of sleep, the world of life into the half-remembered world before life.

Shelley finds the Luciferic island very seductive. In saying so, he is being more honest than many modern writers, anxious to avoid accusations of retreat from reality. It embodies for him all those tendencies which join him to the intensities of Sensibility in imagination and the idealisms of Platonism in thought; or rather, the landscape unbodies itself to blend with them in his mind. Shelley considered, when he came to formulate his theory of poetry, that some such Luciferic movement of the mind was necessary for any art to exist at all.[66] It was this recognition which raised him above empiricism as an ultimate creed and made him the great poet he is. It enabled him to be honest to the full spectrum of experience, particularly those states where our relationship with objectivity is strained, or overstepped. He used the term 'reverie' to describe them, and noted that it is in such states that there originates the 'Platonic' hope of a realisation of the self beyond the limits of chance and change. That hope of radical 'belonging' in the world originates in experience, not just in fantasy or speculation: and therefore, just as he cannot deny the Ahrimanic intimations he received on Mont Blanc, he cannot deny that human existence likewise involves as a part of its essence the contrary, Luciferic movement toward a transcendent ideal. In childhood, he points out, we are nearly all subject to reverie, and many carry the experience on into their reflective years – like Shelley himself. They recapture transiently something of the quality of childhood perception, before we learn to distinguish ourselves from the world. They:

> feel as if their nature were dissolved into the surrounding universe, or as if the surrounding universe were dissolved into their being. They are conscious of no distinction. And these are states which precede, or accompany, or follow an unusually intense or vivid apprehension of life.[67]

It is plain that Shelley knew the condition well.

Recovered at the level of Shelley's 'Intellectual System' of philosophy, the Luciferic state furnished the basis of a second axiom to complement the first (i.e. 'Mind cannot create, it can only perceive'). For Shelley now found himself unable to dissent from 'the conclusions of those philosophers who assert that nothing exists but as it is perceived . . . the solid universe of external things is "such stuff as dreams are made of" '.[68] By a pincer-movement deriving from these two axioms, Shelley vindicates imagination by abolishing the contrast with knowable external things. Things exist only as they are perceived; the mind cannot wilfully create, however, but only perceive. Shelley believes that he has thereby provided sufficient ground both for the truth of imagination and for objective knowledge. If we attempt to look beyond what the mind can perceive, we find ourselves peering into the Ahrimanic void. The Luciferic impulse, with its assertion that things only exist as they are perceived, rescues us from that destructive vision. Yet equally, if we follow the Luciferic impulse entirely and one-sidedly we enter into a fantasy-world where all criteria of objectivity finally break down.[69] Lucifer transports us to an unfallen Paradise, a time before the 'cruel twins':

Error and Truth, had hunted from the Earth
  All those bright natures which adorned its prime,
And left us nothing to believe in, worth
  The pains of putting into learned rhyme.[70]

In his metaphysical sketches, therefore, Shelley approaches philosophically a recognition of the need for both movements, the Luciferic as well as the Ahrimanic, if there is to be any certitude of knowledge. In his poetry, the Luciferic state is explored more profoundly and from a greater variety of perspectives, not just the cognitive – above all, on the level of 'daemonic' reality.

Shelley's rendering of the Luciferic 'reverie', and of the metaphysical hopes it may beget, has interesting analogues among the other English Romantics. How often, indeed, we encounter a similar imaginative projection in Coleridge! But there are also significant divergences. Take Coleridge's celebrated *The Eolian Harp* from the *Effusions* of 1796. There the wind-harp's sighing, moaning, sobbing notes subtly blend themselves (like Shelley's half-heard planetary music) with Coleridge's musings, associations of thought and his feelings for the Sara who leans pensively upon his arm. Gradually he is transported into a Shelleyan reverie, and exclaims:

O! the one Life within us and abroad,
Which meets all motion and becomes its soul,
A light in sound, a sound-like power in light,
Rhythm in all thought, and joyance every where –
Methinks, it should have been impossible
Not to love all things in a world so fill'd.[71]

The eolian harp's exquisite modulations to the varying breeze and the poet's varying mood suggests to him a unifying presence suffusing nature and man:

And what if all of animated nature
Be but organic Harps diversly fram'd,
That tremble into thought, as o'er them sweeps
Plastic and vast, one intellectual Breeze,
At once the Soul of each, and God of all?[72]

But then, suddenly, comes the reversal: Coleridge sees (or thinks he sees, it does not really matter for the guilt is his own) a reproach in Sara's eyes for his Luciferic imaginings, which he proceeds to revile as 'shapings of the unregenerate mind':

> Bubbles that glitter as they rise and break
> On vain Philosophy's aye-babbling spring.
> For never guiltless may I speak of Him,
> Th' INCOMPREHENSIBLE! save when with awe
> I praise him, and with Faith that inly *feels*.[73]

Thus Coleridge reveals once more how firmly he stands within the framework of Judaic 'guilt-culture', transmitted to modern Europe through the medium of orthodox Christianity. He shows too the tension which inevitably exists between Christian orthodoxy and the Romantic determination to experience all possibilities with ultimate intensity. Sensing that his imagination is leading him into the 'incomprehensible', where finite mental criteria of truth and morality no longer apply, Coleridge turns back to confess the limits of human awareness. The Luciferic urge is defeated, called sinful and unregenerate; and the sublimity of God, the unfathomable, who can be known only to awe-struck 'faith', is once again asserted. There is a boundary experience and a painful reversion, known to us under the name of guilt.

This reversion of 'guilt' is the inward pole within the dynamics of Judaic spirituality, just as the doctrine of sublime creation is its outward pole. The teaching of the divine creation annuls the terror of the Ahrimanic, so as to permit a greater degree of individual consciousness – at least in comparison with the older oriental religions: but at the same time, as we have seen, the burden of fear is shifted onto a collective, paternal Deity, so that in another way limitations are still placed on the autonomy of the individual spirit; what is effected is rather a powerful sense of national–religious community. This means in turn that Judaism, having fostered what was in the ancient world an unparalleled freedom in the cultivation of inwardness and private moral responsibility, must also define the limits of individual consciousness from the inner side. And it does so by setting bounds to man's Luciferic aspirations, forcing the quester after God-like knowledge to contract within his own limits in the pain of guilt.

The powerful Judaeo-Christian religious framework still retains a dominating grip over Coleridge's imagination in his poem. It is interesting, however, to contrast the method of *The Eolian Harp* with the pure interior monologue of *Mont Blanc*. For Coleridge does not make his poem a matter purely of his own individual mind. Since his is the Luciferic impulse, as his is the guilt, he inevitably feels reproach against the power which forces him back at the boundary – but in *The Eolian Harp* projects his feelings onto the 'pensive Sara'. We know nothing from the poem of what she really thinks. It is Coleridge who presents her as the 'meek' yet slightly formidable 'Daughter in the Family of Christ', and we feel his ambivalent attitude under the surface.[74] He regards her quite genuinely as his better self; yet the Lucifer in his imagination cannot completely put off its resentment. In the effort to preserve inner integrity, Coleridge comes to the brink of imaginative self-division. Shelley, in contrast, with his view of the dynamic complexity of the mind, can allow internal tensions and contradictions to appear in his imaginings, as in *Mont Blanc*, within the unity of poetic monologue – or, later, in an internalised or psychic theatre.

Shelley is impatient from the start with the collectively imposed limits of the self stipulated by Judaic tradition. He rejects the culture of guilt along with the doctrine of the sublime Creator, and where Coleridge turned back at the boundary, in an act of agonised self-definition, Shelley follows through the exhilaration of Luciferic release toward an absolute of vision. At this inner extreme of human experience, set free from the bounds of objectivity, Shelley's imagination shapes itself into another 'daemonic' presence. That presence finds its essential embodiment for the first time in a poem of 1820: the ode *To a Skylark*.

HARMONIOUS MADNESS: THE *SKYLARK* ODE

Here strong desire soars up toward an invisible source of music, scorning everything earthly and bounded, all the Necessitarian's endless chain of causes and effects. All is spontaneous, unpremeditated, unrestrained in the skylark's joy and flight; all disembodied, illimitable and ideal in its intense invisibility, as it soars higher and higher. From the beginning the bird is out of sight, leaving Shelley free to imagine a pure, discarnate Spirit spreading itself through the scene before him, and to suppose that the source of sound is 'Heaven, or near it'. The spirit in the song is all Luciferic expansiveness, all fire and cloud and air in its ecstatic ascent:

> Higher still and higher
>   From the earth thou springest
> Like a cloud of fire;
>   The blue deep thou wingest,
> And singing still dost soar, and soaring ever singest.[75]

Yet for all the associations of fire, brightness and clarity in these first stanzas, Shelley's experience already leads toward the utmost bounds of awareness. Here consciousness is vivid, but begins to assume the unreal vividness of dream rather than waking. The song seems to float and run over the clouds at the western horizon, lit from beneath by the already 'sunken sun', and so momentarily brightening just as darkness falls.[76] Objective nature melts in the purple of evening around the visionary flight of song, emphasising still further the apparent omnipresence and infiniteness of the sound. And Shelley senses that the 'race' of its 'unbodied joy' is even then just beginning, when visible and tangible reality drops away. The source of the music is occult, hidden from outward perception like a star in the broad daylight.

And being only unbodied thought, only song, this spirit-or-bird finds release from the phenomenal world, luring us toward a transcendent condition in which, as Harold Bloom says, infinite desire is gratified.[77] Here he becomes all but Lucifer himself:

> Keen as are the arrows
>   Of that silver sphere,
> Whose intense lamp narrows
>   In the white dawn clear
> Until we hardly see – we feel that it is there.[78]

As the morning-star fades in the colder light of day, our eyes reach after it ever more yearningly, to the very limits of the perceptible world, straining into the 'intense inane' of the supersensible.

But again we are denied a voice from some sublimer realm. Of the music's spiritual source in secret springs we can only be told: 'What thou art we know not'.[79] We have come to the boundary of knowledge, and the poem resorts to a wonderful series of images of that fact. Their subject being unknowable, the images are all oblique; and each mirrors its own obliqueness in content. In each the source of light, or sound, or scent, or whatever, is hidden – we know only its effects. The rainbow appears when cloud masses dissolve in the sunshine, and the raindrops fall out of nowhere, like the 'rain of melody' that showers down from the invisible bird. The visionary poet, concealed by the sublimity of his conceptions from general understanding, yet has the power sometimes to move the world 'to sympathy with hopes and fears it heeded not'. Some of the other images are more direct:

> Like a high-born maiden
>   In a palace-tower,
> Soothing her love-laden
>   Soul in secret hour
> With music sweet as love, which
>   overflows her bower:
>
> Like a glow-worm golden
>   In a dell of dew,
> Scattering unbeholden
>   Its aereal hue
> Among the flowers and grass, which
>   screen it from the view!
>
> Like a rose embowered
>   In its own green leaves,
> By warm winds deflowered,
>   Till the scent it gives
> Makes faint with too much sweet
>   those heavy-winged thieves.[80]

The poem runs through a crescendo of images, until all must be rejected, since the skylark itself surpasses them. The movement is exactly analogous to the 'wild thoughts' passage of *Mont*

Blanc, ending by confronting again what gave rise to the train of imagery, so that we are swept over the boundary into the bird's transcendent realm.[81]

Here, however, the poet is merely able to point the contrast with human inadequacy, and to question the bird, with no certainty of being answered:

> What objects are the fountains
>   Of thy happy strain?
> What fields, or waves, or mountains?
>   What shapes of sky or plain?
> What love of thine own kind? what ignorance of pain?[82]

Unable to assert finalities of knowledge, the poem resolves itself through the characteristically Shelleyan procedure of questioning. The poet's questions suggest, without asserting, the heart's vision of realisation freed from the shadow of 'sad satiety' which tracks every mortal desire. The skylark's song is a 'keen joyance' such as we imperfect, fallen beings could not attain even by renouncing our long heritage of fear and suffering; likewise its knowledge of death must be certain and deep, but it is inaccessible to us.

Shelley is probably remembering here an occult tradition, preserved by Francis Barrett. It concerns unfallen man, or Adam, 'whose figure or outward form was beautiful and proportionate as an angel', and:

> in whose voice (before he sinned) every sound was the sweetness of harmony and music: had he remained in the state of innocency in which he was formed, the weakness of mortal man, in his depraved state, would not have been able to bear the virtue and celestial shrillness of his voice.[83]

But then the Deceiver 'found that man, from the inspiration of God, had begun to sing so shrilly, and to repeat the celestial harmony of the heavenly country', and brought about the events of the fall. Man was thereupon deprived of his 'celestial shrillness', which his mortal nature could no longer endure. In longing for the virtue of the skylark, therefore, Shelley is longing for the state of Eden when man still copied the 'celestial harmony' or planetary music.

Yet it is to be noted that Shelley does not believe that Eden can be regained. Even if we could put off the burden of hatred, pride and fear, he says, we could still not approach the unsullied love and joy of the bird. What has been done in human history cannot be undone, and even a wrong that has been forgiven is not a wrong that has never been done.[84]

'I go on until I am stopped,' Shelley is reported to have said to Trelawney, '– and I never am stopped.'[85] But having rent the veil of inner experience, and broken through into the Luciferic realm of light and joy, Shelley is forced to concede an ambiguity in his aspiration and achievement. The daemon of hope offers the exuberance and delight of a visionary, supersensible world where no suffering can come, no mutability disquiet, or death punctuate. Yet the record of man's tyranny and atrocity cannot be wiped out as if it had never been. Moreover Shelley senses, in opposition to the bird's Luciferic wisdom, a fuller humanity than the 'blithe Spirit' of the skylark can ever achieve – a humanity learnt through the suffering and the wisdom of 'sad reality':

We look before and after,
   And pine for what is not:
Our sincerest laughter
   With some pain is fraught;
Our sweetest songs are those that tell of saddest thought.[86]

The tone of praise dominates the final stanzas; but there is more than a hint that Shelley, beneath his overt enthusiasm, has sensed the shortcomings of a Luciferic hope. It was, after all, Lucifer's offer of deathlessness and divine knowledge which rendered Paradise delusive – and so let 'killing Truth' destroy it.

5   Wisdom and Love

In truth all is influence except ourselves . . . but the difficulty is for our better nature to maintain itself vigorously, and not to allow the daemons more power than is due.   (Goethe to Eckermann)

It is love – the desire as Shelley defines it for imaginative community – which induced the brave spirit of the 1818 sonnet to lift the 'painted veil' of death and life, overleaping its boundaries in conscious poetic vision. In *Mont Blanc* and the ode *To a Skylark* Shelley was tentatively to resolve his poetic convictions on the side of Ahrimanic fear and Luciferic hope, at the same time being led to question the position he adopts or to show awareness of its ambiguity. In attempting an overall view he introduces a third daemonic power: that of Ἔρως or Love, which brings the other two into dynamic interplay.

> It is that powerful attraction towards all that we conceive, or fear or hope beyond ourselves, when we find within our own thoughts the chasm of an insufficient void, and seek to awaken all things that are to a community with what we experience in ourselves.[1]

Alastor, the long blank-verse meditative poem composed while Shelley was still at Bishopsgate in 1815, was the poet's first extended study of the loving soul in its lonely wanderings. There the haunted poet-hero is finally destroyed by the unresolved forces his aspiration unleashes. Shelley could not yet see, despite the growing clarity of his 'daemonic' vision, how any reconcilement of their energies could be achieved. Consciousness seems to be at the mercy of elemental powers which drive the central figure to interminable wanderings, both physical and psychological. The narrator, speaking from the standpoint of a belief in the sufficiency of the given world, visible and tangible Nature, condemns the poet he describes for his unreal expectations, for which he suffers the Ahrimanic

144

backlash. The hero is caught in a destructive dialectic of the two spirits, in pursuit of the visionary and himself pursued by the daemon of alienation, the spirit of solitude; through the inadequacy of all objects to his desire he suffers the destiny of those who, according to Shelley's Preface, 'perish through the intensity and passion of their search . . . when the vacancy of their spirit suddenly makes itself felt'.[2] Yet the narrator has no alternative to offer, and we suspect that the young hero of the poem images his own unrealised aspirations.

In *Alastor*, therefore, the only vision possible is that 'chasm of an insufficient void', and, anticipating *Mont Blanc*, the poem's uncertainty finds expression in questions of sleep and death:

> Does the dark gate of Death
> Conduct to thy mysterious paradise,
> O Sleep? Does the bright arch of rainbow clouds,
> And pendent mountains seen in the calm lake,
> Lead only to a black and watery depth?[3]

The Luciferic sense of the world as mere image, like a reflection on the surface of water, leads through disillusionment to the 'black and watery depth' of Ahrimanic negation beneath.

Yet Shelley persists in identifying himself imaginatively with consciousness – even when it appears that demands are being made upon it by powers beyond its control, and which it seems unable to fulfil. *Alastor* is one of the darkest of Shelley's poems, despite the fact that in it he for the first time discovered the full strength of his own style. It brought him to an impasse from which there is no obvious way forward or back. *Mont Blanc* and the *Skylark* ode, as we have seen, offered a clarification of the daemonic powers. But in order for him to escape the cul-de-sac of *Alastor* there had to come a further development of Shelley's consciousness, achieved in a poem of the following year which we have not yet mentioned.

A HARMONY IN AUTUMN: *HYMN TO INTELLECTUAL BEAUTY*

In contrast to the indirect and circuitous wanderings of *Alastor*, the *Hymn* is a direct address. We shall not linger over the background of the word 'Intellectual' in the title, except to say that in Shelley's day it had few of the logical and abstract connotations it bears today. Even to Blake, with his vehement opposition to 'Reason' when set against Imagination, the term 'Intellect' was acceptable in a positive sense: the beings of the spiritual world were for him 'Realities of Intellect', and God or Imagination was 'the intellectual foundation of Humanity'. Shelley's 'Intellectual Beauty' is the highest kind of beauty, above the 'unreal shapes' of sense-perception, a spiritual noumenon; yet there is nothing to suggest that it lies in abstract Platonic Forms – indeed, such an interpretation is decisively rejected in the body of the poem.[4]

Since it is a hymn to an unknown God – a divinity not numbered in the familiar pantheons – the poem must first define its subject: a supersensible Power whose shadow sometimes falls invisibly across the thoughts and perceived forms of man's consciousness. The opening lines present a double bafflement in rendering the occult. The Power is unseen, yet it is known by the effect of its shadow sweeping across phenomenal reality. That shadow, however, is also unseen and occult. What, after all, is Beauty? Certainly not a sensible quality that can be predicated of natural objects or outer forms. Nothing can really be said to 'possess' Beauty in that way. It lies more in a 'way of seeing', in a relationship between the object and the beholding consciousness. But that does not mean it falls under our deliberative control: we cannot choose to see or not to see the presence of Beauty by consciously adjusting our relationship to things. There are times when all of us, like Shelley and Coleridge and Wordsworth, would like to feel what we cannot then feel – we see, or hear, and know that we should be able to experience Beauty, but do not.[5] The relationship may therefore be described as one which relates the object of Beauty in some way to something within us, yet not to something in our consciousness directly. Beauty relates perceived things to something in our deeper being, an occult something not immediately describable in terms borrowed from phenomenal reality.

Shelley's figure for that relationship is the falling of a shadow, invisible ('occult') and from an invisible source. The opening stanza associates the shadow with natural scenes and events, but the syntax makes it clear that the presence of Beauty actually visits the beholder, the 'human heart and countenance'. It manifests itself in the objects through the fact that these henceforward become one pole in a comparison whose other term remains indefinable, mysterious, occult:

> Like clouds in starlight widely spread,
> Like memory of music fled,
> Like aught that for its grace may be
> Dear, and yet dearer for its mystery.[6]

On a starlit night, the presence of scattered clouds is revealed only when we notice patches of dark, where the stars are blotted out, though the obstructing clouds are unseen and there is no determinate outline of a 'hole' in our vision; nevertheless, the dark patches are felt as positive presences. Music often makes an especially strong impression upon us when we are no longer hearing it, and perhaps cannot recall a single note or phrase of melody, but only the deep effect. These things, and others, suggest to Shelley that the sense of mystery – a positive relation to the unknown – may form a basis for understanding the Spirit of Beauty, in so far as it can be 'understood' at all.

A profound sense of relatedness, then, at times irrupts into consciousness from the depths of our being as the experience of Beauty. Familiar objects of 'this various world' are transfigured in such moments as by the falling of some tremendous shadow. But the conscious self cannot compel its presence, nor choose to prolong or curtail the experience. The invisible shadow of Beauty moves amongst us 'inconstantly', like 'summer winds that creep from flower to flower'. Behind the image lies the New Testament passage on the *pneuma* – the word in Greek means both Spirit and Wind:

> The *pneuma* bloweth where it listeth, and thou hearest the voice thereof, but knowest not whence it cometh, and whither it goeth: so is every one that is born of the *pneuma*.[7]

This suggests that there may be a spiritual value in the very inconstancy of the Spirit – which indeed gradually emerges as the true theme of Shelley's *Hymn*. By a Shelleyan paradox, when in the second stanza the poet addresses the Spirit of

Beauty directly, it is straight away to lament its absence and to demand: 'where art thou gone?':

> Why dost thou pass away and leave our state,
> This dim vast vale of tears, vacant and desolate?[8]

There is a hint here of *Alastor* and its negative dialectics. But the *Hymn* now takes a different direction of thought, and though it touches on the powers and temptations which impelled the young poet-hero to his doom, manages to attain a tentative resolution of daemonic forces that will allow the survival, even the exaltation, of the conscious imaginative self.

Taking up the theme of Beauty in its largest sense, and the problem of ugliness and evil, the poem moves to consider a first false resolution. There are those, it says, who ask why evil and darkness should exist at all, why all that is good and pleasant does not last for ever, why it is that man should have so great a scope for hatred as well as love, for despair as well as hope. They long to believe in the essential goodness of things: to believe that pain and hate and fear are things that should not be, and have no meaning. Unable to find the comfort they seek in the real world, they ask whether there is not beyond it an ultimate fulfilment of their hope. But the poem replies to these Luciferic projectors with the full force of the poet's scepticism:

> No voice from some sublimer world hath ever
>   To sage or poet these responses given:
>   Therefore the names of Demon, Ghost, and Heaven,
> Remain the records of their vain endeavour –
> Frail spells, whose uttered charm might not avail to sever,
>   From all we hear and all we see,
>   Doubt, chance, and mutability.[9]

The solutions of dogmatic philosophy and religion, like all other attempts to lay hold on ultimate reality by the sheer force of the believing self, appear to the poet all-too-human. Their attempt to dispel 'Doubt, chance, and mutability' leads to a refuge in delusion, a half-willing though unacknowledged blindness to harsh truths. Shelley has seen in *Alastor* where such delusions end, how man's spirit is most open to attack from what it refuses to see. He must accept, therefore, for the integrity of his vision that death and change are deeply entwined in the nature of things, much as man longs Luciferically to possess Beauty for ever and by the power of his own Ego. Could he do so, man would himself become as a God. Still addressing the Spirit of Beauty the poet says:

> Man were immortal, and omnipotent,
> Didst thou, unknown and awful as thou art,
> Keep with thy glorious train firm state within his heart.[10]

The Shelleyan conditionals ('were', 'Didst') subtly make the point of man's need to be conscious of his own actual limits, as well as of his hidden depths and potentialities.

Shelley accepts, then, the full reality of death and change. But he does not falsify the inherently human desire that the vision of the ideal should never fade or die. He still begs the Spirit not to depart, the desire for permanency being all the more poignantly felt as the poet faces the ultimate consequences of his dark acceptance:

> Depart not as thy shadow came,
> Depart not – lest the grave should be,
> Like life and fear, a dark reality.[11]

The poem moves now toward the world of Gothic imagination, through which Shelley had explored the fearful powers which may invade the self in a spectral intensity of terror. A month after the *Hymn*, this strain in Shelley's poetry was to culminate in the Ahrimanic vision of *Mont Blanc*. Here, Shelley looks back upon his history of attempts to penetrate the 'black and watery depth' behind physical nature – in a not so much religious as magical, necromantic search for the sources of ultimate power:

> While yet a boy I sought for ghosts, and sped
> Through many a listening chamber, cave and ruin,
> And starlight wood, with fearful steps pursuing
> Hopes of high talk with the departed dead.[12]

Later, as we have seen, Shelley put his Gothic fantasies to maturer uses. But the attempt to penetrate reality in this direction proves as unsuccessful as the former Luciferic way: 'I was not heard, I saw them not', the poet bluntly says. Followed to its extreme, the Ahrimanic vision too yields no human truth by which man can live; it leaves him trapped within himself, staring out into voidness.

Thus Shelley in the *Hymn* plays off against one another the contrary impulses which in *Alastor* succeeded in wrenching imaginative consciousness asunder. Against the unreal hope of a 'voice from some sublimer world' to make all effortlessly plain, he poses the sceptical awareness of human weakness and man's fathomless powers of self-deception. Against the vision of negation and its helpless gropings in the Gothic void, he poses the seemingly ineradicable human hope of a higher truth. And against the inconstant manifestation of the Spirit of Beauty, when the visible universe is glorified in the shadow of the invisible, he sets a human power of acceptance that can achieve freedom in relinquishing the Luciferic–Ahrimanic attempt to possess truth and beauty absolutely.

Consciousness can achieve final control neither over outer nature nor over the hidden depths of man's being. Yet it can hold itself open, it can bear the burden of fear without fleeing into delusions, it can resist man's desire of self-inflation beyond the bounds of attained reality. And therefore there may be moments when it is illumined, transfigured, even 'consecrated' by the Spirit to whom the *Hymn* is dedicated. Whilst Shelley was musing over the labyrinthine errors of past time, he relates:

> Sudden, thy shadow fell on me;
> I shrieked, and clasped my hands in ecstasy![13]

In the *Hymn* Shelley finds his vocation as in some sense a religious poet – though it is a 'religion' very different from what we ordinarily mean by the word. It has its vigils, certainly, in that constant openness to the presence of infinites in experience which pervades Shelley's thought and life:

> I call the phantoms of a thousand hours
> Each from his voiceless grave: they have in visioned bowers
>   Of studious zeal or love's delight
>   Outwatched with me the envious night:
> They know that never joy illumed my brow
>   Unlinked with hope that thou wouldst free
>   This world from its dark slavery –
>   That thou, O awful LOVELINESS,
> Wouldst give whate'er these words cannot express.[14]

Through the *Hymn to Intellectual Beauty* Shelley discovers a way of fusing the poetry of ultimates with an acceptance of human consciousness in its uncertainties and shortcomings. In the last stanza of the poem, recalling an earlier image of the Spirit of Beauty – 'Like hues and harmonies of evening' – Shelley tempers his delight in pure strong colours, and contrasts with it a poetry of reconciliation. A softening of the pure qualities of absolute vision grants to man's frail and finite imaginative consciousness a unique music, like that sensed in the *Skylark* ode, in contrast to the superhuman melody of the bird, a mingling of sweet song and saddest thought:

> The day becomes more solemn and serene
> When noon is past: there is a harmony
>   In autumn, and a lustre in its sky,
> Which through the summer is not heard or seen,
> As if it could not be, as if it had not been![15]

The autumn harmonies blend the tones of glaring summer and chilling winter, of living and dying – praising the particular glory of what it means to be man: the planetary song accommodated to human ears. That music may often seem an impossibility – but in the *Hymn* Shelley proves for the first time that it can be heard and sung.

The occultist Francis Barrett taught his adepts that 'the sum and perfection of all learning' was 'to live in the fear of God, and in love and charity with all men'.[16] But in dedicating himself to the service of the hidden power of Beauty, Shelley owns his responsibility to a nearer authority:

> Whom, SPIRIT fair, thy spells did bind
> To fear himself, and love all human kind.[17]

A KIND OF OPTIMISM: WISDOM AND LOVE

'Let us believe in a kind of optimism', Shelley wrote, 'in which we are our own gods.'[18]

What he envisaged was not, I think, a manic form of humanism on the way to self-worshipping rationalism, Blake's vision of man adoring his own Spectre – what he himself called the 'dark idolatry of Self'. Writing to Maria Gisborne (in a prose letter this time) he was evidently revolving in his mind a passage from Coleridge's *The Friend*. There Coleridge discusses the importance – even the 'awful duty' – of hope for man's life, describing it as 'an instinct of his nature and an indispensable condition of his moral and intellectual progression'. For Wordsworth too, points out Timothy Webb, hope had been 'the paramount duty that Heaven lays, / For its own honour, on man's suffering heart'.[19] But in Shelley's letter the duty we owe to Heaven is redefined: from his humanistic perspective it becomes 'a solemn duty which we owe alike to ourselves & to the world'.[20] And in a broader sense, taking in man's deepest fears as well as his instinctual hopes, Shelley presents it as the centre of his poetic thought that man must take upon himself the burdens and the aspirations he once shared with God or 'the gods'. The doctrine of creation had enabled man to share the crushing weight of alienation with an Almighty Father; the Olympian ideal had kept alive man's hope with the vision of a superhuman order of fulfilment. Both had held man back, however, from the full sense of his conscious individuality – which Shelley realises is the pivotal point of human freedom.

In the *Hymn to Intellectual Beauty* Shelley first forges an imaginative self, the presence of an 'I' in the poem, able to sustain the terror of the 'black and watery depth', the Ahrimanic vacuity behind nature, without yielding to despair; an 'I' that is strong enough to hold itself open to hope even while the transfiguring Spirit of Beauty seems irrevocably absent from its world. But what is the power which Shelley trusts, which can rise from the inscrutable depths of man's unconscious nature and accord him that strange and uncontrollable, conscious yet self-transcending experience he has described as the vision of Intellectual Beauty? What is that supersensible presence whose shadow falls invisibly across sensible reality? What can it be, this power which is at once united with our own deepest being and yet carries us beyond ourselves – if not the daemonic power of Love?

In *Alastor* it was the impetus of love, understood in Shelleyan terms as the desire for imaginative communion, which set in motion the destructive dialectic of Luciferic and Ahrimanic forces. For there love was perverted, prevented from going forth from itself and turned back in self-love. The youth turns away the human love of the pining Arab maiden to pursue his phantom ideal; the narrator denies his own inner aspirations. Giving himself to the pursuit of a delusory self-projection, the young hero like the Wordsworthian narrator experiences the backlash of the alienated outer world. But just as love can lead to the internal contradiction which destroys conscious integrity when it remains fettered to the principle of Self – so when consciousness attains to the self-overcoming of the *Hymn*, the hidden power of love enables a dialectical balance between hope and fear to be achieved, and with it a balance between self and other that can be the foundation of mutual relationship. It is important to grasp that Shelley's ideal of love is neither naïve and uncritical, nor sentimental and simple. To love rightly, he found, is a difficult and often complicated thing. True love does not seek to possess, being in this respect the reverse of the Luciferic and Ahrimanic aspirations, both of which seek to possess ultimate knowledge or power for the self.

Love therefore is as uncontrollable as the Spirit of Beauty in the *Hymn*, can never be more than partially grasped by conscious wisdom. In its own illimitable essence it reaches into the heights of the 'rare universe' beyond conscious perception or systematic thought. It manifests itself in a powerful occult sympathy – so that Shelley in his essay *On Love* envisions the form of the beloved as:

> a frame whose nerves, like the chords of two exquisite lyres, strung to the accompaniment of one delightful voice, vibrate with the vibrations of our own . . . this is the invisible and unattainable point to which Love tends; and to attain which, it urges forth the powers of man to arrest the faintest shadow of that without the possession of which there is no rest nor respite to the heart over which it rules.[21]

Yet by reaching with an endless striving into the supersensible through love, consciousness need not lose itself in the infinite. If it can balance the daemonic and disruptive powers of Lucifer and Ahriman, consciousness finds itself once more as one term in a reciprocal movement, a new polarity which might be represented at right angles to the established Luciferic-Ahrimanic polarity. Along with Love, in the *Hymn*, are given

'Hope' and 'Self-esteem' – Shelley's reconstituted triad of Christian virtues – replacing the negative triad of 'fear and self-contempt and barren hope' which rule the life of enslaved and unimaginative man.[22]

Figure 6 may help us visualise the interplay of forces Shelley imagines, and draw together some of the thoughts in our interpretation. We must beware, however, of taking its suggestive coordinates too fixedly.

For one thing, we must always remember to think dynamically. Figure 6 is intended to represent fundamental tensions and tendencies in Shelley's imagination, not to establish categories of his thought.

Secondly, we must not be tempted to take Figure 6 in a merely psychological sense, even though it may sometimes be legitimate to stress its psychological aspects. Its four polar terms certainly cannot be understood in the sense of Jungian

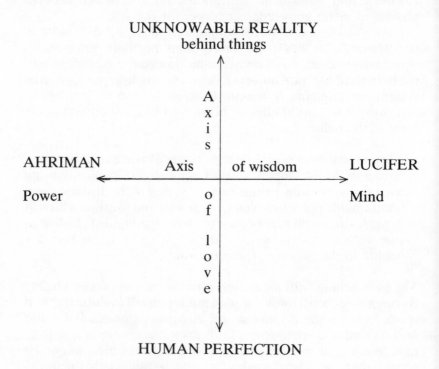

FIGURE 6   *The Shelleyan polarities*

archetypes, or as standing for psychic pressures alone, since all of them involve a relation to objectivity as a crucial part of their meaning. Furthermore, all four terms demand in their imaginative realisation a response from the whole being of man, his cognitive capacities as well as his emotional or unconscious inner nature.[23]

Lastly, it should be realised that Figure 6 represents the forces of Shelleyan imagination in a state of dynamic equilibrium – the configuration belonging especially to the *Hymn*. In other manifestations of that imagination the pattern of tensions will naturally appear different. To represent the destructive constellation of *Alastor*, for example, we might show the love-axis turned anticlockwise until it merges with the horizontal axis: the vision of human perfection is absorbed into Luciferic desire, and reality is acknowledged only in the form of the inhuman Ahrimanic backlash. The healthy polarity between man and cosmic reality is assimilated to the Luciferic–Ahrimanic movement of mutual negation.

Used within proper limits and with imaginative appropriateness, then, such a parallelogram of forces may assist us in clarifying the imaginative energies which give form to Shelley's greater poems. We have seen how in *Alastor* the Luciferic and Ahrimanic complement each other and lead to a psychic disintegration; how in the *Hymn to Intellectual Beauty* Shelley achieves an openness through equilibrium and an 'autumnal' blending. The sense of polarity, and of the added dimension represented by the vertical axis of Figure 6, remain through all of Shelley's later poems, including *Prometheus Unbound* – and even *The Triumph of Life*, where all of the poet's established forms appear to become fluid and undefined once more, as he moves toward a new synthesis, never fully revealed.

In the balancing of forces along the horizontal axis consists the cultivation of conscious wisdom. Yet along that axis we come to grips only with man as a knower, as a being whose attention is turned to understanding the universe around him in his conscious experience. Critics who have treated Shelley in terms of two simple contrary tendencies (scepticism and idealism, realism and fantasy, etc.) have therefore had little chance of comprehending the poet's doctrine of mediating love, which treats of man in his own essential being.

Human consciousness, according to Shelley, is only possible where contrary absolutes are held in creative interplay – but the power which holds them also relates man directly to a greater reality, revealed in those moments of visionary Beauty when the conscious world is overshadowed by the supersensible. The infinite possibilities inherent in these experiences can never, in the modern parlance, be fully 'formalised'. Indeed they are in principle transcendences, our capacities for leaping beyond the known, familiar and defined to new apprehensions, the lived reality in which we know our own being and at the same time know our roots to lie in the unknown, unfathomable immediacy of life.[24] The question, 'What is love?' fades into absurdity: 'What is love? Ask him who lives, what is life? Ask him who adores, what is God?'[25] Shelley values the forces of conscious wisdom highly: without them a life lived out of pure spontaneity would inevitably fall victim to fears and delusions. But without the immediate relationship of essence to essence which is love, man's life would be a self-referent and self annihilating analytics.

In this context it should not appear strange that the axis of love in Figure 6 is not concerned with the human world alone; for Shelley human love is continuous with the hidden sympathies which join us to nature as a whole:

> Hence in solitude, or in that deserted state when we are surrounded by human beings, and yet they sympathise not with us, we love the flowers, the grass, and the waters, and the sky. In the motion of the very leaves of spring, in the blue air, there is often found a secret correspondence with our heart. There is eloquence in the tongueless wind, and a melody in the flowing brooks and the rustling of the reeds beside them, which by their inconceivable relation to something within the soul, awaken the spirits to a dance of breathless rapture, and bring tears of mysterious tenderness to the eyes, like the enthusiasm of patriotic success, or the voice of one beloved singing to you alone. Sterne says that, if he were in a desert, he would love some cypress.[26]

Along the vertical axis of Figure 6, therefore, we approach at its cosmic pole the unfathomable reality of life and the world, the object of Shelley's profound agnosticism. But it is approached here, not through the instruments of conscious mental realisation but as the immediate source of things in which 'we live, and move and have our being', Shelley's unknown God. We are, after all, ourselves a part of that reality in which we live, however baffling and inscrutable it may largely remain to the evidence of our senses and intellect. It presents itself to the imagination in 'secret correspondences' or in 'unconceivable relation' to something in the depths of the soul. It is a paradox to torment philosophers, that they live in practical union with the reality they strive progressively to comprehend.

The axis of love, however, does not cut blindly across the axis of wisdom, ignoring the efforts of conscious progression. Indeed, if the daemons of knowledge and power are given improper rein, love's energy may turn its currents disastrously awry, destroying itself and conscious wisdom alike. On the other hand, for Shelley it is also possible to enter with an imaginatively strengthened and balanced consciousness into love's world of secret sympathies and thinking of the heart. Or rather, one might say that love of its own nature strives from its unconscious origins to awaken within our conscious being. For that 'profound and complicated sentiment, which we call love', is not limited to our organic, sensual being, but: 'is rather the universal thirst for a communion not merely of the senses, but of our whole nature, intellectual, imaginative and sensitive'.[27] In Shelley's dynamic philosophy of mind it is the power of love which at once strives for a plenum of consciousness while at the same time constantly leading man out beyond himself to mark 'the before unapprehended relations of things' and reveal what is lovable in objects that to the custom-bound mind may seem ordinary, drab or even repulsive. Here Shelley also found the germ of a theory of poetry – and much else besides.[28]

Above all, it afforded him a notion of morality that broke with the 'normative' view of ethics, deriving in his time from the Enlightenment and epitomised in the views of Hume and Kant. They presented the demands of ethics as fundamentally unrelated to man's actual situation: as an 'ought' of moral obligation which can never be derived from the 'is' of how things are (Hume); or as a 'categorical imperative' of practical reason whose ground cannot be questioned (Kant). But for Shelley:

> The great secret of morals in love; or a going out of our own nature, and an identification of ourselves with the beautiful

which exists in thought, action, or person, not our own. A man, to be greatly good, must imagine intensely and comprehensively; he must put himself in the place of another and of many others; the pains and pleasures of his species must become his own. The great instrument of moral good is the imagination; and poetry administers to the effect by acting upon the cause. Poetry enlarges the circumference of the imagination by replenishing it with thoughts of ever new delight, which have the power of attracting and assimilating to their own nature all other thoughts, and which form new intervals and interstices whose void for ever craves fresh food. Poetry strengthens that faculty which is the organ of the moral nature of man, in the same manner as exercise strengthens a limb.[29]

Shelley's philosophy of 'moral imagination' and love is at once a fulfilment and a transcendence of the ethics of Sensibility and the 'man of feeling'.[30] It shares the 'aesthetic' emphasis on sympathy and identification with another's situation; but goes beyond the ponderous moral deliberations of Sensibility in its view of the active imagination and the acceptance of man's divided, mixed nature. In a passage which seems to have been important to Shelley, Paul wrote to the Corinthians of love that it 'suffereth long, and is kind . . . beareth all things, believeth all things, hopeth all things, endureth all things'.[31] The vision of 'Intellectual Beauty' depended upon an acceptance of the fact of darkness and death inextricably mixed in the actual world – without such acceptance beauty would be only a bright delusion. Likewise in Shelley's ethics, love must accept and endure the inevitable presence of evil. Those who pass judgement upon themselves by the codes of categorical moral philosophy must ultimately destroy themselves as human beings in barren self-contempt and despair. The moral imagination redeems us with a power of self-acceptance – and of self-transformation.[32]

Love, as the moving agency of moral life and, in the conscious imagination, as the spring of 'Intellectual Beauty', furnished Shelley with a path forward between the twin absolutes of wisdom. His doctrine of love is unsentimental: it does not merely idealise the beloved, but rather resembles that Christian love which bears and endures imperfections. Its hope is not the deluded hope of the Luciferic idealist, a 'barren hope' denied by the nature of things; its endurance is not based on an Ahrimanic nihilism. It permitted Shelley 'a kind of optimism' about man and the universe, the ability of man's spirit to make sense of the world and his existence, to transform himself and rise above seemingly insurmountable practical and metaphysical obstacles. It rescued him from 'the wisdom of a high despair' such as has claimed many modern thinkers. At the same time – to return to the passage from Coleridge in *The Friend* which Shelley quoted, a passage where for once Coleridge does not speak out of the values of the Judaic heritage, but out of a more purely Christian confidence – it enabled him to 'temper the desire of improvement with love and a sense of gratitude for what we already are'.[33]

Shelley's new resolution of the daemonic forces results in the imagination of a new archetype of human consciousness, a Promethean attitude to the world and the 'divinity' of man. That consciousness is projected most fully in *Prometheus Unbound* itself, the centrepiece of Shelley's poetic *oeuvre*.

We witness its birth-pangs of the soul, however, in another poem that was to be published in the same volume.

PROLOGUE TO REGENERATION: *ODE TO THE WEST WIND*

Winters and summers, spring and summer seasons roll round in their course with their own qualities, their own characters, their own fruits. For the earth is schooled by heaven to clothe the trees after they have been stripped, to colour the flowers anew, to cover the earth again with grass, to bring forth the seeds which have been destroyed, and not to bring them forth until destroyed. A wonderful plan! The defrauder becomes a preserver, making away in order to restore, losing in order to safeguard, spoiling in order to renew, reducing in order to enlarge; for indeed this process restores to us things far richer and finer than those which it brought to an end; by a ruin which is in truth a profit, an injustice which yields a dividend, a loss which is a gain. I might sum it up by saying that renewal is a universal principle. Whatever you meet with has before existed; whatever you have lost returns to existence. All things return after they have disappeared; all things begin when they have ceased to be; they come to an end in order that they may come to be. Nothing perishes but with a view to restoration. Thus the whole order of things, this order of revolution, bears testimony to the resurrection of the dead. (Tertullian of Carthage, *De resurrectione carnis*, 12)

Stirb and werde!
(Goethe)

To move from the *Hymn to Intellectual Beauty* of 1816 to the *Ode to the West Wind* of three years later is to experience the shift from discovery to affirmation. Shelley's voice has grown in confidence as well as in power, and Shelley's mind has succeeded in further unifying the conflicting energies of his imagination – finding in the westerly storm-wind of Italy an image capable of profoundly satisfying them all and bringing them within a single dynamic complex of poetry. He has learnt a great deal from the huge projects of the intervening years: the sprawling failure of *Laon and Cythna* (1817), his first attempt at an integral epic vision; the gathering triumph of *Prometheus Unbound* (begun in September 1818 and still in progress). Yet the *Ode*, composed in the autumn of 1819, represents a deepening and intensification of the themes of the *Hymn*, not a new departure. It resumes many of the concerns of its predecessor: but the pace has changed from lyrical Andante to urgent Allegro, expressing now the sense of something struggling into existence. The revelation of Beauty no longer descends upon a 'passive youth', but upon a Promethean imagination striving to be free of its chains.[34]

The poem commences with the immediacy of invocation. There is no descriptive prelude as in the *Hymn*. The poet calls upon the hidden power of the *pneuma*, Wind and Spirit, the 'unseen presence' which brings life-in-death or death-in-life, herding the autumn leaves like hordes of the dead or dying. The *Hymn* invoked an 'awful shadow', only to lament its absence in the universe of death: now Shelley sees deeper, to a total pattern in which transfiguration and destruction are aspects of one creative movement. The inherence of evil and death is no longer simply accepted alongside the manifestation of Beauty; it is affirmed. The revelation of Beauty in the 'before unapprehended relations of things' is only possible if we are prepared to leave behind what is old and faded from its first imaginative splendour. To stand still is to atrophy; destruction is a necessary moment in the creative flux of transformation.

Shelley's occult energy, his 'Wild Spirit' moving everywhere through phenomenal reality like the wind through autumn leaves, is both destroyer and preserver; and the first stanza of the poem celebrates both aspects equally, almost as if it were mathematically possible to pose the one against the other and estimate the balance:

O Wild West Wind, thou breath of Autumn's being,
Thou, from whose unseen presence the leaves dead
Are driven, like ghosts from an enchanter fleeing,

Yellow, and black, and pale, and hectic red,
Pestilence-stricken multitudes: O thou,
Who chariotest to their dark wintry bed

The winged seeds, where they lie cold and low,
Each like a corpse within its grave, until
Thine azure sister of the Spring shall blow

Her clarion o'er the dreaming earth, and fill
(Driving sweet buds like flocks to feed in air)
With living hues and odours plain and hill:

Wild Spirit, which art moving everywhere;
Destroyer and preserver; hear, oh, hear![35]

The symmetry of death and birth, autumn and spring, in these lines make it seem temporarily that Shelley is ready to be consoled by a purely natural vision, the promise of nature's flourishing once more after winter's deprivations. It seems that he will deny for the sake of that vision the irreversible human reality of death. The seeds lie cold and low in the ground, but they are only 'like' human corpses in their graves. They do not die, and wake from sleep along with the 'dreaming earth' itself in the spring.[36] Being unindividualised fragments of the pervading life of nature, what could they know of the pain of mutability?

But with man it is different: 'They die – the dead return not', as Shelley had movingly written in his poem *Death*.[37] If there were no more to the poetry of the *Ode* we should mistrust its stormy rhetoric. But in the second stanza Shelley expands his vision from the earthly scene with the leaves before him to take in the vaster commotion of the skies. The Wind's power now reaches from the far boundary of the horizon to the zenith's height overhead. The clouds, borne with unusual rapidity on the 'aery surge' of the streaming Wind, reflect and magnify the image of the swirling, decaying leaves, and the parallelism suggests that we have lifted our attention from the finite world into the macrocosm. The cloud-masses are more precarious bodies than the leaves, despite their larger scale, more suggestive of the dissolution that is to come when the impending storm finally breaks. As 'angels' of rain and lightning, they are at once the literal 'messengers' (Greek *angeloi*) of the oncoming tempest, and implicitly apocalyptic angels heralding an eschatological destruction.

The rhetoric of the poem, besides admirably generating the tension of a Mediterranean squall, now clearly becomes the bearer of an aspiration which cannot remain content with the natural vision of the first stanza. The energy of the *pneuma* strains toward Dionysian ecstasy, an intense exhilaration transcending the bounds of the mundane object-world. The comparison of the inrushing stream of storm clouds to the floating hair of the Maenad introduces into the stanza a sense of overwhelming power that must inevitably burst the finite vessel into which it is poured – even when that vessel is the whole dome of the visible earth and sky! The fact of destruction and dissolution in the natural world is now admitted in its full force, without an attempt at consoling the natural man. Shelley calls upon the Spirit which annihilates 'the dying year' in the act of emergence upon a higher level of reality:

> Thou dirge
> Of the dying year, to which this closing night
> Will be the dome of a vast sepulchre,
> Vaulted with all thy congregated might
>
> Of vapours, from whose solid atmosphere
> Black rain, and fire, and hail will burst: oh, hear![38]

The necessity of death and change is here honestly acknowledged and affirmed.

Shelley's account of the pain of transitoriness in the *Ode* is very different from that in the *Hymn*. In the earlier poem Beauty came and went, and the recipient consciousness permitted itself to be borne along in the succession of experience, enabled to bear the intervening pain by grace of the inconstant visitations of the Spirit. In the *Ode to the West Wind* Shelley no longer allows himself to be carried along on the flow of life through light and dark, beauty and desolation. He plunges actively into life, embracing the need of change and becoming in a constant dying and rebirth. The bleak intervals of abandonment by the presence of Beauty assume their ultimate meaning on a higher level as workings of the Spirit in a total pattern of transformation – a rite of passage: an initiation.

In the third stanza, however, Shelley quite suddenly turns from the acceptance of death and change to wistful reminiscence. He recalls with genuine pathos (yet without being wholly seduced by it) an alternative possibility of transcendence – a Luciferically intensified natural reality translated into the purity of the image:

> Thou who didst waken from his summer dreams
> The blue Mediterranean, where he lay,
> Lulled by the coil of his crystalline streams,
>
> Beside a pumice isle in Baiae's bay,
> And saw in sleep old palaces and towers
> Quivering within the wave's intenser day,
>
> All overgrown with azure moss and flowers
> So sweet, the sense faints picturing them![39]

This is not simply, in Harold Bloom's terms, 'the best of the old order' that is to be swept away in the apocalyptic fury of the Wind;[40] it is the order of nature made metaphysical in the mirror of imaginative desire. Yet compared to the awakening blast of the Wind it has only the vividness of dream. Consciousness faints in its excess or fades in its 'intenser day'. The quivering reflection on the summer sea epitomises Shelley's imagery, which we have noticed before, of the bright but inessential floating surface-picture – and suggests that we shall find the Ahrimanic 'black and watery depth' below. But here consciousness is not to be lured into the self-destroying dialectic: the Luciferic harmony is blended into the symphonic complexity of the *Ode*, but instead of the inscrutable dark abyss beneath the image, we are shown another mysterious working of the Spirit, penetrating even to the ocean depths through occult sympathy:

> while far below
> The sea-blooms and the oozy woods which wear
> The sapless foliage of the ocean, know
>
> Thy voice, and suddenly grow gray with fear,
> And tremble and despoil themselves.[41]

'The phenomenon alluded to at the conclusion of the third stanza', explains Shelley in a note to the *Ode*, 'is well known to naturalists. The vegetation at the bottom of the sea, of rivers, and of lakes, sympathises with that of the land in the change of seasons, and is consequently influenced by the winds which announce it.'[42] In the context of Shelley's address to the 'unseen presence' of the *pneuma*, however, the well-known natural phenomenon becomes something of deep strangeness and mystery – natural science becomes occult science – anticipating the elemental worlds portrayed in *Prometheus Unbound*.

In all three stanzas Shelley has been calling to the Wind, 'striving' with the Spirit in prayer, as he later says. In the fourth of the *Ode*'s stanzas he attacks the problem of his own fixity and intractability before the Spirit's power. The elements of nature, since they do not seek their own identity, share the impulse of the Spirit's strength without the resistence of selfhood. Even Shelley himself, if he could regain the Wordsworthian raptures of his childhood –

and could be

The comrade of thy wanderings over Heaven,
As then, when to outstrip thy skiey speed
Scarce seemed a vision[43]

– might succeed in identifying himself unreflectively with the Wind. But that, he knows, can no longer be. A man cannot put aside the weight of experience and step back into the world of innocence. Shelley sees also the 'shades of the prison-house' which have darkened around him, the closedness and intransigence which have become part of his very identity. It is because of these that he cannot yield himself like a leaf, or cloud or wave to the surge of the *pneuma* but must struggle in the agony of prayer. Unlike the spiritually translucent objects of nature, Shelley can move toward the longed-for identity with the Wind only by a painful casting out of the intransigent elements in his psyche, in a death and regeneration. Yet, torn and bleeding, Shelley's lower self forms the chaos of raw material from which his higher imaginative identity must be shaped.

Shelley's vision differs once again, therefore, from Blake's idea of a 'Last Judgment' which happens 'whenever any Individual Rejects Error & Embraces Truth'. The individual then realises his identity with the divine–human Imagination and puts off the outer, inessential man, acknowledging it as only a 'State' through which his true 'identity' has passed.[44] But Shelley is not prepared to give up the 'connexion' of personal history in this dualistic manner. In his version of apocalypse the visionary expansion of consciousness and the dying, changing selfhood exist in dynamic tension and in virtually continuous process of rebirth.

Thus in the final stanza of the *Ode* there is no mystical union though there is achievement. There is still striving and aspiration; still the pain of change and impermanence. Shelley does not dissolve his identity in the omnipresent Spirit, but rather calls upon the Spirit to be his spirit: 'Be thou me, impetuous one!' He survives as an imaginative consciousness even his near encounter with the occult power of inspiration, destroyer and preserver.[45] He is definitely not translated into a Platonic 'sublimer world' – he remains in the realm of death and becoming, his leaves falling and decaying like those of the forest. Therefore the planetary music of his closing song cannot be the absolute intensity either of destruction or of an Elysian dream. It is again the mingled, autumn music of the human condition, even amidst the glory of Promethean apocalypse:

> Make me thy lyre, even as the forest is:
> What is my leaves are falling like its own!
> The tumult of thy mighty harmonies
>
> Will take from both a deep, autumnal tone,
> Sweet though in sadness.[46]

The *Ode to the West Wind* is Shelley's most powerful demonstration among his shorter poems that visionary rebirth need not be understood as the negation of man's consciousness, but as its dynamic fulfilment in a process of spiritual growth. In the last lines of the poem the initiatory themes of regeneration and apocalypse finally emerge into explicitness. Shelley calls upon the 'Spirit fierce':

> Drive my dead thoughts over the universe
> Like withered leaves to quicken a new birth!
> And, by the incantation of this verse,
>
> Scatter, as from an unextinguished hearth
> Ashes and sparks, my words among mankind!
> Be through my lips to unawakened earth
>
> The trumpet of a prophecy! O, Wind,
> If Winter comes, can Spring be far behind?[47]

Shelley discovers in the *Ode* the true centre of his poetry, the unifying impulse which will hold together the tensions of his mind and imagination. In *Prometheus Unbound* he was already making of it a vision of the universe. It is the power of imaginative transformation, an elevating power enabling us to bear the godlike burden of ultimate perspectives that open up beyond the 'painted veil', a power that exalts but also burns and destroys in the fierceness of its love.

6 Riders in the Chariot

EARTH-CHILD AND MOON-CHILD: *PROMETHEUS UNBOUND*

Shelley's greatest and most original achievement, the 'lyrical drama' *Prometheus Unbound*, was composed in a period of about a year from autumn 1818 to the latter part of 1819, with perhaps a few later additions. Yet in many ways it contains the whole of his life's wisdom – concentrated into a highly unusual and Shelleyan form, for which the only modern parallel in matters of form may be the Second Part of Goethe's *Faust*.

Richard Cronin has said that *Prometheus* is a drama of 'modes of perception', and so it is, so long as we realise that a mode of perception is not passivity but an active expression of the inner state of the perceiver.[1] Since Shelley himself remarked that he had drawn much of the imagery 'from the operations of the human mind', all serious critics of the play have begun from the recognition that the personae, and even the natural settings of the scenes, are directly linked with aspects of the mind or self of Prometheus. More exactly, we may describe *Prometheus Unbound* as daemonic or psychic theatre, where inner complexities as well as outward orientations of the mind can be played out in poetic imagination.

Holding to our old coordinates, we may point to the fundamental opposition within the play, in imagery intensified by the personal tragedies and joys of Shelley's life in Italy, between the 'icy rocks' of Act I, the spiritless Ahrimanic world:

> Black, wintry, dead, unmeasured; without herb,
> Insect, or beast, or shape or sound of life[2]

and the redeemed valley of Asia, Prometheus' lost heart, the setting of Act II, Scene i. The white star of morning leads us

beautifully to her far-off place of exile, a Luciferic intermingling
of nature and the 'transforming presence' of her solitary spirit:

> rugged once
> And desolate and frozen, like this ravine;
> But now invested with fair flowers and herbs,
> And haunted by sweet airs and sounds, which flow
> Among the woods and waters, from the aether
> Of her transforming presence.[3]

Any reading of the play must be sensitive to these underlying
modes of experience, which interact in the poetic and dramatic
structure of the work.

In *Alastor* the daemonic principles were brought together in
destructive interplay, culminating in the hero's death on the icy
Caucasian summits. When *Prometheus Unbound* begins, its
central figure has already reached this condition: Asia is exiled
and unattainable, and Prometheus suffers the 'torture and
solitude' of the Ahrimanic alienation. Like the youth who
awakens in the cold morning light in *Alastor*, he finds that the
visionary gleam of nature, with whose spirit he communed in the
days before his ideal of love was parted from him, has fled – and
he asks:

> Oh, rock-embosomed lawns, and snow-fed streams,
> Now seen athwart frore vapours, deep below,
> Through whose o'ershadowing woods I wandered once
> With Asia, drinking life from her loved eyes;
> Why scorns the spirit which informs ye, now
> To commune with me?[4]

Shelley's answer has grown, however, in power and complexity
since 1815. The opening Act of *Prometheus Unbound* shows the
mind trapped in landscapes of its own fabrication, the victim of
its own confusions. The drama follows the unravelling of those
confusions both in conscious struggle, through the dawning
realisation by Prometheus that he has locked himself in an
unreal battle against 'absolute' tyranny, and in the unconscious
depths to which Asia brings transfiguring light.

Prometheus is the victim of the kind of static moral
consciousness which Shelley sought to replace with the moral

instrument of imagination. Setting himself against the world-tyrant, Jupiter, he accepts the torment of alienation in a dead, soul-piercing landscape. Through his devotion to an unattainable ideal, he exposes himself to Luciferic temptations, and in refusing them condemns himself to what seems infinite suffering. He cannot see that his defiance perpetuates the struggle with no possibility of advance; he cannot see that Jupiter is thus guaranteed his reign over the unwilling spirit; he cannot see, in short, that 'the tyrant of the world' is his own creation, a part of himself with which he refuses to come to terms. The action of the play begins when Prometheus withdraws his curse and commences the real inner work of transformation – a regeneration like that described in the *Ode to the West Wind*, bringing unity back to his divided self.

At the beginning of the drama, then, Jupiter appears as a blurring of Luciferic and Ahrimanic; or better, he is a Luciferic creation of Prometheus' own mind masquerading in the form of a separate reality. And because he is inwardly divided and confused, Prometheus cannot appear yet as the true type of human perfection which he is 'destined' to be,[5] but as an ambivalent mixture of that and Lucifer. It is fascinating to note that Coleridge, for whom human perfection had been historically represented in Christ, saw in the figure of the mythical Prometheus a kind of Christ and Lucifer in one – an illuminating remark which forms a point of departure more valid than any of the efforts of Shelley's critics to pin down the symbolic meaning of the central figure in his play.[6] In the course of the dramatic action, Prometheus will be purified into an image of Christ-like suffering and perfection.[7]

In Asia's world at the beginning of the play, consciousness is contrastingly depicted in retreat from the world-out-there, the loneliness of her magic valley providing an escape from the dark powers of external reality; Luciferic and Ahrimanic here stand in powerful opposition. As the action proceeds, Prometheus' struggle for self-knowledge has to be complemented by the mind's overcoming of its own isolation, by that projection over the 'chasm of an insufficient void' which is love, the search for relationship. Asia must undertake a mental journey to the deep to put her questions to the ultimate source of hidden Power.

The events of *Prometheus Unbound* thus extend beyond the 'painted veil', the illusory static universe from which we begin.

Prometheus in his suffering sees the veil torn away, revealing the depths of the human psyche, the full extent of the transformation that can and must be achieved. Asia passes through 'the veil and the bar / Of things which seem and are' on her journey to the 'remotest throne'.[8] Adjusting to these vaster perspectives, consciousness sees clearly the nature of the opposing daemonic forces, imaged in the false Luciferic heaven-world of Jupiter with his attendant deities, and in the Ahrimanic abyss of Demogorgon. As in the *Hymn to Intellectual Beauty* and the *Ode to the West Wind*, the daemonic powers can be played off against each other by an awareness which is born and sustained in their confluence and the dynamic equilibrium between them.[9]

It is in the superb lyrical Act IV – now acknowledged as an integral part of Shelley's careful construction – that the poet attempts to depict a regenerated consciousness and the transfigured reality which it beholds. But it is especially important to realise that the 'apocalyptic' vision of Act IV emerges organically from the imaginative structures fashioned and transmuted in the earlier Acts; it is a coherent outcome of the inner development we have summarised from Acts I, II and III. The cosmic changes which the poet envisages reflect the changing consciousness of Promethean humanity, connected vitally with the surrounding universe through love. Shelley's doctrine of macrocosm and microcosm, which pervades his vision of a humanised cosmos, is not to be understood as a quasi-Platonic speculation. It arises from his teaching of love. 'Wouldst thou think that toads, and snakes, and efts, / Could e'er be beautiful?'[10] They can be, if we look deeply enough within ourselves to find that nothing need finally be alien to our awakened humanity.

We gain an invaluable insight into the structure of Promethean consciousness if we consider, in a little more detail, the visions of Ione and Panthea. In these it becomes evident that through the imagery of Earth and Moon, Shelley is returning again to ultimate questions, cosmic in scope – and attempting to incorporate and humanise further elements of religious thought from Judaism and Christianity, reworking the imaginative solutions of earlier modes of vision.

It is of course typical of Shelley that, even in apocalypse, he should offer no single compelling perspective, but a double prospect upon reality. The visions appear through two openings in the forest; and the rivulets below point subtly to their complementary rather than contradictory nature, 'like sisters / Who part with sighs that they may meet in smiles', suggesting that the duality of vision is the key to a deeper eventual unity. Ione's vision is as follows:

> I see a chariot like that thinnest boat,
> In which the Mother of the Months is borne
> By ebbing light into her western cave,
> When she upsprings from interlunar dreams;
> O'er which is curved an orblike canopy
> Of gentle darkness, and the hills and woods
> Distinctly seen through that dusk aery veil,
> Regard like shapes in an enchanter's glass;
> Its wheels are solid clouds, azure and gold,
> Such as the genii of the thunderstorm
> Pile on the floor of the illumined sea
> When the sun rushes under it; they roll
> And move and grow as with an inward wind;
> Within it sits a winged infant, white
> Its countenance, like the whiteness of bright snow,
> Its plumes are as feathers of sunny frost,
> Its limbs gleam white, through the wind-flowing folds
> Of its white robe, woof of ethereal pearl.
> Its hair is white, the brightness of white light
> Scattered in strings; yet its two eyes are heavens
> Of liquid darkness, which the Deity
> Within seems pouring, as a storm is poured
> From jagged clouds, out of their arrowy lashes,
> Tempering the cold and radiant air around,
> With fire that is not brightness; in its hand
> It sways a quivering moonbeam, from whose point
> A guiding power directs the chariot's prow
> Over its wheeled clouds, which as they roll
> Over the grass, and flowers, and waves, wake sounds,
> Sweet as a singing rain of silver dew.[11]

The passage deserves careful reading. In the first part, Shelley conducts us into a 'moony' world of half-awakened dreams. Consciousness here draws into its own inwardness of will: the shape-shifting clouds move magically, impelled from within by pneumatic power; the dark eyes of the Moon-child suggest the Deity within. All our attention is directed on the mystic depths of inwardness, and the objective universe fades into seeming unreality. Seen through the canopy of darkness, the forms of outer landscape appear distantly 'like shapes in an enchanter's glass'. There is a Luciferic suspension of objective awareness, replaced in the 'ebbing light' by a mystical harmony, the music-making clouds faintly recalling the 'rain of melody', the 'Sound of vernal showers / On the twinkling grass', and the 'Rain-awakened flowers' of the *Skylark* Ode.

Yet the Luciferic tendency is not given free rein. Indeed the final effect is of self-control and 'guiding power'. In achieving that control Shelley makes surprising use of imagery and themes from Jewish mysticism, which of course had long devoted itself to the problem of attaining to the inwardness of divine vision while resolutely holding the Luciferic tempter at bay. Ione's vision, as Harold Bloom in particular has emphasised, is Shelley's meditation on *Ma'aseh Merkavah*, the 'Work of the Chariot', one of the central strands of Jewish mysticism and esotericism from Old Testament times onward.[12]

Elements of *Merkavah* mysticism appear especially in Ezekiel, Daniel and the New Testament Apocalypse. Shelley has drawn upon all of these, and perhaps knew in addition the recently rediscovered *Book of Enoch* which caused much discussion and fascinated, among others, Blake.

In Ezekiel the theophany of Yahweh and the manifestation of his glory (*kavod*) is still partly described in the storm-imagery prevalent throughout the ancient Near East:

> And I looked, and, behold, a stormy wind came out of the north, a great cloud, with a fire infolding itself, and a brightness round about it, and out of the midst thereof as the colour of amber, out of the midst of the fire.[13]

He beholds the *Hayyoth*, the Living Creatures who minister to the divine Throne, which moves upon mysterious wheels:

> And when the Living Creatures went, the wheels went beside them. . . . Whithersoever the spirit was to go, they went; thither was the spirit to go, and the wheels were lifted up beside them; for the spirit of the Living Creature was in the

wheels. . . . And over the head of the Living Creature was the likeness of a firmament, like the colour of the terrible crystal, stretched forth over their heads above. . . . And above the firmament that was over their heads was the likeness of a throne, as the appearance of a sapphire stone: and upon the likeness of the throne was a likeness as the appearance of a Man. . . . This was the appearance and the likeness of the glory of Yahweh.[14]

Much of Shelley's imagery is already present here; but for the one who is seated upon the Throne–Chariot we need also to look at the related vision of Daniel.

Daniel sees dream-images, monstrous beasts rising out of the sea; and then:

I beheld till thrones were placed, and one that was Ancient of Days took his seat: his raiment was white as snow, and the hair of his head like pure wool; his throne was fiery flames, and the wheels thereof burning fire.[15]

There comes to him, 'with the clouds of heaven', one 'like unto a Son of Man', on whom the Ancient of Days bestows everlasting dominion.

In the Apocalypse much of the imagery recurs – but with a difference which probably prompted Shelley's imagination to a decisive change. There is a vision of the *Merkavah*; but before it, near the very beginning of the revelation, comes the appearance of the figure all in white. Now, however, there is no paternal, authoritative figure such as the Ancient of Days conferring power on the Son of Man. The one 'like unto a Son of Man' announces in his own right: 'I am the first and last, and the Living One; and I was dead, and behold, I am alive for evermore.'[16] The God who became Man and even suffered death has replaced the hoary divinity of the Old Testament and assumed his own throne.

To Shelley the God of Moses was mainly subsumed under the conception of the tyrant Jupiter, rather as to Blake he had suggested Urizen, God of abstract rules and repressive morality. Hence, although Shelley counters the Luciferic tendency of the mind with all the apparatus of an Old Testament theophany, it is not in the end the God of Mosaic law whom he enthrones among the clouds. The 'guiding power' he invokes – following the lead of the New Testament 'Son of Man' – is that of still unrealised human possibility imaged in the child. In its dark, lustrous eyes he sees more hope than in any code of morals handed down on Sinai. They feed the hope that man may ultimately be 'king over himself', rather than receiving authority from a transcendent Father.

Something similar and yet very different happens in Panthea's vision:

> And from the other opening in the wood
> Rushes, with loud and whirlwind harmony,
> A sphere, which is as many thousand spheres,
> Solid as crystal, yet through all its mass
> Flow, as through empty space, music and light;
> Ten thousand orbs involving and involved,
> Purple and azure, white, and green, and golden,
> Sphere within sphere; and every space between
> Peopled with unimaginable shapes,
> Such as ghosts dream dwell in the lampless deep,
> Yet each inter-transpicuous, and they whirl
> Over each other with a thousand motions,
> Upon a thousand sightless axles spinning,
> And with the force of self-destroying swiftness,
> Intensely, slowly, solemnly roll on,
> Kindling with mingled sounds, and many tones,
> Intelligible words and music wild.
> With mighty whirl the multitudinous orb
> Grinds the bright brook into an azure mist
> Of elemental subtlety, like light;
> And the wild odour of the forest flowers,
> The music of the living grass and air,
> The emerald light of leaf-entangled beams
> Round its intense yet self-conflicting speed,
> Seem kneaded into one aereal mass
> Which drowns the sense. Within the orb itself,
> Pillowed upon its alabaster arms,
> Like to a child o'erwearied with sweet toil,
> On its own folded wings, and wavy hair,
> The Spirit of the Earth is laid asleep,
> And you can see its little lips are moving,
> Amid the changing light of their own smiles,
> Like one who talks of what he loves in dream.[17]

The imagery here is related primarily to the outer cosmos: the fathomless universe of space with its tens of thousands of orbs and spheres, revolving invisibly about their gravitational centres. More precisely, the vision stands for man's efforts to comprehend the world of stars and planets, his speculations on celestial mechanics. Such conjectures are mocked by Raphael in Milton's *Paradise Lost*, where men vainly try;

> to model Heav'n
> And calculate the Starrs, how they will wield
> The mightie frame, how build, unbuild, contrive
> To save appearances, how gird the Sphear
> With Centric and Eccentric scribl'd ore,
> Cycle and Epicycle, Orb in Orb.[18]

Man's struggle to comprehend the inhumanly vast universe, the Angel strongly implies, can only be partially successful, and God's wisdom makes all human calculation seem folly. Milton's primordial pair risk the derision of the Creator: but in Shelley's world the interstellar spaces of the 'lampless deep' hold more daunting Gothic terrors – 'unimaginable shapes' out of the dreams of ghosts. From one point of view the cosmic system is seen as a great whirlpool whose centre is vacuity, sucking in the phenomenal world of things and objects and battering them down into a single overwhelming mass, in whose confusion consciousness shrivels or is drowned. Its 'intense yet self-conflicting speed' cancels out reality in the force of 'self-destroying' motion, recalling the grinding down of things in the later part of *Mont Blanc*. As in that earlier poem, there is a 'bright brook' of things and phenomena which flows through the adverting mind – and is consumed, shattered into a vapour 'of elemental subtlety'.

Yet the Ahrimanic terror of destruction and vacuity is held in check. The grinding down of empirical reality, the shattering of impressions and the horrors of interplanetary space are offset by certain positive effects. From the destructive cycles of material nature is regenerated, as Wilson Knight has observed, the spiritual – consciousness, meaning.[19] 'Intelligible words and music wild' are kindled from the whirling annihilation. And again there is a child. The Earth-child has already appeared as a speaker in Act III: but each of its manifestations has to be treated with imaginative independence. Here its smiling sleep provides an assurance at the centre of being, which the Ahrimanic fears at the stellar periphery and the mind-stunning eolian harmonies of the cosmic spheres can do nothing to disrupt. In a masterly poetic comment, Ione adds to her sister's vision of the child: "Tis only mocking the orb's harmony'.[20] 'Mocking', of course, means primarily 'imitating': the changing aspects of the heavens are mirrored in the expression of the slumbering child. But the child's serenity also 'mocks' the vastness and geometric complexity of the spatial universe. It may be infinitely large and incomprehensibly complex – but the sleeping infant is replete with infinities far more significant. Hegel was likewise to dismiss the mere endlessness of the universe, and contrast it with the 'true infinity' of self-determining consciousness or individuality.[21]

The bright–dark eyes of the Moon-child counteracted the impulse toward Luciferic self-absorption. The slumbering smiles of the Earth-child prevent man from losing himself in the outer spaces, pointing to a harmonious relationship with the unconscious depths within. In *Julian and Maddalo*, consciousness was disintegrated and the maniac muttered in his restless sleep. On the other hand, Maddalo's infant daughter provided an image of hope and integration. Now, in Panthea's vision, Shelley fuses 'open' consciousness with infant hope, in the marvellous image of the Earth-child moving its 'little lips': 'Like the one who talks of what he loves in dream'.[22] If we seek in visionary tradition for something comparable to Panthea's experience and imagery, we find its best analogue, I believe, in the *Christos Pantokrator* of Byzantine symbolism. Paul had written to the Colossians and other communities of Christ's victory and authority over the cosmic powers – the archons, or sinister world-rulers in the heavenly spaces of early Christian and Gnostic literature. In later times, Christ was represented in an icon-like posture of blessing, enthroned above the spheres of the universe below – as *Pantokrator*, ruler of the cosmic totality. The idea proved useful in a completely new way to the Deists and Newtonians of the eighteenth century, who conceived God as presiding over a well-regulated universe running by natural law, finding little or no occasion to intervene by more miraculous events. By adopting the old title, and citing those passages in the New Testament where Christ receives all authority in heaven and earth, they hoped to show that their Deistical belief harmonised with Christian revelation.[23]

Shelley's response was more subtle and imaginative. Once more he rejects the notion of a benevolent supreme Ruler, as he rejected the paternal Deity of the Old Testament. Or rather, he does not reject the imaginative core of truth in these older visions so much as bring them humanistically up-to-date. He acknowledges the need for imaginative solutions to the issues they raise – but the assurance Christians and Deists derived from the *Pantokrator*, Shelley again finds more sufficiently in his infant child and its human potentialities. In his concern with ultimates, Shelley is a religious poet. In him the humanism of the eighteenth century attains, as it does somewhat differently in Blake, to a religious dimension.

The two-fold visions of Earth-child and Moon-child are crucially important to the understanding of *Prometheus Unbound*. They show that in the new age Shelley imagines, man's nature is not miraculously altered by some divine decree. The tendencies that formerly worked destructively in his consciousness are still present. They are, however, subdued and held in quiet control by the power of equilibrium at the centre of man's psyche, serving a higher harmony in a humanly recreated world.

DECAYING DREAMS: *THE TRIUMPH OF LIFE*

> *Shelley dreamed it. Now the dream decays.*
> (R. S. Thomas, 'Song at the Year's Turning')

> *For there is no deformity but saves us from a dream.*
> (W. B. Yeats, *The Phases of the Moon*)

A retrospect of those amazing years since 1815 shows a development and maturing of Shelley's poetic vision which is scarcely believable over so short a space of time. The tentative explorations of *Alastor*, where the way forward had still not been discerned, led to the powerful affirmations of *Prometheus Unbound*. But in accordance with his commitment to the principle of death and rebirth, Shelley still leaves his vision open to fresh uncertainties. Few affirmations seem possible on the subject of Shelley's incomplete fragment *The Triumph of Life*, on which he was working immediately before his unanticipated death. His death added a last irony to the title. In the poem the 'Triumph' is a hideous pageant, like that which the Roman emperors used to celebrate after a victory, driving their humiliated captives and their plunder in procession for all to see; and 'Life' – but it is hard to answer the question which brings to an end the fragment we possess.

In the fragment we have two visions. We recognise points of contact with the earlier Shelley in both: but the poet is evidently rethinking many of his own conclusions, calling in question the foundations he himself had progressively laid down. Moreover, since he did not live to finish the poem (which leaves the impression of a substantial work commencing) it is not possible to tell precisely what new direction Shelley would have taken. The fragment of *The Triumph* is both frustratingly inconclusive as it stands, yet apparently closed within its own contradictions, so that there is no obvious room for further development. No doubt Shelley's solution would have been different from anything we can predict on the basis of what he left, since it would have been offered as a solution to the seemingly insoluble predicament of the figures in the poem. There had been similar crises before: we remember the impasse of *Alastor*, which heralded the great positive phase of Shelley's writing that culminated in *Prometheus Unbound*. We cannot know what vision he would have hammered out in response to the doubts expressed in the extant *Triumph*, though we can see that the cost of vision in terms of suffering and endurance seemed to him greater than he had ever before realised.

The dawn sequence comprises many familiar Shelleyan elements. There is the 'inverted' simile of the opening lines, where the invisible component takes precedence over the familiar natural one, giving the sense of a world which is a reflection of some occult original:

> Swift as a spirit hastening to his task
> Of glory and of good, the Sun sprang forth
> Rejoicing in his splendour.[24]

But the birth of light has the usual coldness and bleakness of Shelley's dawns: the narrator has been kept awake all night by his thoughts, and his weariness invests the returning day with a feeling of toil and imposition. The stars have faded with the 'cone of night', yet the contrast is not now between fading ideal and harsh reality, but beween the restlessness of sleepless night and the burdens of the day. An oppressive weight pervades the description of the slow change. As in Shelley's earlier poetry, consciousness finds itself in the midst of immensities, cosmic processes which in their vastness threaten the finite ego:

> before me fled
> The night; behind me rose the day; the deep
> Was at my feet, and Heaven above my head.[25]

It is the pressure of these hugely weighted forces which propels consciousness into an intermediate state, a 'strange trance' which 'was not slumber': 'And then a vision on my brain was rolled.'

The 'tenour' of the first vision is Ahrimanic. A great stream of people hurries aimlessly back and forth, starting at their shadows or walking wrapped in their own gloom, flying in fear or seeking to manipulate the fears of others. The way is 'Thick strewn with summer dust' – recalling the passage from Wordsworth quoted in *Alastor*:

> The good die first,
> And those whose hearts are dry as summer dust,
> Burn to the socket![26]

The whole landscape is one of 'visionary dreariness', and the path one 'where flowers never grew'. But the ironic description of mankind's 'serious folly' is interrupted by a theophany, a *Merkavah* vision heralded by a blinding light 'intenser than the noon', blotting out the sun as he the stars. Yet its terrible glare is icy cold. Perhaps Shelley knew the recently translated *Book of Enoch*, in which the writer beholds in a vision the heaven of the Moon, fashioned of crystal and flame:

> And I entered into that house, and it was bright as fire and cold as ice: there were no delights of life therein: fear covered me, and trembling took hold upon me.[27]

The *Merkavah* vision recapitulates many of the features of the Moon-child in *Prometheus Unbound* – but with a ghastly twist:

> Like the young moon
>
> When on the sunlit limits of the night
> Her white shell trembles amid crimson air,
> And whilst the sleeping tempest gathers might –
>
> Doth, as the herald of its coming, bear
> The ghost of its dead mother, whose dim form
> Bends in dark aether from her infant's chair, –
>
> So came a chariot on the silent storm
> Of its own rushing splendour, and a Shape
> So sate within, as one whom years deform,
>
> Beneath a dusky hood and double cape,
> Crouching within the shadow of a tomb.[28]

'Shelley's old antitheses', remarks Wilson Knight, 'are breaking down.'[29] It no longer seems possible to distinguish opposites: the Moon-child seems here to have fallen victim to and merged with the Ahrimanic daemon. The Promethean man who carries the crushing psychic burdens of estrangement and 'divine' self-control as the price of his achieved individual consciousness, though he is enthroned in majesty like a god, finds cosmic evil irrevocably enwoven in his own being. The figure in the chariot is declared to be 'Life': in short, such ensnarement is now declared to be inevitable simply through the nature of life in the actual world. Man must act and take responsibility in the world, beyond the limits of himself, and therefore must bear evils it is not in his power to remedy. 'Good' and the 'means of good' are irreconcilable.

The crowd – the 'million' – are dragged along behind the Chariot in 'maniac dance', sucked into the vortex of Life, maddened and intoxicated, tortured by Life's 'agonising pleasure' until they fall dead or senseless. Maidens and youths pursue their frantic destruction, the aged dance hideously and without dignity to where they fall, 'and corruption veils them as they lie'. The Triumph includes among its captives many even of the great thinkers of the past, 'phantoms of an elder day', and former lights of Shelley's intellectual development: Plato, Aristotle, Bacon – as well as emperors and kings and religious leaders. All compromised with the world. Indeed, they had to do so to achieve the good; but thereby at the same time they opened the way to the evil. Shelley adds a striking image in which opposites again break down: the 'men divine' who produced on the foundation of Christianity the outrages of the Inquisition and 'rose like shadows between man and God', by eclipsing the true light of spiritual vision, taught the world to worship the eclipse, 'still hanging over heaven', as the sun itself. In the battle with Life no one can be a conqueror. There escape her domination only those

> sacred few who could not tame
> Their spirits to the conquerors – but as soon
> As they had touched the world with living flame,
> Fled back like eagles to their native noon.[30]

The poet is 'struck to the heart' and, without expecting any answer, asks the meaning of the figure in the Chariot.

The voice which answers 'Life' issues from the hideously deformed remnant of 'one of those deluded crew'. In the most explicitly Dantean episode in the poem, he declares himself to have been Rousseau. He becomes for the present a guide through the Inferno: but once more in the breakdown of oppositions, he is also its victim. What follows is Shelley's most penetrating analysis of the failure of Sensibility ('I / Am one of those who have created,' Rousseau declares, even 'If it be but a world of agony').[31] Rousseau himself now understands his failure, and the failure of those like him:

> their lore
> Taught them not this, to know themselves; their might
> Could not repress the mystery within,
> And for the morn of truth they feigned, deep night
> Caught them ere evening.[32]

Rousseau comprehends the whence and how of his dreadful fate; but the meaning, the 'why', remains inscrutable. Perhaps a clue to the projected development of the poem lies in the turning back of the question on the passive seer, demanding that he should 'from spectator turn / Actor or victim in this wretchedness'. He might then be able to teach Rousseau what he now asks from him. The hint is not developed, however, in the fragment as we now have it.

Instead, Rousseau relates his own vision, the Luciferic counterpart of the first. The setting is a contrary landscape to the blighted region of the first one – a mountain valley, and a cave:

> And from it came a gentle rivulet,
> Whose water, like clear air, in its calm sweep
>
> Bent the soft grass, and kept forever wet
> The stems of the sweet flowers, and filled the grove
> With sounds, which whoso hears must needs forget
>
> All pleasure and all pain, all hate and love,
> Which they had known before that hour of rest.[33]

The 'oblivious spell' of the place fills the mind with thought-dispelling 'magic sound'; a 'light diviner than the common sun' leads to the second, Luciferic theophany.

The 'Shape all light' has perplexed many commentators, who were unable to decide whether its role in the poem is fundamentally positive or negative. From our point of view, we may see in it a variant of Shelley's characteristic Luciferic images – though again there are radical new compressions of thought which seem to fuse former opposites. The 'silver music' which the Shape strews upon the dusky grass looks back to *Prometheus Unbound* and the vision of both Earth-child and Moon-child in their musical progressions. More sinister, the Shape appears to be not only the glimmering star / fading coal but also the chill dawning light:

> And all the gazer's mind was strewn beneath
> Her feet like embers; and she, thought by thought,
>
> Trampled its sparks into the dust of death;
> As day upon the threshold of the east
> Treads out the lamps of night, until the breath

Of darkness re-illumine even the least
Of heaven's living eyes – like day she came,
Making the night a dream.

Yet a little later:

the fair shape waned in the coming light,
As veil by veil the silent splendour drops
From Lucifer.[34]

Shelley's old antitheses confusingly merge: and the effect on
Rousseau is to suspend him 'between desire and shame', from
which state he finally asks the identity of the Shape.

Her answer, however, is to betray him immediately to the
vision of the Triumphal Chariot. Yet he continues to feel the
unseen presence of the Shape, like that of the morning-star
during the day or the 'ghost of a forgotten form of sleep'. It
glides beside his path, silent as a spectre. Meanwhile in the final
part of the extant poem Shelley puts his daemonology and
eidolon-theory to horrific use: the cold light of the Chariot
purges away the youth and beauty of its victims, producing
eidola 'numerous as the dead leaves blown / In autumn evening
from a poplar tree'. They populate the air thickly with phantoms
'in a thousand unimagined shapes'. These no longer inhabit the
'lampless deep', as in *Prometheus Unbound*, kept at bay by the
power of the Earth-child, but swarm in the broad daylight over
the sunny streams and grassy shelves, or crowd around corrupt
humanity.

And there the fragment breaks off, with the impassioned
question 'Then what is life?'

We do also learn, however, that love is exempt from the
'transfiguring' power of the Chariot's 'creative ray':

How all things are transfigured except Love;
For deaf as is a sea, which wrath makes hoary,

The world can hear not the sweet notes that move
The sphere whose light is melody to lovers.[35]

Rousseau declares the theme worthy of Dante, whom Love led
serene through Hell and Heaven – and perhaps it would have

been the continuing theme of Shelley's Dantean final poem. It is impossible to say. There are no hints as to how love might make itself felt in the nihilistic world of the Luciferic–Ahrimanic forces. In their universe action is possible only by incurring a weight of evil that seems ultimately beyond man's control or remedy; wisdom can be won from the delusion of man's dreams only at the cost of a deformity that almost goes beyond the limits of the human. Yeats was to solve the problem in *A Vision* by invoking the lunar cycles of rebirth. Perhaps, with his own later thought taking a cyclical direction in *Prometheus* and *Hellas*, Shelley too was contemplating an extension of man's field of action to a multiplicity of lives. He had experimented with the idea of reincarnation before; but there is no trace of it in *The Triumph*.

Thus Shelley's last testament calls in question the highest wisdom of his own most assured poetry. But this in the end is not a turning upon himself in disillusion. Rather it is a development in harmony with his own determination to forge a poetry of visionary self-consciousness from the encounter with the daemonic forces beyond the painted veil. It would have been stale wisdom indeed which, formulated by a man in his twenties, should have served unchanged a life charged with the potential to expand and deepen its experience. Demogorgon returns at the end of *Prometheus Unbound* to announce that the victory may have to be won again. In all his later verse Shelley pits his imagination directly against the greatest obstacles possible. For the imagination is inherently dynamic, and would inevitably make an enemy of its own stasis unless given the 'purer nutriment', the challenge of a universal vision. In his last moments of clarity, Goethe's Faust says:

> Here wisdom speaks its final word and true,
> None is of freedom or of life deserving
> Unless he daily conquers it anew.
> With dangers thus begirt, defying fears,
> Childhood, youth, age shall strive through strenuous
>   years.[36]

Shelley died, still in youth, in the midst of striving to conquer anew those dangers which seemed to him an intrinsic part of life; there is no doubt, however little we are able to see the direction of his latest thought, that he also considered them the empowering conditions of man's imaginative and moral growth. He died whilst extending the domain of his imagination into regions darker than any he had explored, but which the poet always demands as the ground of his peculiar victory, however partial, achieved at whatever cost of suffering and deformity, without which there would be perhaps no poem.

7 The Christian Spirit

Have this mind in you, which was also in Christ Jesus: who, being in the form of God, did not account equality with God as something to be grasped, but poured himself out, taking the form of a servant, coming-to-be in the likeness of men; and being found in fashion as a man, he humbled himself, becoming obedient even unto death.

(Paul, Letter to the Philippians, 2:6–8)

'Poets, not otherwise than philosophers, painters, sculptors and musicians', wrote Shelley, 'are, in one sense, the creators, and, in another, the creations of their age. From this subjection the loftiest do not escape.'[1] Shelley himself is a case in point. We have already remarked that Shelley's commitment to the English and French philosophers of the Enlightenment, his imperviousness to the new German dialectics, held back the unfolding of his mind on the theoretical plane; no doubt this also permitted him to develop certain unique facets of his own imagination. From a more general point of view, one might suggest that Shelley's passionate intellectual humanism, in whose name he espoused the ideals of freedom, self-consciousness and patient love, fuelled some of his greatest poetry, but also, in its specific historical form, blinded Shelley to certain profound and significant aspects of his own work. Above all, his fidelity to the 'atheistic' humanism of the eighteenth century seems to have prevented Shelley from ever realising the full extent of the congruence between his own imaginations and the Christian spirit.

Yet the atheist poet undoubtedly struck a Christian note in many of his central utterances and clearest thoughts. As he developed, he even became fascinated by 'the Christian mythology', and adapted its religious symbols to his own creative vision in *Prometheus Unbound* and elsewhere. The man who could write verse such as the following is a strange spectacle for a positivist revolutionary:

186

> Resist not the weakness,
> Such strength is in meekness
> That the Eternal, the Immortal,
> Must unloose through life's portal
> The snake-like Doom coiled underneath his throne
> By that alone.[2]

We are therefore invited to consider how far Shelley's individual imagination is in its characteristic structures and predilections conformable to the Christian type – and thence to look at two related questions: firstly, how did such a congruence come about, in defiance of the poet's atheistic convictions; and secondly, how did Shelley progress in his conscious evaluation of his spiritual stance. It may be best to take the last problem first.

CROSS-PURPOSES

The gradual alteration in Shelley's opinion of Christianity (and of its founder) has been ably traced before.[3] The change was palpable. Anyone who reads the *Notes* to *Queen Mab* and then the *Essay on Christianity*, may come to his own conclusions about that. We soon find ourselves asking, however, whether Shelley was thereby fundamentally altering his own attitudes, moving away from the rebellious position of his younger days, or whether he was realising, and starting to acknowledge, the deeper similarities which went beyond the distaste the contemporary manifestations of Christianity inevitably evoked – the social apparatus of 'state religion' against which Blake also fumed. In this book I have attempted to trace the forms of Shelley's imagination from his earliest serious explorations through to his mature work. If I have been at all successful it must be clear that there was no radical change of direction in Shelley's imaginative life, but rather growth and deepening. Hence I shall argue that the characteristic structures we have examined can in fact be illuminatingly compared with those implied by the Christian spirit, employing the terms we have established in earlier chapters. The question posed by Robert Browning, as to whether Shelley's conscious revaluation of

Christianity would in due course have proceeded to the point of intellectual acceptance, must be left – since it is intrinsically unanswerable – unanswered.

We shall accordingly be less concerned here with Shelley's opinion of Christian doctrine than with patterns of imaginative coherence. The Romantic poets aspired to present a vision of life and the meaning of things, which was essentially a religious undertaking. Some came to regard their Romanticism in the light of an adjunct to their Christian belief; others offered rival conceptions. All of them saw a need for something new, more immediate than traditional faith. But from our perspective it appears that Shelley did not so much rival the Christian spirit, violently opposed though he was to the letter of its interpretation by his contemporaries, as renew the vesture through which the Christian spirit manifests itself, giving the essential values and emphases of Christianity a form adequate to the mental and physical realities of his day.

Perhaps this approach best explains the fact that the immature Shelley's distorted image of Christianity is inextricably involved with his own still blurred apprehension of his basic imaginative categories. At the time of *Queen Mab* he treats Christianity as though it were a parody of his own vision. Yet this is primarily because his own terms of reference (Luciferic, Ahrimanic, etc.) have not yet crystallised into the configuration whose clarity we know from later poems. We represented the mature constellation in Figure 6. In the diagram suggestive of *Queen Mab* (Figure 7), I use traditional names drawn from religious language to facilitate the discussion. Any *Weltanschauung* that seeks to engage us fully and humanly must somehow deal with those possibilities of relationship, of inward and outward orientation, most adequately summed up in the rich mythological figures of Lucifer and Ahriman. It must also find room for an image of human perfection, whether or not represented as achieved, which we may call 'Christ'. (I do not mean that every image of human perfection has been modelled on Christ, or resembled him in any way whatsoever, even if Shelley's does. I mean that as for the Christian, Christ stands in a definitive relationship with himself and with reality, so in any philosophy there must be an implied position where man is properly himself and in right connection with the world. It might also be said that at the very least Christ is one of the most

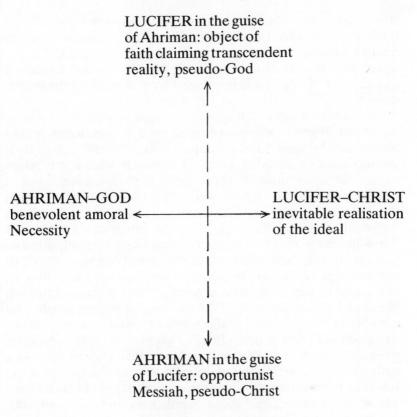

LUCIFER in the guise
of Ahriman: object of
faith claiming transcendent
reality, pseudo-God

AHRIMAN–GOD
benevolent amoral
Necessity

LUCIFER–CHRIST
inevitable realisation
of the ideal

AHRIMAN in the guise
of Lucifer: opportunist
Messiah, pseudo-Christ

FIGURE 7 *'Queen Mab'*

adequate imaginations we have of such an ideal.) Any ultimate
world-view must also finally give some idea of the reality itself
with which we stand in human relationship: that reality is
theologically called God, specifically, God the Father. (Again,
not every conception of ultimate reality is at all like the
traditional God the Father. A philosophy may have as its 'God'
a categorically unknowable Somewhat, or a dogmatic Nothing.
Nevertheless it is partly by its 'God' that it will be judged in its
adequacy or otherwise as a human vision of things.)

In order to represent Shelley's imaginings in *Queen Mab*,
however, we must envisage these categories not yet clearly
sorted out. We might say, for instance that Ahriman appears in
the guise of Lucifer: that is to say, purely material trickery is

represented as being at the bottom of a 'supernatural', divine quality. With this Luciferically disguised Ahrimanic figure Shelley arrives at his opportunist Messiah, a pseudo-Christ, which is all that he can yet see in the New Testament figure – a mockery of man's ideal, motivated by a concealed desire for power.

Conversely, Lucifer appears in the guise of Ahriman: that is, an object of pure faith purports to be a transcendent reality above and beyond all experience. Thus Shelley arrives at a pseudo-God, a delusive paternal Jehovah who is really an excuse for opportunists to tyrannise over their fellows.

The interesting point, however, is that these distortions which Shelley sees in orthodox Christianity, go hand in hand with his own confusions and blurrings of his later categories. For his own 'God' has merged with Ahriman – according to his definition of that reality as a 'benevolent amoral Necessity': a power fatal to any concept of human freedom is yet supposed to solve all human ills by a quasi-natural necessity. The correlate of this is a blend of Lucifer and 'Christ' at the pole of human ideals: the supposedly inevitable realisation of man's best nature irrespective of any moral effort or painful struggle. Thus the young Shelley had a religion of perfectibility at cross-purposes with the hypocritical Christianity he saw in the worst of his religious contemporaries. But the re-evaluation of Christianity which gradually came about went hand-in-hand with the separating out of his own imaginative polarities.

HUMANISM AND MYTH

Shelley achieved the clarification of his own vision through exploring at their sources the great myths of good and evil, of error and illumination, from East and West. Now Christianity itself originally came into being in a meeting of East and West, from which emerged the prototype of a new religious consciousness. Indeed the main spiritual streams which fed emergent Christianity were precisely those which, by their intrinsic power, later fascinated Shelley. They were above all the Judaic (with its sense of moral consciousness struggling against Luciferic temptation), and the Iranian (which was

mainly involved in the struggle against Ahrimanic alienation).
The Judaic background was obviously reflected in the
acceptance of the Old Testament as part of the new scripture,
and in the Jewish setting of the Event of Golgotha itself. But it
was not out of mainstream Judaism that Christianity arose.
Rather the way was paved by the esoteric baptising sects on the
fringes (geographical and spiritual) of Judaism – groups like the
Essenes, for instance, who were strongly influenced by non-
Jewish ideas, especially those of Iranian dualism. Long
historical links with Iran led to a fruitful meeting of faiths, as we
can see from the many Iranian images and concepts in Jewish
apocalyptic writings. 'So it was out of a Judaism enriched by five
centuries of contact with Zoroastrianism', writes Mary Boyce,
'that Christianity arose in the Parthian period, a new religion
with roots thus in two ancient faiths, one Semitic, the other
Iranian. Doctrines taught perhaps a millennium and a half
earlier by Zoroaster began in this way to reach fresh hearers.'[4]
The Zoroastrians themselves expected the Saoshyant or Saviour
and, as Mary Boyce points out, longing for his advent must have
grown stronger in the dark period following Alexander's
conquest of the Iranian Empire. Gnostic writings (in which the
Iranian influence remained strongest) clearly identified Jesus
with the reborn Zarathustra. In the newly discovered and
translated Gnostic library from Nag Hammadi, as Jack Lindsay
observed, we meet traditions 'of Zoroaster changing his
appearance so as to be identified with the prophet Seth, son of
Adam, and of . . . Saoshyant becoming a form of Jesus'.[5]

Iranian dualism represents a particularly radical way of
establishing equilibrium among the contending daemonic urges.
It does not do so in the modern, self-conscious manner, but in an
oriental mode which gives little importance to the conscious self.
Man is certainly represented as a fighter on the side of Ohrmazd
and his light-beings against the alienating power of Ahriman.
But the ego is not the crucial battleground on which the struggle
depends; rather it is the cosmic dimension which is continually
stressed in the myths and visions of Zoroastrianism. All
available psychic resources are bent against the Ahrimanic, so
that Ohrmazd can be regarded, from the standpoint of our
categories here, as a God, Christ and Lucifer in one. Man has his
ultimate meaning as a creature of light, such as he was made in
the beginning, before he descended to the material realm to help

battle against Ahriman. And man's aspiration to a godlike state is not treated as a temptation, but enlisted in the struggle: the initiate, either in mystic experience or after death, is offered the hope of entering the Boundless Light. It is scarcely a wonder, with all these combined forces, that Zoroastrian mythology regards the final defeat of Ahriman as inevitable.[6]

We have examined the spiritual configuration of Judaism, with its central doctrine of creation, in an earlier context. There the terror of the Ahrimanic void was subsumed in the attitude of sublime wonder at the marvels of creation, and the moral life was directed to the overcoming of the Luciferic urge – again with the strong conviction of ultimate success. Judaism thus permitted man a much greater sense of inwardness and individuality, even though this was limited by the sense of the paternal authority of God over his special people, and depended on a large degree of national solidarity. It nevertheless represented a decisive step in the development of individual consciousness, away from older oriental forms.[7]

Both Zoroastrianism and Judaism achieved a stable and enduring configuration of inner forces. When their constellations came together, on the other hand, some unstable religious forms emerged – of which the most notable is Gnosticism. In the Gnostic world-view, the material world is no longer experienced as one moment in a cosmic struggle whose eventual outcome is the victory of Light, as it was for the Zoroastrians. The material world appears to be self-existent, radically separate from the spiritual. In this respect, the Gnostic shares the world-experience of Judaism, with its sense of the inert 'finished work' of the world. But the Gnostic remains too 'oriental' in attitude to accept the Jewish evaluation of the individual moral self and the God of the Law. The Judaic World-Creator merges for him with Ahriman, the power behind the inert outer world. Hence originates the Gnostic figure of the Demiurge, the deluded World-Creator who originates an anti-spiritual creation, and breathes into man the 'counterfeit spirit' of individual consciousness, an illusion which prevents man from realising his identity with the Cosmic Man in the world of light. Man achieves his salvation through knowledge (Greek *gnosis*) when he sees that he does not belong in essence to the material world and identifies himself with the spiritual, making a radical break with his lower 'self'.[8]

Gnosticism resolves the daemonic conflict in the most desperate fashion: by attempting to assert a radical separation, even when this means a split in the vision of the Godhead. It occupies a fascinating position in the history of consciousness, with its modern sense of the estranged outer world, combined (or rather juxtaposed, one should say) with an orientalising spirituality. Above all, it provides a key to certain of the stages of Romanticism, where oriental and 'primitivist' ideas, from Iran and elsewhere, helped poets enter domains of imaginative experience and give them a new importance that challenged many of the cultural and religious assumptions of their time. A 'Gnostic' stage where contrary realities are felt in this way can be detected in several European poets – Goethe, Baudelaire, in England above all Blake with his elaborate Gnostic mythology.[9] It is not surprising that Shelley touches for a certain time upon a Gnostic, rather Blakean mythology. The seventh section of *Queen Mab* shows a Gnostic God–Devil of a Jehovah as the oppressor of an exiled, rebellious spark of spiritual light condemned to wander the alien earth – Ahasuerus. There is even a Gnostically retold version of the creation-story from Genesis, like that in Blake's *Book of Urizen*. Shelley's 'omnipotent Fiend' announces:

> From an eternity of idleness
> I, God, awoke; in seven days' toil made earth
> From nothing; rested, and created man:
> I placed him in a Paradise, and there
> Planted the tree of evil, so that he
> Might eat and perish.[10]

This is Shelley at his closest to Blake; but it is a mythological line Shelley soon abandoned.[11]

In Christianity, as opposed to Gnosticism which influenced and existed alongside it, the Iranian and Semitic elements no longer stand in uneasy conjunction, but are absorbed into a new synthesis. In fact we meet there for the first time the 'cross' configuration which stands for the equilibrium of the conscious self amidst the daemonic powers, and expresses many of the formative tensions behind Shelley's imaginings. Christian thought sets out to resolve the same critical problems – the tension between paternal 'authority' and individual ethics, between acceptance of the natural world and the human desire for ultimate knowledge. The Christian response to these questions was epitomised in the doctrine of the Incarnation. This was the way in which mythology could be made identical with history, the natural made once more a moment in the evolution of the spiritual, the individual consciousness potentially a revelation of the divine: 'God became as we are that we might be as he is. . . . The Word was made man in order that we might be made divine.'[12] Already here we have a deep humanism, an evaluation of the moral ego which may attain to the status of the divine, going far beyond the tentative individualism cultivated in Judaism or anywhere else in the ancient world.

At the same time, it is a humanism that is not achieved through the denial of ultimate perspectives – though it does turn the ancient world's idea of religion inside out. Man need not abnegate his individuality in order to be absorbed into God, as in the ancient East. Each individual, with his unique gifts, may become part of the 'body of Christ'. The doctrine of the Incarnation, hammered out in the first centuries of Christendom, marked as important a step in the historical evolution of consciousness as the Judaic discovery of the doctrine of creation. Indeed, it was perhaps a vastly greater one. From a certain standpoint, indeed, it is hard to see anything in the secular humanism of the West but a disintegrated after-image of Paul's 'Christ in you'.

Shelley never fully admitted the extent to which his humanism coincided with the spiritual structure of Christianity. Nevertheless it is startling to find how far he was prepared to go in adopting, on occasion, Christian terminology. Quite rightly does Stuart Curran conclude:

> Acknowledging in the preface to *The Cenci* that 'Imagination is as the immortal God which should assume flesh for the redemption of mortal passion,' the poet who paradoxically began his career by admitting to the 'Necessity of Atheism' testifies to the faith that informs his major works. In justifying that faith for later generations, Shelley proved himself the greatest religious poet in the English language between Blake and Yeats.[13]

'Faith' may be not exactly the right word here. But Shelley's 'incarnational' view of poetics endorses Curran's general conclusion; it belongs with the other Christian emphases in his imagination's world. Above all it justifies man's taking upon himself the existential burdens borne by God or the gods in earlier stages of consciousness. This, as we know, means a confrontation with the opposed tendencies of Lucifer and Ahriman, and it is important to note that the distinction was still clearly understood by some of the Church Fathers, notably those who like Clement of Alexandria were still in touch with the early esoteric traditions. Clement writes in his *Miscellanies* (*Stromateis*): 'The face of evil looks in two directions: on the one hand it works by cunning lies and deceit, and on the other through brute force.'[14] However, adds Clement, the Word has appeared in man and thus given us the possibility of evading both.

We may thus briefly delineate the structure of spiritual forces that will serve to represent the Christian constellation, though we must also admit that Christianity evolved into many different things in different times and places. A point that needs brief comment is the theological introduction of the Holy Spirit, the presence of God in human consciousness, which in turn allows the placing of Christ at the pivotal centre-point of the whole diagram (Figure 8). In Shelley's vision too, we argued, the conscious self cannot itself compel the revelation of beauty and truth, but only hold itself in readiness, give itself as the vehicle of a reality making itself known. So in Christian spirituality, the working of Christ can by no means be represented wholly within the sphere of consciousness, even though it does require a conscious act of faith on the part of the believer. Christ works in the deeper nature of the soul, and on that working depends the sending of the Spirit, the Paraclete.

Having argued that Shelley arrived, through his own imaginative growth, at a vision close to that of Christianity, which he never accepted, it remains to suggest what advantages he might have obtained from a frank recognition. For certainly he might have progressed in some important respects further than he actually did. He might, for instance, have been able to transcend that sense of history as essentially cyclical (which persists in *Hellas*), or as an up-hill struggle against the powers of inertia and tyranny (*Prometheus Unbound*). He might, instead

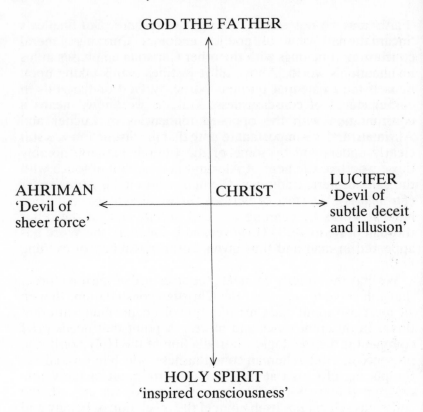

GOD THE FATHER

AHRIMAN   CHRIST   LUCIFER
'Devil of   'Devil of
sheer force'   subtle deceit
                                  and illusion'

HOLY SPIRIT
'inspired consciousness'

FIGURE 8   *The Christian 'theological' model*

of rejecting earlier modes of vision as false ontologies, in the eighteenth-century manner, have begun to grasp the historical transformations of thought and awareness.

Here we become speculative. But it was from an inadequate sense of history that Romanticism ultimately suffered, and which a 'Romanticism come of age' would have to supply.[15] And that it might have learnt from Christian spiritual history, *Heilsgeschichte.* The Christianity that resulted from such a confluence would also, of course, have been a radical extension of existing Christian thought. It would have had to rise to the challenge of a vastly intensified humanism: the feeling for man's moral autonomy that is expressed in the impulse of Romanticism. It would have had to meet the challenge of the

Ahrimanic expansion of technology, the Industrial Revolution, and the new understanding of material nature. Christianity had risen to similar challenges several times in the course of its history. But now, though Coleridge made brilliant efforts to keep the whole Romantic issue within the framework of Judaeo-Christian conceptions, the breakthrough did not come. In the nineteenth century as a whole, art, science and religion went their separate ways.

Notes

NOTES TO THE INTRODUCTION: THE PAINTED VEIL

1. The image of the 'veil' came to Shelley partly through Platonic sources, though it is older and played a part in the ancient Mystery religions from which Plato derived it: see Neville Rogers, *Shelley at Work* (Oxford, 1956) pp. 120ff. His interpretation of the sonnet (pp. 122–3), however, is too simple in its Platonic faith. The veil may be the sacred veil of Isis, which 'no mortal hath ever lifted': John Beer pointed out to me that the Romantics encountered this image in the popular school-handbook of mythology, Tooke's *Pantheon*.

   'Lift not the painted veil' may profitably be read in conjunction with 'Ye hasten to the grave' (1820), which presents a converse view illustrating the complexity of Shelley's attitude.
2. Cf. Shelley's remarks in the Preface to *Alastor*. The poem represents, he says, 'a youth of uncorrupted feelings and adventurous genius led forth by an imagination inflamed and purified through familiarity with all that is excellent and majestic, to a contemplation of the universe. He drinks deep of the fountains of knowledge, and is still insatiate. The magnificence and beauty of the external world sinks profoundly into the frame of his conceptions, and affords to their modifications a variety not to be exhausted. . . . But the period arrives when these objects cease to suffice' (*The Complete Poetical Works of Percy Bysshe Shelley*, ed. Neville Rogers, vol. II (Oxford, 1975) p. 43).
3. William Wordsworth, *The Poetical Works of William Wordsworth*, ed. E. de Selincourt and H. Darbishire, vol v (Oxford, 1952) pp. 3–4.
4. William Blake, letter to Thomas Butts dated 25 April 1803: in W. Blake, *Complete Writings*, ed. Sir Geoffrey Keynes (Oxford, 1972) pp. 822–3.
5. 2 Cor. 12:2–4. Shelley's penchant for choosing his self-descriptions from the language of the New Testament is noted by M. H. Abrams, *Natural Supernaturalism* (New York, 1971) pp. 439–40. For Shelley's 'constant perusal' of the Bible see also p. 33 and p. 485 n38; and for parallels between Shelley and traditional Christian 'inspiration' see Harold Bloom, *Shelley's Mythmaking* (Cornell, 1959) pp. 36ff.
6. See the Romantic material on this subject assembled by Abrams, *Natural Supernaturalism*, pp. 377ff.
7. Wordsworth wrote confidently in the manuscript Prospectus to *The Recluse*

   > Of truth, of Grandeur, Beauty, Love, and Hope,
   > And melancholy Fear subdued by Faith.

But the vision of splendour soon faded. Shelley's *Laon and Cythna* (1817) was an epic devoted explicitly to establishing 'how far a thirst for a happier condition of moral and political society survives, among the enlightened and refined, the tempests which have shaken the age in which we live' (*Complete Poetical Works*, vol. II, p. 99), an age Shelley characterised as 'an age of despair'.

8. Wordsworth, *Resolution and Independence*, ll. 48–9, in *Poetical Works*, ed. E. de Selincourt, vol. II (Oxford, 1944) p. 236.

9. *On Life*: written, conjectured Rossetti, in 1815; see *Shelley Complete Works*, ed. R. Ingpen and W. E. Peck, vol. VI (reprinted New York, 1965; the 'Julian Edition') p. 193.

10. Ibid.

11. I think especially of the paintings of John Martin, of which the best known are probably *Manfred on the Jungfrau* (City Museum and Art Gallery, Birmingham) and *The Bard* (Paul Mellon Collection).

12. For Blake art works by penetrating to the essence of things, 'melting apparent surfaces away, and displaying the infinite which was hid' (William Blake, *The Marriage of Heaven and Hell*, in *Complete Writings*, ed. Sir Geoffrey Keynes (Oxford, 1972) p. 154). On the dissolution of the actual in Shelley's imagining see the brilliant essay by D. J. Hughes on 'Potentiality in *Prometheus Unbound*', *Studies in Romanticism*, XI (1963); reprinted in R. B. Woodings, *Shelley: Modern Judgments* (London, 1969) pp. 142–61.

13. Eccles. 1:14 *passim*.

14. The scientifically minded Shelley may well have had in mind sunspots, which are actually bright masses only appearing as 'blots' because the surrounding area of the sun is still brighter.

NOTES TO CHAPTER 1: CONTRARY LANDSCAPES

1. Harold Bloom, *The Visionary Company* (New York, 1971) p. 282.

2. *Queen Mab* (1813) displays absolutely no premonitory sign of Shelley's future lyrical energy. Its heavy, ornamented verse labours in the tradition of Erasmus Darwin and the epics of Southey. The outward paraphernalia of the dream-vision alone imitates Spenser, except in one or two moments where dogmatism temporarily blinks. All Shelley's boyhood obsessions are crowded in: the snippets of science in the Darwinian notes which outbulk the poem; the atheism; the radical politics; the Wandering Jew. The elements which exist in electrifying tension in the adult Shelley are all heaped together in an ill-assorted jumble of ideas. The influence of the poem in reform circles was nevertheless astonishing: see Richard Holmes, *Shelley: The Pursuit* (London, 1976) pp. 208ff.

3. *Queen Mab*, VI, 197–8.

4. La Mettrie, *L'Homme Machine* (1748), followed by *L'Homme Plante* (the series sounds capable of indefinite extension); Baron d'Holbach, *Système de la Nature* (1770). Shelley began a translation of the latter work in 1812, when most of *Queen Mab* must have been written: see A. M. D. Hughes, *The Nascent Mind of Shelley* (Oxford, 1947) p. 153.

5. *Queen Mab*, v, 76–7. Cf. William Godwin, *Enquiry Concerning Political Justice*, ed. S. Kramnick (Harmondsworth, 1976) p. 756 ('Beware of reducing men to the state of machines') and p. 758 ('a clockwork uniformity'). The positive view of technology predominates, however.
6. *Prometheus Unbound*, I, 21–2.
7. *The Triumph of Life*, ll. 182ff. and 77–8. Compare too the figure impaled on the tree in the prose fragment *The Assassins*. It is interesting to pose the relationship of these images, particularly that in the *Triumph of Life* passage, to Dryden:

> Stay, I fancy
> I'm now turn'd wild, a Commoner of Nature;
> Of all forsaken, and forsaking all;
> Live in a shady Forest's *Sylvan* scene,
> Stretch'd at my length beneath some blasted Oke;
> I lean my head upon the Mossy Bark,
> And look just of a piece, as I grew from it:
> My uncomb'd Locks, matted like *Misleto*,
> Hang e're my hoary Face . . .
> (John Dryden, *All for Love*, I, 252–60)

8. Cf. John Locke, *Essay Concerning Human Understanding*, Bk II, ch. 1, para. 3:

> First, our senses, conversant about particular sensible objects, do convey into the mind several distinct perceptions of things, according to those various ways wherein those objects do affect them; and thus we come by those ideas we have, of yellow, white, heat, cold, soft, hard, bitter, sweet, and all those which we call sensible qualities; which when I say the senses convey into the mind, I mean they from external objects convey into the mind what produces there those perceptions.

9. Cited in Rudolf Steiner, *The Riddles of Philosophy* (New York, 1973) p. 79.
10. *The Letters of Perry Bysshe Shelley*, ed. F. L. Jones, vol. I (Oxford, 1964) pp. 99–100; letter 82, dated 11 June 1811.
11. Sir William Drummond, *Academical Questions* (1805): for his influence on Shelley see Hughes, *The Nascent Mind*, pp. 241–3. 'Academical' refers to the fact that the New Academy, successor to the Old Academy of Plato, was the home of the ancient Sceptics.
12. *On Life*, in *Complete Works*, ed. R. Ingpen and W. E. Peck, vol. VI, (reprinted New York, 1965; the 'Julian Edition') p. 197: 'But cause is only a word expressing a certain state of the human mind with regard to the manner in which two thoughts are apprehended to be related to each other.'
13. Ibid.
14. Cf. also *Queen Mab*, IV, 101–3 which pictures:

> The meteor-happiness, that shuns his grasp,
> But serving on the frightful gulf to glare,
> Rent wide beneath his footsteps.

15. *On Life*, in *Complete Works*, vol. VI, p. 196.
16. Approaching the matter from the opposite direction, A. O. Lovejoy rightly says that

> the force of the monistic pathos is in some degree intelligible when one considers the nature of the implicit responses which talk about oneness produces. It affords, for example, a welcome sense of freedom, arising from a triumph over, or an absolution from, the troublesome cleavages and disjunctions of things. . . . The deliquescence of the sense – the often so fatiguing sense – of separate personality . . . which comes in various ways . . . is also capable of excitation, and of really powerful excitation, too, by a mere metaphysical theorem. (A. O. Lovejoy, *The Great Chain of Being* (Harvard, 1964) p. 13).

Conversely, trance states or other modifications of consciousness may suggest an idealist universe, in terms as direct as those of Bishop Berkeley. For example, Humphry Davy experimented with the inhaling of nitrous oxide, and reports how he soon 'lost all connection with external things; trains of vivid visible images rapidly passed through my mind, and were connected with words in such a manner, as to produce perceptions perfectly novel. I existed in a world of newly connected and newly modified ideas.' On waking he exclaimed, 'Nothing exists but thoughts! – the universe is composed of impressions, ideas, pleasures and pains!' (*Collected Works of Sir Humphry Davy*, vol. III (London, 1839–40) pp. 289–90).

17. A. E. Taylor, *Elements of Metaphysics* (London, 1961) pp. 381–2.
18. See David Newsome, *Two Classes of Men: Platonism and English Romantic Thought* (London, 1974).
19. The fullest study of Shelley's Platonism is that by J. A. Notopoulos, *The Platonism of Shelley* (Durham, NC, 1949), a book marred by a certain monomania about its central conviction and by the notion that Shelley's changing affinity with the Greek philosopher can be plotted on a multiple graph. An excessive belief that Shelley was 'basically' a Platonist spoils the work of several other scholars too. Notopoulos reprints Shelley's translations of Plato; and *The Banquet of Plato* is now also available in Richard Holmes' anthology, *Shelley on Love* (London, 1980) pp. 113–72.
20. Notes on *Queen Mab*, in *Complete Poetical Works*, ed. Neville Rogers vol. I (Oxford, 1972) p. 319.
21. Notopoulos distinguishes direct Platonism (= reading Plato), indirect Platonism (= reading those who have read Plato) and natural Platonism (= thinking what Plato thought without having read Plato).
22. *Queen Mab*, II, 71–2. It is a cosmic vista 'at whose immensity / Even soaring fancy staggers' (I, 266–7).
23. Ibid., II, 91ff.: the realm of 'all prevailing wisdom, when it reaps / The harvest of its excellence'.
24. Ibid., II, 94–6.
25. Ibid., II, 13–21. Cf. also I, 94ff., prophetic of the later Shelley with its reference to the fading morning star.
26. Compare with the following Neville Rogers' alternative interpretation, *Complete Poetical Works*, vol. I, p. 381.

27. Hence Shelley's recurrent argument that there is no choice except between atheism and revealed religion: deistical arguments from nature up to God are rejected. In his poetry and later writing, however, the choice is formulated as between starting from above or starting from below, and the problem is how to relate the two movements.

28. Compare Shelley's account of a particular landscape which had been reflected in dreams:

> After the lapse of many years I have dreamed of this scene. It has hung on my memory, it has haunted my thoughts, at intervals, with the pertinacity of an object connected with human affections. I have visited this scene again. Neither the dream could be dissociated from the landscape, nor the landscape from the dream, nor feelings, such as neither singly could have awakened, from both. (*Speculations on Metaphysics*, in Shelley, *Complete Works*, ed. R. Ingpen and W. E. Peck, vol. VII (New York, 1930) p. 67)

29. *Julian and Maddalo*, ll. 15–17.

30. We shall discuss this imagery later. Contrary to the statements of W. B. Yeats, however, the fading star did not come to Shelley charged with already fixed associations. Within Shelley's poetry it became the focus for a wealth of poetic intimations, which derive their meaning from the matrix of his imagination. The essay on *The Philosophy of Shelley's Poetry* meanwhile stands as a remarkable testimony to what Shelley would have thought had he been W. B. Yeats. The essay is readily available in Yeats, *Selected Criticism and Prose* (London, 1980) pp. 53–79.

31. Cf. Earl Wasserman, *Shelley: A Critical Reading* (Baltimore, 1971) pp. 140–1.

32. As anatomised by Richard Holmes, *Shelley: The Pursuit*, p. 642.

33. In his *Coleridge's Poetic Intelligence* (London, 1977), John Beer has suggested, however, that Coleridge's underlying concepts of 'primary consciousness' etc. developed earlier, before he visited Germany, and retained certain distinguishing features. His work is therefore incidentally valuable for the light it throws on sources of Romantic thought accessible to Shelley in England. There is no dispute, though, about the stimulation Coleridge gained from contact with parallel developments in German thought, facilitating a profound extension of his own philosophy.

34. Represented for Shelley especially by Calderon, Rousseau and Dante. It is noteworthy that Shelley was strongly motivated in translating when he felt he could do nothing creative; he had an urge to bring European poetry *into English*.

35. Shelley worked seriously at reading Goethe in German, and translating him, only in the last year of his life.

36. Coleridge's masterpieces of poetry are, with few exceptions, notable for the suspension of waking consciousness: the supposed opium dream of *Kubla Khan*, the repressed energies apparent in *Christabel*, the magnetic eye and obsessive narration of *The Ancient Mariner*, etc.

    By contrast, for an 'inside' survey of Coleridge's philosophy see Owen Barfield, *What Coleridge Thought* (Oxford, 1971).

37. Cited in C. E. Pulos, *The Deep Truth* (Lincoln, Nebraska, 1962) p. 46.
38. *On Life*, in Shelley, *Complete Works*, vol. VI, p. 196.
39. Ibid. Cf. the anxiety in the image of the soul, in *Queen Mab*, II, 61–2, 'immured / Within the prison of itself', despite being there 'resigned / To pleasurable impulses' (59–60).
40. *On Life*, in Shelley, *Complete Works*, vol. VI, p. 196.
41. Pulos, in *The Deep Truth*, first demonstrated Shelley's consistent study of the Sceptical tradition, exploding the idea (of Mary Shelley and others) that he had been a fugitive from French dogmatism into Berkeley's Immaterialist doctrines, and showing the importance of Drummond and Hume.
42. See the chapter 'Angels and Critics', in Timothy Webb, *Shelley: A Voice Not Understood* (Manchester, 1977) pp. 1–32.
43. Harold Bloom, 'Introduction' to *Selected Poetry and Prose of Shelley* (New York, 1966) p. xviii.
44. Wasserman, *Shelley: A Critical Reading*.
45. *Shelley's Letters*, vol. I, p. 150; letter 118, date 16 October 1811.
46. Wasserman, *Shelley: A Critical Reading*, p. 4.
47. Richard Cronin, *Shelley's Poetic Thoughts* (London, 1981). See particularly the chapter 'Realism and Fantasy', pp. 39–76. Cronin is, with Wasserman, our most sensitive reader of Shelley's verse thus far.
    Totally unacceptable is M. H. Abrams' picture of Shelley. Basing himself upon a single passage in a note to *Hellas*, Abrams interprets the 'vatic' poet in Shelley as his public *persona*, a deliberately assumed bardic voice; whilst the doubting, uneasy questioner is Shelley in his private character. Quite apart from laying extraordinary weight upon a single late footnote, this is not a practicable way of understanding Shelley's poems. These convince us that visionary and sceptic are densely interwoven aspects of his personality and thought, manifested in private and public alike. Cf. M. H. Abrams, *Natural Supernaturalism* (New York, 1971) pp. 439–40.
48. Cronin, *Shelley's Poetic Thoughts*, p. 201.
49. Blake was referring to the dispute between God and the Devil, Heaven and Hell. 'For this history has been adopted by both parties' (William Blake, *The Marriage of Heaven and Hell*, in *Complete Writings*, ed. Sir Geoffrey (Oxford, 1972) Keynes p. 150).
50. Though it might be debated how far the rationalist or the realist enterprise is strictly viable on its own theoretical terms.
51. Shelley reveals his uncompromising nature in a brief parenthesis, with a stark enunciation of the principle that 'a medium ought not to be adopted' (*Shelley's Letters*, ed. F. H. Jones, vol. II, p. 339; letter 656, dated 15 August 1821). He advocated in his poetic thought neither one extreme, nor the other, nor a sorry compromise – but a dynamic openness to the potential of experience.
52. Not everyone, however, finds it congenial. 'No one', writes John Holloway for example, 'ought to feel so passionately, so intensely as this, and yet move in thought with such virtuosity . . . over his work seen as a whole, the price is a fatiguing intensity of intellectual and emotional response, within a range which is fatiguing in its narrowness'. Cited in R. B.

Woodings, *Shelley: Modern Judgments* (London, 1969) p. 27. Yet he is not altogether just to Shelley. Not only, as Woodings suggests, is Shelley's range much broader than lyrical anthologies tend to show, but the rewards of making the effort – as in climbing a mountain peak and adjusting to the rarified air – far outweigh, for this reader at least, the exhaustion incurred.
53. Cronin, *Shelley's Poetic Thoughts*, pp. 189-90, 192–3.
54. *Adonais*, ll. 491–2.

NOTES TO CHAPTER 2: LITERARY POWERS

1. G. M. Matthews points out how Palgrave and Tennyson, in anthologising 'The Invitation', actually cut out the middle section to make the poem conform to their notion of a Shelleyan lyric: G. M. Matthews, *Shelley*, Writers and their Work Series (London, 1970) p. 7.
2. Richard Cronin, *Shelley's Poetic Thoughts* (London, 1981) p. 245.
3. R. G. Cox, *From Donne to Marvell* (Harmondsworth, 1970) p. 113.
4. *Prometheus Unbound*, III, iv, 193–204.
5. Fragment *On the Symposium*; see Richard Holmes (ed.), *Shelley on Love* (London, 1980) p. 113.
6. William Godwin, letter to Shelley, dated 10 December 1812; in *The Letters of Percy Bysshe Shelley*, ed. F. L. Jones, vol. I (Oxford, 1964) pp. 340–1.
7. Cf. Earl Wasserman, *Shelley: A Critical Reading* (Baltimore, 1971) pp. 363ff.
8. See Harold Bloom, *The Visionary Company* (Cornell, 1971).
9. *Peter Bell the Third*, l. 319.
10. See Cronin's perceptive reading of *The Mask of Anarchy*, in *Shelley's Poetic Thoughts*, pp. 39–55.
11. *Peter Bell the Third*, ll. 273–7 and 293–7. The passage at *Prelude* (1805) XIII, 107–2 can certainly be read as a declaration of obsessive self-satisfaction!
12. On which see now Ann Thompson, 'Shelley's "Letter to Maria Gisborne": Tact and Clutter', in M. Allott (ed.), *Essays on Shelley* (Liverpool, 1982) pp. 144–59.
13. *Adonais*, ll. 381–5.
14. Akenside, *The Pleasures of Imagination*, II, 311–15.
15. Samuel Taylor Coleridge, Sonnet *To the Rev. W. L. Bowles* (written 1794); on the link with Akenside see George Dekker, *Coleridge and the Literature of Sensibility* (London, 1978) pp. 152ff.
16. Richard Sulivan, *View of Nature*, vol. II (1794) p. 92; cited in John Beer, *Coleridge's Poetic Intelligence* (London, 1977) p. 45.
17. On the importance of Chatterton in this context, and the parallel role played elsewhere by Otway and others see Dekker, *Coleridge and the Literature of Sensibility*, pp. 58ff.
18. In his Oxford period, if we are to believe reports, Shelley sometimes spent as many as sixteen hours a day reading.

19. After his schoolboy ventures in prose fiction, however, Shelley never managed to complete a prose romance or novel, though he started several. Perhaps the longer form could not keep pace with his astonishingly rapid inner growth. Especially for the younger Shelley, his prose fragments are sometimes more revealing than his derivative early political verse.

20. A general discussion of the Sensibility movement is in Basil Willey, *Eighteenth-Century Background* (London, 1940); a valuable article is R. S. Crane, 'Suggestions Toward a Genealogy of the "Man of Feeling" ', in *ELH*, 1 (1935) 205–30; and on the transition to Romanticism, the collection of essays *From Sensibility to Romanticism*, ed. F. W. Hillis and Harold Bloom (Oxford, 1965) has much of interest.

21. See G. D. Stout, 'Yorick's Sentimental Journey: a Comic *Pilgrim's Progress* for the Man of Feeling', in *ELH*, 30 (1963) 395–412.

22. L. Sterne, *A Sentimental Journey*, ed. A. Alvarez (Harmondsworth, 1967) p. 111.

23. *Shelley's Letters*, vol. I, p. 480; letter 353, dated 12 July 1816.

24. Ibid., 493–4; letter 356, dated 18 July 1816.

25. Thomas Love Peacock, *Nightmare Abbey*, ed. R. Wright (Harmondsworth, 1969) p. 46. *Werter and Charlotte: A German Story* was rendered into English by an anonymous translator and published in London in 1786; the slightly later version of Goethe's novel made by Graves, *The Sorrows of Werter*, appeared in London in 1794, and was probably the one Shelley knew.

26. See S. P. Atkins, *The Testament of Werther in Poetry and Drama* (Cambridge, MA, 1949); Dekker, *Coleridge and the Literature of Sensibility*, pp. 77ff.

27. *Shelley's Letters*, vol. I, p. 577; letter 432 to William Godwin, dated 11 December 1817. Mary Shelley adapted the passage in her Note on *Laon and Cythna*, in *The Complete Poetical Works of Percy Byssche Shelley* ed. Neville Rogers, vol. II (Oxford, 1975) p. 273.

28. *Charles the First*, Scene I, 18–20. The idea is developed in many Sensibility writers. Mary Wollstonecraft writes of 'a certain kind of elevation' of the mind: 'We see what we wish, and make a world of our own – and, though reality may sometimes open a door to misery, yet the moments of happiness procured by the imagination may, without a paradox, be reckoned among the solid comforts of life' (Mary Wollstonecraft, *The Wrongs of Woman*, ed. J. Kinsley and G. Kelly (Oxford, 1980) pp. 188–9.

29. Preface to *Laon and Cythna*, in *Complete Poetical Works*, vol. II, p. 100.

30. Sterne, *A Sentimental Journey*, p. 138.

31. Ann Radcliffe, *The Mysteries of Udolpho*, ed. B. Dobrée (Oxford, 1970) pp. 79–81.

32. Mary Wollstonecraft, *The Wrongs of Woman* and *Mary* are both mentioned in the diary where Mary Shelley kept a record of her husband's reading. See also *Shelley's Letters*, vol. I, pp. 400, 405.

33. Mary Wollstonecraft, *Vindication of the Rights of Woman*, ed. S. Kramnick (Harmondsworth, 1975) p. 158. 'All Rousseau's errors in reasoning', she later asserts, 'arose from sensibility . . . reflecting on the sensations to which fancy gave force, he traced them in the most glowing colours, and sunk them deep into his soul' (p. 189).

34. Robert Southey, cited in Dekker, *Coleridge and the Literature of Sensibility*, p. 90.
35. Bodleian MS Shelley adds. e. 11, p. 78.
36. Wollstonecraft, *The Wrongs of Woman*, p. 163.
37. William Blake, *Book of Urizen*, 14, 51–4:

> & Pity began,
> In anguish dividing & dividing,
> For pity divides the soul
> In pangs, eternity on eternity.

38. William Blake, *Milton*, 9, 46.
39. The history and, to some extent, the sources of Gothic have been treated in two excellent though very different books: Eino Railo, *The Haunted Castle* (London, 1927); and more recently, David Punter, *The Literature of Terror* (London, 1980).

   A not very illuminating account of Gothic elements in Shelley is provided by John V. Murphy, *The Dark Angel* (London and New Jersey, 1975).
40. Railo, *The Haunted Castle*, p. 43; and see pp. 40ff for the general theme.
41. Ibid., pp. 38ff.
42. Above all, Railo speaks constantly in terms of a 'horror Romanticism'. None of the Gothic writers, however, present a properly Romantic vision, though horror was undoubtedly one of the crystallising elements in the fusion of cultural forces from which Romanticism came into being.
43. D. G. Halliburton, 'Shelley's "Gothic" Novels', in *Keats–Shelley Journal*, 16 (1967) 39–49 (43).
44. On Shelley's homosexual or bisexual leanings, cf. Richard Holmes, *Shelley: The Pursuit* (London, 1976) esp. pp. 14–15, 295, 431ff., 566.
45. Punter, *The Literature of Terror*, esp. pp. 45, 59, 127–8.
46. Thomas Carlyle, *Goethe's Helena* (1828).
47. See Joseph Warren Beach, *The Concept of Nature in Nineteenth-Century English Poetry* (New York, 1966). The Romantics' concern with, and knowledge of, the cosmological tendencies of science has been more widely recognised of late. See, for example, Beer, *Coleridge's Poetic Intelligence*, which includes discussion of Coleridge's extensive use of 'scientific' imagery; Geoffrey Durrant, *Wordsworth and the Great System* (Cambridge, 1970) argues against oversimplifying Wordsworth's anti-scientism; Donald Ault's interesting but speculative *Visionary Physics* (Chicago, 1974) examines some of the ways Blake tried to create an imaginative counter-science to that of Newton.
48. William Blake, *Auguries of Innocence*, ll. 109–10.
49. *Refutation of Deism*, in Shelley, *Complete Works*, ed. R. Ingpen and W. E. Peck, vol. VI (reprinted New York, 1965; the 'Julian Edition'), p. 48.
50. M. Horkheimer and Th. Adorno, *Dialectic of Enlightenment* (London, 1973).
51. Punter, *The Literature of Terror*, p. 27; and generally, pp. 99ff. On Blake, cf. A. J. Welburn, 'Blake's Cosmos', in *Journal of English and Germanic Philology*, 80 (1981) 39–53. On the cosmic image in Romanticism see also Bernard Blackstone, *The Lost Travellers* (London, 1962) pp. 17ff.

A work in which we seem to witness the crucial transition of Gothic magician to Gothic scientist is of course Mary Shelley's *Frankenstein* (written 1817). It would be fascinating to know how big a part Shelley played in its production!

52. W. Hazlitt, 'William Godwin', in *The Spirit of the Age* (1825), ed. E. D. Mackerness (London and Glasgow, 1969), pp. 35–6.

53. And for that very reason no doubt appeared to Shelley to sum up the philosophical wisdom the poet had painfully struggled to synthesise for himself. Godwin continued to develop, however, after writing the *Enquiry*, and moved away from the rationalism and Necessitarianism it embodied towards an acknowledgment of the power of feeling. His novel-writing must have helped to produce broader psychological insights into motivation and character. His 'sentimental education' is traced in G. Kelly, *The English Jacobin Novel* (Oxford, 1976).

54. Hazlitt, 'William Godwin', in *The Spirit of the Age*, p. 48.

55. *Remarks on Mandeville*, in Shelley, *Complete Works*, vol. vi, p. 220.

56. For a historian's view of the Rosicrucians see Frances Yates, *The Rosicrucian Enlightenment* (London, 1972); important texts are collected in Paul M. Allen (ed.), *A Christian Rosencreutz Anthology* (New York, 1968). The 'Rosicrucian' ideas of *St Leon* derive from a strange satire on longevity called *Hermippus Redivivus*, remembered now (if at all) from I. Disraeli's *Curiosities of Literature* (London, 1791). Its translator, Dr J. Campbell, describes its 'serious Irony' as befitting those 'who are inclined to see how far the Strength of human Understanding can support philosophical Truths, against common Notions and vulgar Prejudices'. The 'Truth' for which it ironically contends is man's power of never dying, asserted by Hermippus, Roger Bacon *et al.*, proved by a 300-year-old Yogi in Bengal, and moreover: 'This is certain, that the Society of the *Rosicrucians* openly claimed it as one of the Privileges of their illustrious Body' (p. 83). The instance of Gualdi (pp. 84ff) is clearly behind Godwin's plot in *St Leon*. See J. H. Cohausen, *Hermippus Redivivus* (London, 1744); discussion in Kelly, *The English Jacobin Novel*, pp. 209–36.

Shelley probably also read *Hermippus*, which may have contributed to some of the imagery in *The Sensitive Plant*.

57. E. M. Sickels, 'Shelley and Charles Brockden Brown', in *PMLA*, 45 (1930) 1116–28; Punter, *The Literature of Terror*, pp. 189ff.

58. Like David Seed, in his article 'Shelley's "Gothick" in *St Irvyne* and After', in Allott (ed.), *Essays on Shelley*, pp. 39–70.

59. *St Irvyne, or the Rosicrucian*, ch. vii.

60. Holmes, *Shelley: The Pursuit*, p. 293; and see in his index under 'Shelley: fantasy and horror'.

61. Radcliffe, *The Mysteries of Udolpho*, pp. 49–50.

62. Ibid., p. 626. A voice from a distinctly less sublime world than either hero or heroine wish to inhabit.

63. As observed by David Seed, 'Shelleys "Gothick" ', in Allott (ed.), *Essays on Shelley*, p. 60.

64. Holmes, *Shelley: The Pursuit*, p. 246; and generally see pp. 243ff.

65. *The Assassins*, in Shelley, Complete Works, vol. vi, p. 157.

66. Ibid., p. 163.
67. Ibid., p. 158.
68. Ibid., pp. 158–9.
69. Ibid., p. 160.
70. Ibid., p. 159.
71. Ibid., p. 157.

NOTES TO CHAPTER 3: OCCULT QUALITIES

1. C. Grabo, *A Newton Among Poets* (Chapel Hill, NC, 1935); Desmond King-Hele, *Shelley: His Thought and Work* (London, 1971).
2. On the vulcanism see especially G. M. Matthews, 'A Volcano's Voice in Shelley', *Journal of English Literary History*, xxiv (1957) 191–228; reprinted in R. B. Woodings, *Shelley: Modern Judgments* (London, 1969) pp. 162–95.
3. *Speculations on Metaphysics*, in Shelley, *Complete Works*, ed. R. Ingpen and W. E. Peck, vol. vii, p. 117.
4. Thus for example the natural-scientific readings of *The Cloud* and the volcanic passages need to be supplemented by thoughts along other lines. G. Wilson Knight shows how the symbolic equivalences in the former render the Cloud a centre of identity like the human 'I am', so that its transmutations are felt on the human level as experiences of death and rebirth (with perhaps a hint of reincarnation): see G. Wilson Knight, *The Starlit Dome* (London, 1959) pp. 198–9. Earl Wasserman has shown the connection between the volcanoes and Shelley's conception of an occult 'Power', about which we shall say more later: see Earl Wasserman, *Shelley: A Critical Reading* (Baltimore, 1971) pp. 330–46 *passim*.
5. Grabo, *A Newton Among Poets*, p. 3.
6. R. Ingpen, *Shelley in England* (New York, 1917), p. 48.
7. *Hymn to Intellectual Beauty*, ll. 49ff.
8. See Richard Holmes, *Shelley: The Pursuit* (London, 1976) pp. 3ff.
9. T. J. Hogg, *Life of Shelley* (London, 1906) p. 54.
10. *The Letters of Percy Bysshe Shelley*, ed. F. L. Jones, vol. i (Oxford, 1964) p. 227; letter 159, dated 10 January 1812.
11. Thomas De Quincey, *Suspiria de Profundis*, 'The Palimpsest'. In his *De resuscitationibus* Paracelsus says:

> If a thing loses its material substance, the invisible form still remains in the light of Nature, and if we can reclothe that form with visible matter, we may make that form visible again. . . . By alchemical means we may recreate a magnetic attraction in the astral form, so that it may attract from the elements those principles which it possessed before its mortification, and incorporate them and become visible again. (Cf. Franz Hartmann, *Paracelsus* (New York, 1973) pp. 46, 205 and note).

Athanasius Kircher is reported to have resurrected a rose from its ashes in the presence of Queen Christina of Sweden in 1687.

Cf. *A Defence of Poetry*, in Shelley, *Complete Works*, vol. VII, p. 114.
The starting-point for Shelley's researches on alchemical resuscitation
was probably the entry on 'Spectral Flowers' in R. Southey and Samuel
Taylor Coleridge's *Omniana* (ed. R. Gittings, Fontwell, 1969). Southey
cites an account by Gaffarel:

> Though plants, he says, be chopt in pieces, brayed in a mortar, and even
> burnt to ashes; yet do they nevertheless retaine, by a certaine secret and
> wonderfull power of nature, both in the juyce and in the ashes the selfe
> same forme and figure that they had before: and though it be not there
> visible, yet it may by art be drawne forth and made visible to the eye, by
> an artist.

A certain Polish physician is said to have

> kept in glasses the ashes of almost all the hearbes that are knowne: so
> that, when any one out of curiosity, had a desire to see any of them, as
> for example, a rose, in one of his glasses, he tooke that where the ashes
> of a rose were preserved; and holding it over a lighted candle, so soon as
> ever it began to feele the heat, you should presently see the ashes begin
> to move; which afterwards issuing up, and dispersing themselves about
> the glasse, you should immediately observe a kind of little dark cloud;
> which dividing itself into many parts, it came at length to represent a
> rose; but so aire, so fresh, and so perfect a one, that you would have
> thought it to have been as substantial, and as odoriferous a rose as any
> that growes on the rose tree. (From *Unheard of Curiosities* (Oxford,
> 1650), in *Omniana*, pp. 213–14)

See further Jacques Marx, 'Alchimie et palingénésie', *Isis*, 62 (1971)
274–89; A. G. Debus, 'A Further Note on Palingenesis', *Isis*, 64 (1973)
226–30. The reconstitution of a flower by alchemical means had been
referred to in poetry before, by the ingenious Sir William Davenant. See
Gondibert, ed. Gladish (Oxford, 1971) I, iv, 4. Also in Davenant, *Shorter
Poems*, ed. Gibbs, 'The Christians Reply to the Philosopher', stanza 2. In
Davenant, it serves as an image of poetry itself.

12. Charles Nicholl, *The Chemical Theatre* (London, 1980) p. 5. See also
    B. L. Knapp, *Theatre and Alchemy* (Detroit, 1980).
13. See Goethe, *Die Wahlverwandtschaften*, ed. Nisbet and Reiss (Oxford,
    1971) pp. xvff. and pp. 270–1 n35 with addendum p. 282. For alchemical
    background to Goethe, cf. Alice Raphael, *Goethe and the Philosopher's
    Stone* (London, 1965); also D. Gray, *Goethe the Alchemist* (Cambridge,
    1952).
14. *Peter Bell the Third*, ll. 339–44.
15. As is claimed by Timothy Webb, *Shelley: A Voice Not Understood*
    (Manchester, 1977) pp. 236–8.
16. *The Sensitive Plant*, ll. 59–69.
17. Paracelsus, *De origine morborum invisibilium*. The passage is obviously
    related to the ideas behind 'the violet in the crucible'.
    There is much fascinating material in Walter Pagel, *Das medizinische*

Weltbild des Paracelsus: seine Zusammenhänge mit Neuplatonismus und Gnosis (Wiesbaden, 1962). For a modern, sympathetic study of Paracelsus' thought see Johannes Hemleben, *Paracelsus* (Frauenfeld and Stuttgart, 1973). He concurs with the remark of W.-E. Peuckert that 'one must read Paracelsus extensively before one realizes that he can genuinely think and express himself'.

For the influence of Paracelsus on Shelley see E. Ebeling, 'A Probable Paracelsan Element in Shelley's Poetry', *SP*, xxxii (1935) 508–25.

18. *The Sensitive Plant*, ll. 130–3.
19. See Carlos Baker, *Shelley's Major Poetry: Fabric of a Vision* (Princeton, 1966) pp. 66–7. Stuart Curran, *Shelley's Annus Mirabilis* (San Marino, CA, 1975) pp. 88–90 and pp. 227–9 n81 explores Newton's influence more deeply.
20. For Barrett's influence on Bulwer-Lytton, Eliphas Levi and others, see the discussion in E. M. Butler, *Ritual Magic* (Cambridge, 1979) pp. 254–7. Information about Barrett's disciples outside London, in Cambridge, comes from Montague Summers' vast knowledge of magical and occult affairs, though without precise source-references: see the passage cited in Butler, *Ritual Magic*, p. 257. Kathleen Raine has taken up the suggestion that Blake may have been in touch with Barrett and his circle some time around 1789. Certainly Fuseli, a friend and admirer of Blake, had contributed to Barrett's *Conjuror's Magazine*. See Kathleen Raine, *Blake and Tradition*, vol. i (London, 1969) p. 103 n12.
21. Timothy d'Arch Smith, 'Introduction' to Francis Barrett, *The Magus* (Secaucus, NJ, 1980) pp. ie–v.
22. Barrett advises vegetarianism: see, for example, Barrett, *The Magus*, vol. i, p. 11. The passage quoted on its spiritual effects is from vol. ii, p. 71.
23. *Mont Blanc*, ll. 49–52.
24. R. Southey, *Joan of Arc*, ix, 8–10.
25. Thomas Love Peacock, *Memoirs of Shelley*, cited in *The Complete Poetical Works of Percy Bysshe Shelley*, ed. Neville Rogers, vol. ii (Oxford, 1975) p. 336.

Barrett (*The Magus*, vol. ii, p. 57) discusses the 'innumberable daemons', and tells us that the 'ancient *theologians* of the Greeks' reckoned amongst them the Alastores, described as 'bearing ill-will to men' and spreading calamities, plagues and famines. Their connection with the river Styx is interesting in view of the important part played by the dark river in the hero's death in *Alastor*.

26. On the *eidola* see Barrett, *The Magus*, vol. i, pp. 79ff; and cf. the remarks on vision at p. 33. On Magian lore see vol. ii, pp. 143ff; also vol. i, p. 107 where Barrett says: 'Magicians do constitute three Princes of the world – Oromasis, Mithris, Araminis; *i.e.* God, the mind, and the spirit', which is actually a quotation from Ficino's *Theologia Platonica*, iv, 1. On toads, see Barrett, *The Magus*, vol. i, p. 25 and generally to p. 27.
27. See S. Foster Damon, *A Blake Dictionary* (London, 1973) p. 322, *sub* 'Paracelsus'. Damon quotes the passage from the *Archidoxis* on the imagination being 'the sun of man. . . . The whole heaven, indeed, is nothing but an imagination. . . . Even as (man) imagines himself to be, such he is, and he is also that which he imagines.' Cf. Barrett, *The Magus*,

vol. I, p. 7 where it is said that 'each mortal creature possesses a Sun and system within himself', together with other Paracelsian material. Cf. Hartmann, *Paracelsus*, p. 13 for the schema whereby Paracelsus asserted that man can reach God through the Soul; Christ through Faith; and the Holy Ghost through Imagination.

28. Barrett, *The Magus*, vol. II, p. 13; p. 26 on the 'magnetism of all things begotten in the imagination of man'; p. 28 on the inefficacy of rites without imagination ('no sympathetic remedies, magnetical or attractive, but from the idea of phantasy of the operator impressing upon it a virtue and efficacy from the excited power of his own soul').

29. See Robert Darnton, *Mesmerism and the End of the Enlightenment in France* (Cambridge, Ma, 1968) pp. 10ff. Cf. John Beer, *Coleridge's Poetic Intelligence* (London, 1977), pp. 72–3. Shelley's fascination with balloon airships, incidentally, was second only to his love of boats: see Holmes, *Shelley: The Pursuit*, pp. 149 (on the early poem 'To a Balloon, laden with Knowledge'), 308, 504, 561, 604, etc.

30. Ernst Lehrs, *Man or Matter* (London, 1951) pp. 48ff; for details of eighteenth-century electrical speculations see P. C. Ritterbush, *Overtures to Biology* (Yale, 1964). John Wesley's comment is cited in Grabo, *A Newton Among Poets*, pp. 94–5. Hegel regarded 'electricity' with some distrust as 'an occult agent, like the occult properties assumed by the Scholastics'.

31. Barrett, *The Magus*, vol. I, Preface; p. 1; p. 8. On the significance of the conception of *magia naturalis*, cf. Frances Yates, *Giordano Bruno and the Hermetic Tradition* (London, 1964) pp. 62ff.

32. Shelley, Preface to Mary Shelley, *Frankenstein, or The Modern Prometheus* (1818). Victor's occult learning, described in Chapter 2 of the book, is founded upon Agrippa's *De occulta philosophia*, and the works of Paracelsus and Albertus Magnus – Barrett's main authorities!

33. For occult themes in Godwin, see G. Kelly, *The English Jacobin Novel* (Oxford, 1976) pp. 209ff; Mary Wollstonecraft cites Swedenborg in the *Vindication of the Rights of Woman*, ed. S. Kramnick (Harmondsworth, 1975) p. 117, where she is probably thinking of Emanuel Swedenborg's *Delights of Wisdom Concerning Conjugal Love* (1768).

34. See in particular A. L. Morton's study *The Everlasting Gospel: A Study in the Sources of William Blake* (New York, 1966), also included in his collection of essays *The Matter of Britain* (London, 1966); and A. J. Welburn, 'The Gnostic Imagination of William Blake', PhD thesis, University of Cambridge, 1980, pp. 60ff. Wider background is in M. H. Abrams, *Natural Supernaturalism* (New York, 1971) esp. pp. 141ff.

35. Holmes, *Shelley: The Pursuit*, p. 709.

36. Thomas Medwin, *Life of Shelley*, p. 270.

37. Wollstonecraft, *Vindication of the Rights of Woman*, pp. 300ff. There are in fact several references to magnetism in Shelley's notebooks.

38. Darnton's *Mesmerism and the End of the Enlightenment* represents a new approach to Mesmer in his historical role. See also M. M. Tatar, *Spellbound* (Princeton, 1978).

39. See the interesting assessment by two of Charcot's pupils: Alfred Binet and Charles Féré, *Animal Magnetism* (London, 1898). The occult

background of the pioneers of the psychoanalytic movement has not been properly investigated, though James Webb, who has made a special study of occult traditions claims that 'there is evidence which suggests that Freud had a closer contact with the occultists of Vienna than has ever been admitted, and in the school of analytical psychology stemming from C. G. Jung, attention swung back to a consideration of topics treated by alchemy, Swedenborg, and the Gnostics' (James Webb, *The Harmonious Circle* (London, 1980) p. 535). For Jung see now the collection of his papers issued as C. G. Jung, *Psychology and the Occult* (Princeton, 1977), which includes Jung's MD dissertation on the psychology of occult phenomena (1902).

40. Binet and Féré, *Animal Magnetism*, pp. 3ff includes Mesmer's twenty-seven propositions published in 1779. The background of his theories was astrological, modelled after the idea of planetary influence, as is shown by his earlier thesis 'On the Influence of the Planets in the Cure of Diseases' (1766). For a time, Mesmer identified his ethereal fluid with the bearer of physical magnetism, but later changed his opinion and declared 'animal magnetism' to be a distinct kind. He abandoned the use of steel traction instruments and confined his technique to passes with the hand. The close analogy between the workings of physical and animal magnetism, however, was retained.

41. *Epipsychidion*, ll. 91–104.

42. Darwin: Grabo, *A Newton Among Poets*, p. 41 and cf. 50; Swedenborg: Emanuel Swedenborg, *Principia . . . Being New Attempts Toward A Philosophical Explanation of the Elementary World* (1734) (trans. Revd Augustus Clissold, London, 1846).

43. Desmond King-Hele, *Shelley: His Thought and Work* (London, 1971) pp. 193–5. *Prometheus Unbound*, IV, 463–6. King-Hele offers no source for Shelley's idea of a magnetic, polar attraction between Earth and Moon, rather than a gravitational one. W. Hildebrand, *Shelley's Polar Paradise* (Salzburg, 1974) emphasises parallels with Coleridgean polarity-concepts in Shelley's poetry. Hegel may also be reckoned among those thinkers for whom the idea of 'magnetism' provides the exemplar for fundamental spiritual and physical conceptions, as is pointed out by Findlay in his Introduction to the *Naturphilosophie: Hegel's Philosophy of Nature*, trans. A. V. Miller (Oxford, 1970) p. xx; cf. p. 163 (magnetism as the sensible demonstration of the Notion).

44. See Binet and Féré, *Animal Magnetism*, pp. 33ff.

45. Beer, *Coleridge's Poetic Intelligence*, p. 81 cites a note Coleridge made at the end of his copy of K. C. Wolfart's *Mesmerismus* (Berlin, 1814): 'I think it probable, that Animal Magnetism will be found connected with a Warmth-Sense.'

Beer concludes that animal magnetism was implicated in much of Coleridge's thought, in the ideas of fancy and imagination, genius and talent, reason and understanding. 'In each case,' he says, 'the distinction receives its true Coleridgean impress only when set in the context of psychological theories which locate the basic source of imagination, genius and reason at the level of organic being that is known chiefly to the primary consciousness' (Beer, *Coleridge's Poetic Intelligence*, p. 225).

Wordsworth too in *Lyrical Ballads* had explored psychosomatic states, especially in *The Idiot Boy* and *Goody Blake*, and other writers were looking to animal magnetism to provide images of mind and body – e.g. Balzac in the novels belonging to his *études philosophiques* and Edgar Allan Poe in *Mesmeric Revelation* and other tales. Cf. D. V. Falk 'Poe and the Power of Animal Magnetism', in *PMLA*, 84 (1969) 536–46.

46. Medwin, *Life of Shelley*, pp. 270ff.

Shelley's account of the division of consciousness in the magnetic state is remarkably similar to Hegel's conclusion that it involves 'a separation of psychical life from objective consciousness', and therefore a *rapprochement* with organic process: *Philosophy of Mind* from the *Encyclopaedia of Philosophical Sciences* (Oxford, 1971) p. 107, paragraph 406. Hegel further commented (p. 116): 'But if my psychical life separates itself from my intellectual consciousness and takes over its function, I forfeit my freedom which is rooted in that consciousness, I lose the ability to protect myself from an alien power, in fact, become subjected to it.'

47. William Law, cited in Beer, *Coleridge's Poetic Intelligence*, p. 71.

48. *Prometheus Unbound*, II, iii, 70.

49. Hogg, *Life of Shelley*, p. 51.

50. *Speculations on Metaphysics*, in Shelley, *Complete Works*, vol. VII, p. 62.

51. Ibid., p. 63.

52. Ibid., p. 62.

53. *Journal at Geneva*, in Shelley, *Complete Works*, vol. VI, p. 147.

54. Ralph Cudworth, cited in K. V. Thomas, *Religion and the Decline of Magic* (Harmondsworth, 1978) p. 706.

55. Holmes, *Shelley: The Pursuit*, pp. 294–5.

56. See David Hume, *A Treatise of Human Nature* (1735), Part IV, *Of the Sceptical and Other Systems of Philosophy*, Sections V (*On the Immateriality of the Soul*) and VI (*Of Personal Identity*).

57. *Speculations on Metaphysics*, in Shelley, *Complete Works*, vol. VII, p. 61. This passage is necessarily ignored by those who wish to see Shelley as a Platonist – necessarily, because I take it to be the essence of what has gone by the name of Platonism that mind can be considered pure. In his dynamic view of mind, Shelley can be called neither materialist nor idealist; he looks forward, however sketchily, to a genetic epistemology of the type that Goethe was also groping for: see Rudolf Steiner, *Theory of Knowledge Implicit in Goethe's World-Conception* (New York, 1968); also the remarks of Lehrs, *Man of Matter*, pp. 96–7.

58. *Speculations on Metaphysics*, in Shelley, *Complete Works*, vol. VII (New York, 1930) p. 61.

59. J. P. Eckermann, *Conversations with Goethe*, trans. J. Oxenford (London and New York, 1970), 4 February 1829. Interestingly, Goethe asserts this as a doctrine of 'common sense' as against philosophy and its logical proofs.

60. 'History of ideas' seems an inadequate frame of reference in which to treat such a shift in consciousness. Cf. Owen Barfield, 'History of Ideas: Evolution of Consciousness', in *History, Guilt, and Habit* (Chapel Hill, 1979); and his earlier collection of essays, *Romanticism Comes of Age* (London, 1966).

61. Neville Rogers, *Shelley at Work* (Oxford, 1956) pp. 68ff; and generally

pp. 64–90. Rogers' interpretation is not unchallenged, for example Richard by Holmes, *Shelley: The Pursuit*, pp. 187ff, but it has the support of Shelley's intimates, Hogg and Peacock, and the evidence of a strange drawing (reproduced by Rogers).

Particularly important daemonic references in Shelley's poetry are the Paracelsian picture of the gnomes drinking quicksilver in the *Letter to Maria Gisborne*, ll. 57–65, and the strange fragment 'Wine of the Fairies' (1819). The disturbing, fantastic quality of the latter points the contrast between Shelley's elementals and the 'literary' use made of the 'Rosicrucian doctrine of spirits', for example by Pope in *The Rape of the Lock*, or the artificial machinery of elemental spirits in Erasmus Darwin. Daemonic presences in the longer poems will be considered in their due place in our discussion; frequently they constitute an integral part of the imaginative structure.

62. See Holmes, *Shelley: The Pursuit*, pp. 714–15.
63. Ibid., p. 723.
64. Beer, *Coleridge's Poetic Intelligence*, pp. 79ff.

   It is noteworthy that, without reference to background movements of thought, Wolfgang Clemen in his *Shelleys Geisterweet* (Frankfurt, 1948) came to some of the same insights into Shelley's sense of 'daemonic' forces. 'The whole of nature', he observed, 'is not understood in Shelley in terms of existence, but activity. It is not what things are, but what comes forth from them, streaming out as a power proceeding from them, as action, that touches Shelley's poetic imagination and takes on life in his language' (p. 22). He thus also came to see that a sense of concealed, elemental presences constantly accompanied the poet's picture of the natural world. 'So it becomes clear that his whole study of nature is so deeply imbued with the sense of the spirit-world, that the forces of nature quite spontaneously take the form of spirits' in Shelley's later works (p. 45). Natural science tends to become occult science.

65. The *topos* of soul-harmony in Sensibility and its relation to the tradition of Platonic world-harmony has been studied in detail in George Dekker, *Coleridge and the Literature of Sensibility* (London, 1978) pp. 101–41.
66. *Epipsychidion*, ll. 83–6, 89–90.
67. *Defence of Poetry*, in Shelley, *Complete Works*, vol. VII, p. 116.
68. Ibid., p. 117.
69. Denis Donoghue, *Yeats* (London, 1971) p. 45.
70. Cited in Curran, *Shelley's Annus Mirabilis*, p. 44.

NOTES TO CHAPTER 4: ON THE DEVIL AND DEVILS

1. The chief account of the dualist myth in the sacred literature of Zoroastrianism is contained in the book known as the *Bundahishn*, although there are innumerable scattered references and retellings elsewhere. A modern translation is included in R. C. Zaehner's useful little anthology *The Wisdom of the Magi* (London, 1975) pp. 34ff. The many paradoxes contained in the myth, for example with regard to

Ahriman's co-eternity with Ohrmazd but ultimate defeat and annihilation, evoked both many heresies (such as subordinating Light and Dark to a higher principle called Zervan; or, possibly, accepting Ahriman as a God alongside Ohrmazd) and much ingenious philosophical argument. It may be that Ohrmazd was regarded as being limited in space by Ahriman's power, but as being infinite in time: whereas Ahriman, whose essence is retardation, must finally vanish when all time is rolled up into eternity. The subtle, almost 'evolutionary' concept of time in Zoroastrianism, however, was not grasped by eighteenth-century antiquarians or orientalists, and is only beginning to be fully understood by scholars today.

2. See in general J. Duchesne-Guillemin, *The Western Response to Zoroaster* (Oxford, 1958). The classic work on dualism in the Christian Middle Ages is still S. Runciman, *The Medieval Manichee* (Cambridge, 1947); on the later descendants of Manichaeism see especially D. Obolensky, *The Bogomils* (Cambridge, 1948).

Southey made free use of Indian–Iranian mythological material in his epic *The Curse of Kehama* (1810), which from its length may be described as regrettably complete; regrettably incomplete is Thomas Love Peacock's proposed epic *Ahrimanes*, of which more later. Wordsworth and Byron were strongly influenced by the older notion about early Persian religion, best represented by Thomas Hyde's *Historia religionis veterum Persarum* (1700), once a standard authority. This represented the ancient Zoroastrians as nature-worshippers pure and simple, a view also adopted by Goethe in his account of them in the *Noten* to the *West-Östlicher Divan*. Thus Byron:

> Not vainly did the early Persian make
> His altar the high places and the peak
> Of earth-o'ergazing mountains, and thus take
> A fit and unwall'd temple, there to seek
> The Spirit in whose honour shrines are weak,
> Uprear'd of human hands. Come, and compare
> Columns and idol-dwellings, Goth or Greek,
> With Nature's realms of worship, earth and air,
> Nor fix on fond abodes to circumscribe thy pray'r!
> (Lord Byron, *Childe Harold's Pilgrimage*, III, 91)

And thus Wordsworth, on:

> the Persian – zealous to reject
> Altar and image, and the inclusive walls
> And roofs of temples built by human hands –
> To loftiest heights ascending, from their tops,
> With myrtle-wreathed tiara on his brow,
> Presented sacrifice to moon and stars,
> And to the winds and mother elements,
> And the whole circle of the heavens, for him
> A sensitive existence, and a God.
> (William Wordsworth, *The Excursion*, IV, 671–9)

On these passages, cf. Stuart Curran, *Shelley's Annus Mirabilis* (San Marino, CA, 1975) p. 226 n77.

Blake contrastingly knew that the Persian system, or 'Manichaean doctrine' as it was indiscriminately called, was founded upon 'two principles'; and he agreed with Henry Crabb Robinson that it was 'rational' (evidently Crabb Robinson's term, not Blake's). In confirmation, Blake 'asserted that he did not believe in the *omnipotence* of God – The language of the Bible on that subject is only poetical or allegorical(.) Yet soon after he denied that the natural world is any thing. It is all nothing and Satan's empire is the empire of nothing.' There is no inconsistency here; but it is plain that Blake interpreted dualism in a Gnostic rather than a genuinely Zoroastrian way. See Henry Crabb Robinson, in Bentley, *Blake Records* (Oxford, 1969) pp. 316, 543.

Iranian mythology makes few earlier appearances in English literature. Ohrmazd – or 'Orozmades' – figures in Nathaniel Lee's *The Rival Queens or Alexander the Great* (1677) ii, i as well as in Gray's juvenile 'Lines Spoken by the Ghost of John Dennis', l. 41 (where, however, it apparently refers to Gray's nickname at Eton).

3. The most readily available account of *Ahrimanes*, in particular relation to Shelley, is Carlos Baker, *Shelley's Major Poetry: Fabric of a Vision* (Princeton, 1966) pp. 67ff; and see K. N. Cameron, 'Shelley and *Ahrimanes*', in *Modern Language Quarterly*, 3 (1942) 287–96. The surviving fragments of the poem are printed in *The Works of Thomas Love Peacock*, ed. H. F. B. Brett-Smith and C. E. Jones, vol. vii *Poems and Plays* (London, 1931) pp. 265–86

4. John Frank Newton, *Three Enigmas Attempted to be Explained* (London, 1821) p. 96. Newton ascribes the origin of this idea to the philosopher Epictetus.

5. Here Newton is in sympathy with the development of 'conspiracy theories' of history in such thinkers as Barruel and others. His examples, on the other hand, are particularly extreme. One of the 'Enigmas' considered is the reason for the exile of the poet Ovid in AD 8. Ovid seems to have offended, by his libertine writings, an Emperor even then exiling his daughter for adultery. But for Newton, nothing will do save that Ovid must have betrayed the Mysteries of Eleusis in an obscure passage of his didactic works.

Secret societies have, of course, sometimes been important agents in political and historical events. Particularly in times of stress, war or the threat of war, secret enclaves flourish; they represent a closing of ranks, and often assume a strongly nationalistic, indeed obsessive character. With the obsession also goes the conviction that all the world is actually controlled from behind the scenes by a handful of *illuminati*.

6. On the Zodiac of Dendera see Curran, *Shelley's Annus Mirabilis*, pp. 88–90 and 227–9 n81. On the real Hindu Zodiac see the article by Robert Powell and Peter Treadgold, 'The Sidereal Zodiac. III: The Indian Zodiac', *Mercury Star Journal* 5 (1979) 3, 117–22.

7. *Alastor*, ll. 117–20.

8. A convenient history of cuneiform studies is in Chaim Bermant and Michael Weitzman, *Ebla* (London, 1978) pp. 70ff.

9. *Laon and Cythna*, VII, xxxii, 3109–14.
10. On older ideas of the 'mystical' language of hieroglyphics see the fascinating book of E. Inversen, *The Myth of Egypt and Its Hieroglyphics* (Copenhagen, 1961) and the key text, *Hieroglyphics of Horapollo*, trans. G. Boas (New York, 1950).

    Hippolytus, for his analysis of Pythagorean thought in his *Philosophoumena*, brings together the traditions that 'Pythagoras came to Zaratas [= Zoroaster] the Chaldaean, who explained to him that there are two original causes of things, father and mother, and that father is light, but mother darkness . . . (and) that there are two daemons, the one celestial and the other terrestrial', etc. (*Philosophoumena*, I, ii).
11. Bermant and Weitzman, *Ebla*, p. 72; Curran, *Shelley's Annus Mirabilis*, p. 68; for the details of the recovery and the man who effected it see R. Schwab, *Vie d'Anquetil-Duperron* (Paris, 1934).
12. A. M. D. Hughes, *The Nascent Mind of Shelley* (Oxford, 1947) pp. 184–5; Curran, *Shelley's Annus Mirabilis*, pp. 225–6 n71; J. A. Notopoulos, *The Platonism of Shelley* (Durham, NC, 1949) p. 198.

    To Curran's Iranian references should be added the *Vision of Arda Viraf*, trans. J. A. Pope (London, 1816).
13. Frances Yates, *Giordano Bruno and the Hermetic Tradition* (London, 1964) pp. 15f. and p. 15 n1. The character of Renaissance syncretism is well brought out by Edgar Wind, *Pagan Mysteries in the Renaissance* (Harmondsworth, 1967) pp. 17ff. (chapter on 'Poetic Theology').
14. Newton, *Three Enigmas*, p. 113. I am grateful to Professor Michael Dummett for occasional discussions of de Gebelin and his role in the history of the Tarot. De Gebelin speculated equally wildly, though less influentially, upon a great range of subjects, from etymology to the zodiac.
15. Francis Barrett, *The Magus*, vol. II (London, 1801) pp. 143–9. Barrett's rambling and inconclusive survey of traditions about Zoroaster is a model of restraint in comparison with the history related in an earlier 'Rosicrucian' manual, *The Count de Gabalis* (English editions, 1680) by the Abbé Montfaucon de Villars, whose improbabilities led to Alexander Pope's scathing remark in the Preface to *The Rape of the Lock*, that '*Le Comte de Gabalis*, . . . both in its title and size, is so like a novel that many of the fair sex have read it for one by mistake.' According to the Abbé, Zoroaster was the child of the Salamander (fire-spirit) Oromasis and Vesta, who turns out to have been the wife of Noah. He reigned on earth as a monarch of unsurpassed wisdom, and was then spirited away by his father to the realm of the Salamanders.
16. Barrett, *The Magus*, vol. II, pp. 147–8n.
17. Thomas Love Peacock, *Nightmare Abbey*, ed. R. Wright (Harmondsworth, 1969) ch. 1, p. 45.
18. Peacock, *Ahrimanes*, in *Works*, vol. VII, pp. 265ff.
19. *On the Devil and Devils*, in Shelley, *Complete Works*, ed. R. Ingpen and W. E. Peck, vol. VII, p. 87.
20. Johannes Opsopoeus, *Oracula Magica Zoroastris*, 1st edn (1599), including the commentaries of Gemistus Pletho and of Michael Psellus. Other versions of the oracles could also have been available to Shelley.

Patricius published an edition in 1593, *Zoroaster et eius 320 oracula Chaldaica*, and this Latin text was reproduced in Thomas Stanley's *The History of the Chaldaic Philosophy* (1701) with English versions of the *scholia* of Pletho and Psellus. There was another edition by Jacobus Marthanus (1689); and Thomas Taylor, having translated the *Oracles* for the *Monthly Magazine*, published his rendering in 1806. In an important note to *The Friend*, ed. Barbara E. Rooke (London and Princeton, 1969) vol. I (1818 version) p. 516 (not in original 1809–10 version), Coleridge discussed, along with flower-apparitions and related topics, the *Chaldaean Oracles*, perhaps forming the starting-point for Shelley's researches.

21. The *Chaldaean Oracles* originate, most probably, from the second century AD and presuppose the existence of developed Gnostic systems of thought. Cf. Yates, *Giordano Bruno*, p. 18; E. R. Dodds, *The Greeks and the Irrational* (Berkeley and Los Angeles, 1951) pp. 283–311; and now M. Tardieu, 'La gnose Valentinienne et les Oracles Chaldaiques', in B. Layton (ed.), *The Rediscovery of Gnosticism*, vol. I (Leiden, 1981) pp. 194–237.

22. The authority of the *Chaldaean Oracles* was accepted by the Cambridge Platonists, for instance by Henry More in his tract on *The Immortality of the Soul* (1659) and by Ralph Cudworth in the *True Intellectual System of the Universe* (1678). Cudworth apparently knew other sources on Zoroaster, however: see Yates, *Giordano Bruno*, pp. 423–4, 427–8.

23. *Chaldaean Oracles*, 181 (Proclus, *De providentia*).

24. Ibid., 64 (Proclus, *In Cratylum*). Cf. for the whirlwinds, etc. 63 and 23 (Proclus, *In Parmenidem*), 24 (*Theologia Platonis*, ll. 171–2).

25. Ibid., 185: 'Theurgists fall not so as to be ranked among the herd that are in subjection to Fate' (Johannes Lydus, *De mensibus*).

    On Gnostic–magical efforts to be free of *heimarmene* see the important article of E. Petersen, 'La liberation d'Adam de l'Anangké', *Revue Biblique*, 55 (1948) 199ff; and the discussion of Hans Jonas, *The Gnostic Religion* (Boston, 1963) pp. 241–65.

26. For similar 'Gnostic' experiences underlying Blake's imagery see A. J. Welburn, *The Gnostic Imagination of William Blake'* Cambridge, 1980, pp. 174–9.

27. *Chaldaean Oracles*, 145–6 (Synesius, *de Insomniis*).

28. Curran, *Shelley's Annus Mirabilis*, p. 226 n76. The tradition is Zervanite, i.e. belonging to the heresy which treated Ohrmazd and Ahriman as opposite principles subordinate to a higher unity. For a modern discussion of the myth, cf. Geo Widengren, *Mani und der Manichaismus* (Stuttgart, 1961) p. 49.

29. Democritus, *Fragments*, cited in J. Lindsay, *The Origins of Alchemy in Graeco-Roman Egypt* (London, 19770) p. 93; and the 'summation' cited in C. E. Pulos, *The Deep Truth* (Lincoln, NB, 1962) p. 9.

30. Pliny, *Natural History*, XXIV, 99.

31. Ibid., XXIV, 102; XXXV, 5.

32. Diogenes Laertius, *Lives of the Philosophers*, IX, 34–5; Clement of Alexandria, *Stromateis*, I, 304; Pliny, *Natural History*, XXIV, 17; XXV, 2; XXX, 2, 8–11; Aulus Gellius, *Noctes Atticae*, X, 12, 13–18.

33. For Synesius' view of Democritus see Lindsay, *Origins of Alchemy*, p. 100; and for the story from the *Physica* see pp. 102–3. Cf. Pliny, *Natural History*, xx, 2.

34. Pliny, *Natural History*, xxx, 2; cf. Diogenes Laertius, *Lives of the Philosophers*, ix, 38 and Lucian of Samosata, *The Pathological Liar*, 32–3.

35. Cf. Lindsay, *Origins of Alchemy*, p. 95.

36. Ibid., pp. 94–6.

37. Columella, *De re rustica*, vii, 5, 17.

38. Harold Bloom, *Shelley's Mythmaking* (Cornell, 1959) pp. 19–35; and his *The Visionary Company* (Cornell, 1971) pp. 293–6; Earl Wasserman, *Shelley: A Critical Reading* (Baltimore, 1971) pp. 222–38.

39. Yi-fu Tuan, *Landscapes of Fear* (Oxford, 1980) p. 206.

40. Ibid., p. 55.

41. *On Life* in Shelley, *Complete Works*, ed. R. Ingpen and W. E. Peck, vol. vi (reprinted New York, 1965; the 'Julian Edition') p. 196.

42. R. G. Woodman, *The Apocalyptic Vision in the Poetry of Shelley* (Toronto, 1964) p. 62.

43. Yi-fu Tuan, *Landscapes of Fear*, pp. 204–5.

44. John V. Murphy, *The Dark Angel* (London and New Jersey, 1975) p. 129.

45. Shelley, *Complete Works*, ed. R. Ingpen and W. E. Peck, vol. ix (New York, 1926) pp. 182ff.

46. This phrase, originally encountered by Shelley as a *marginalium* in Charles Lloyd's copy of the works of Berkeley, was taken up by the poet and used in several of his essays. Shelley intended even to use it for an essay title. See Wasserman, *Shelley: A Critical Reading*, p. 135. In *Speculations on Metaphysics* the idea is formulated as the first (and anti-Berkeleyan) axiom of mental philosophy, 'We can think of nothing we have not perceived'. In this form it can clearly be traced back to Locke's *'Nihil in intellectu quod non prius in sensu'*.

47. Wasserman, *Shelley: A Critical Reading*, p. 235. Cf. I. J. Kapstein, 'The Meaning of Shelley's *Mont Blanc*', *PMLA*, 62 (1947) 1046–60.

48. Wasserman, *Shelley: A Critical Reading*, p. 238.
      On *Mont Blanc* and Coleridge's *Hymn* see the remarks of Harold Bloom, *Shelley's Mythmaking*, pp. 11ff.

49. Samuel Taylor Coleridge, *Hymn before Sun-rise, in the Vale of Chamouni*, quoted in Coleridge, *Poems*, ed. J. Beer (London and New York, 1974) p. 290, ll.62–3.

50. Samuel Taylor Coleridge, *The Friend*, ed. Barbara E. Rooke (London and Princeton, 1969) pp. 45–6.

51. Ibid., p. 46.

52. Cf. H. Corbin, 'Cyclical Time in Mazdaism and Ismailism', in J. Campbell (ed.), *Man and Time*, Eranos, no.3 (London, 1958) pp. 116–17; from the original self-existent, divine state of the world (*mēnōk*), according to the *Bundahishn*, is formed a second 'visible, material state, but of a matter which is in itself wholly luminous, a matter immaterial in relation to the matter we actually know' (called *gētīk*). The activity of Ahriman produces as a next stage the impure state of 'mixture' (*gumečishn*), the world in which we now live.

53. Cf. the interesting discussion in Owen Barfield, *Saving The Appearances* (New York, 1965) pp. 107–15 (chapter on 'Israel').
54. *Škand-Gumanik Vičar*, ed. and trans. Jean de Menasce (Fribourg, 1945) pp. 185–201.
55. The problems of authorship and the origins of the treatise are discussed in J. W. H. Atkins, *Literary Criticism in Antiquity*, vol. II (London, 1952) ch. 6. For an overall survey of the influence of 'the sublime' on modern literature, see S. Monk, *The Sublime: A Study of Critical Theories in Eighteenth-Century England* (New York, 1935).
56. M. H. Abrams, *The Mirror and the Lamp* (Oxford, 1953) pp. 72–8.
57. Ibid., p. 76.
58. Edmund Burke, *Philosophical Enquiry into the Origin of the Sublime and the Beautiful* (1756) p. 57.
59. Richard Holmes, *Shelley: The Pursuit* (London, 1976) p. 342. On Shelley's peculiar use of the term *'atheos'*, however, see Neville Rogers, *Shelley at Work* (Oxford, 1956) pp. 58ff; Timothy Webb, *Shelley: A Voice Not Understood* (Manchester, 1977) p. 140.

   The topic has recently been treated by A. Leighton, *Shelley and the Sublime* (Cambridge, 1984). However, she fails to take account of Shelley's radical critique of the traditional Judaeo-Christian sublime; nevertheless her book has many points of importance and critical sensitivity.
60. Holmes, *Shelley: The Pursuit*, p. 340.
61. Shelley's continuing openness to the idea of God is stressed by Timothy Webb, *Shelley: A Voice Not Understood*, p. 161.
62. Rudolf Steiner, *Three Streams in Human Evolution* (London, 1965) pp. 16–17.
63. Genesis 3:5. Here we have an old form of the tradition. Later, in post-Old Testament times, the myth grew up that Lucifer had himself aspired to God-like knowledge and power beyond the proper reach of his nature. The Jewish apocryphal literature circulated under the authority of Enoch played a great role in this development: see D. S. Russell, *The Method and Message of Jewish Apocalyptic* (London, 1964) pp. 249–62. The developments were taken further in early Christianity, on which see generally J. B. Russell, *Satan, The Early Christian Tradition* (Cornell, 1981).
64. Isaiah 14:12. On the Ugaritic background see N. K. Sandars, Introduction to *Poems of Heaven and Hell* (Harmondsworth, 1971) pp. 65–8. The king was Nebuchadnezzar II; the modern suggestion is that in the rites of the 'sacral kingship' celebrated in Babylon, the king would indeed have claimed to ascend into the starry heaven and become a 'bright shiner' like Bel Marduk, his divine prototype. Canaanite mythology, moreover, contains figures such as Shahar (the god of Dawn), a high god El, and a sacred mountain Saphon, all mentioned in Isaiah's satire. The background is certainly correct, but detailed links are still difficult to define. The whole can be compared with the treatment of the king of Tyre by the mocking Ezekiel 28:12–18: see F. H. Borsch, *Son of Man in Myth and History* (London, 1967) pp. 104–6.

For Shelley's perplexity see his essay *On the Devil and Devils*, in *Complete Works*, vol. VII, p. 103.

For developments of the Lucifer-image in poetry see the account of C. Patrides in *Milton and the Christian Tradition* (London, 1966) pp. 91–3.

65. See *Epipsychidion*, ll. 422ff. The passage quoted is ll. 445–56.

66. Compare with the image of the disappearing star the passage in the *Defence of Poetry* which argues that 'the mind in creation is, as a fading coal, which some invisible influence, like an inconstant wind, awakens to transitory brightness'.

67. *On Life*, in Shelley, *Complete Works*, vol. VI, pp. 195–6.

68. Ibid., p. 196.

69. Shelley ought to have been sympathetic to the fundamental proposition of Kant's dialectical thought: 'Without the sensuous faculty no object would be given to us, and without the understanding no object would be thought. Thoughts without content are void; intuitions without conceptions, blind' (I. Kant, Introduction to *Critique of Pure Reason*, Part II, Transcendental Logic). In fact, Shelley never advanced beyond the stage of seeing in Kant a meaningless jumble of philosophical terms. As he reveals in *Peter Bell the Third*, he was prepared to take Sir William Drummond's verdict on Kant and swallow it whole (*Peter Bell the Third*, ll. 518–32). In practice, Shelley (rather like Goethe) evolved a world-view analogous in many ways to Kant's – though from certain perspectives it would be better to say that, also like Goethe, his was a Kantianism turned inside-out. In the crucial matter of the attitude to the limits of knowledge, for instance, what for Kant marked an upper limit of rational enquiry became for the Romantic poets the starting-point for a new departure. What for Kant was a limitation inherent in the nature of things was for the Romantics a condition imposed by the temporary limits of man's organisation. What for Kant was an argument for faith in the Beyond was for the Romantics a call for the self-transformation of man, a summons to further development.

70. *The Witch of Atlas*, ll. 51–4.

71. Samuel Taylor Coleridge, *Poems*, ed. J.B. Beer, pp. 52–3. *The Eolian Harp*, ll. 26–31.

72. *The Eolian Harp*, ll. 44–8.

73. Ibid., ll. 56–60.

74. Cf. the interpretation of Harold Bloom, in *The Visionary Company*, pp. 200–2.

75. *To a Skylark*, ll. 6–10. In passages such as this, intense consciousness begins to fuse the impressions of the different senses: the same happened we recall in the 'reverie' of Coleridge's *The Eolian Harp*. The effect is frequent and important in Shelley: see in particular Glenn O'Malley, 'Shelley's "Air-prism": the Synesthetic Scheme of *Alastor*', in R. B. Woodings (ed.), *Shelley: Modern Judgments* (London, 1969) pp. 72–86.

76. Another version of the 'fading coal'!

77. Bloom, *The Visionary Company*, p. 303.

78. *To a Skylark*, ll. 21–5.

79. Ibid., l. 31.

80. Ibid., ll. 41–55.
81. Cf. the analysis of the movement in *Mont Blanc*, above (pp. 121–2).
82. *To a Skylark*, ll. 71–5.
83. Barrett, *The Magus*, vol. I, p. 14.
84. It may be illuminating to contrast Shelley's attitude once more with that of another Romantic, Blake.

In Blake's *Milton* there is a justly famous passage on the ascent of the larks; each lark for Blake is a 'mighty Angel' and messenger to Eden, despite the diminutive appearance of the bird. The underlying significance of the bird and its expansive song is much the same as in Shelley's ode. In Blake's vision the lark exemplifies a disproportion between visible smallness and the world of sound which oversteps objective limits and 'opens into Eternity'. Likewise the 'precious Odours' of the flowers contradict the 'so small a center' from which they come, showing that infinite Eternity there too 'expands /Its ever during doors that Og & Anak fiercely guard' (W. Blake, *Milton*, pl. 31, 46ff; pl. 35, 61–pl. 36, 12). More daring than the sceptical Shelley, however, and without his concern for self-consciousness, Blake believes that imagination should enter boldly into object-free perception. For Shelley the experience intimates a momentary apprehension of a joy more absolute than is humanly attainable. But for Blake, what is humanly attainable can itself be expanded beyond the limits of the conscious self. The twenty-eighth lark flies free into Eden and the primally Human at the climax of the poem.

For Coleridge, in more general terms, the 'disproportion of human passions to their natural objects' suggested a third response: namely, he turned it into a metaphysical argument, considering it 'among the strongest internal evidences of our future destination' (*The Friend*, vol. I, p. 35; cf. p. 36 n2 and pp. 105–6). He may have been recalling Sir John Davies' 'Dedication' to *Nosce Teipsum* (*The Poems of Sir John Davies*, ed. Robert Krueger (Oxford, 1975) p. 3):

> The strongest and the noblest argument
> To prove the Soule immortall, rests in this;
> That in no mortall thing it finds content,
> But seeks an object that aeternall is.

85. E. J. Trelawney, *Records of Shelley, Byron and the Author* (Harmondsworth, 1973) p. 111.
86. *To a Skylark*, ll. 86–90.

It is absurd of Mario Praz to find in this passage Romantic 'algolagnia': it is rather the pursuit of 'pure' intensities of sensation which leads to the enjoyment of pain, not the balanced and sane awareness Shelley intimates here.

NOTES TO CHAPTER 5: WISDOM AND LOVE

1. Richard Holmes (ed.), *Shelley on Love* (London, 1980) p. 71.
2. Preface to *Alastor*, in *The Complete Poetical Works of Percy Bysshe*

Shelley, ed. Neville Rogers, vol. II (Oxford, 1975) p. 44. On the theme of 'pursuing and pursued' see Neville Rogers, *Shelley at Work* (Oxford, 1956) p. 70 and plate IIa.

3. *Alastor*, ll. 211–15.

4. For Blake's use of 'Intellect' see William Blake, *A Vision of the Last Judgment*, in *Complete Writings*, ed. Sir Geoffrey Keynes (Oxford, 1972) p. 615; *Jerusalem*, pl. 91, 10.

   Wasserman's approach to defining 'Intellectual Beauty' is partly Platonic, partly based upon Shelley's philosophical prose. He describes the *Hymn* as one of the poet's 'speculations'. 'Intellectual' turns out to mean pertaining to 'a divinity of mind only', to be sharply divorced from the 'Power' apprehended in *Mont Blanc*: Earl Wasserman, *Shelley: A Critical Reading* (Baltimore, 1971) pp. 190–2. Bloom too is trapped into seeing the *Hymn* as a symmetrical 'spiritual' counterpart to the 'material' *Mont Blanc*, though he rejects the Platonic reading and emphasises Christian parallels: Harold Bloom, *Shelley's Mythmaking* (Cornell, 1959) pp. 36ff. But the meaning of 'Intellectual Beauty' must be derived from the poem, and above all from the poem's centrality within the structure of Shelley's imagination.

5. The theme above all, of course, of Coleridge in *Dejection*; cf. also Wordsworth in the *Immortality* ode, *Tintern Abbey*, etc.

6. *Hymn to Intellectual Beauty*, ll. 9–12.

7. John 3:8.

8. *Hymn to Intellectual Beauty*, ll. 16–17.

9. Ibid., ll. 25–31.

10. Ibid., ll. 39–41.

11. Ibid., ll. 46–8.

12. Ibid., ll. 49–53.

13. Ibid., ll. 59–60.

14. Ibid., ll. 64–72.

15. Ibid., ll. 73–7.

16. Francis Barrett, *The Magus*, vol. II (London, 1801) p. 198. Cf. vol. I, p. 58. Possible backgrounds of Shelley's idea are discussed in Wasserman, *Shelley: A Critical Reading*, p. 195 n29.

17. *Hymn to Intellectual Beauty*, ll. 83–4.

18. *The Letters of Percy Bysshe Shelley*, ed. F. L. Jones, vol. II, p. 125, letter to Maria Gisborne, dated 13–14 October 1819.

19. Cited in Timothy Webb, *Shelley: A Voice Not Understood* (Manchester, 1977) p. 175; and see Samuel Taylor Coleridge, *The Friend*, ed. Barbara E. Rooke, vol. I (London and Princeton, 1969) pp. 252–3.

20. *Shelley's Letters*, vol. II, p. 125, letter to Maria Gisborne, dated 13–14 October 1819.

21. Holmes, *Shelley on Love*, p. 72.

22. *Hymn to Intellectual Beauty*, l. 37; the negative triad appears in *Prometheus Unbound*, I, 9.

23. I do not assert that a psychological comparison with some of the four-fold 'mantra' patterns turning up by Jung would necessarily be unprofitable. Nor do I think the importance of four-fold patterns in Romantic imagination, noted by Blackstone, uninteresting. But the poles of

'Lucifer' and 'Ahriman', for example, represent forces which demand from the psyche an attitude to actuality, in a positive or negative sense; and one or the other may predominate in a particular cultural mythology. A Shelleyan freedom to hold their powers in equilibrium is a higher development, perhaps we might say, rather than a radical quality of the mind.

24. It is interesting to see these ideas worked out in philosophical terms by Rudolf Steiner, whose world-view has been characterised by Owen Barfield in his book aptly entitled *Romanticism Comes of Age* (London, 1966); see especially the chapter on 'Rudolf Steiner's Concept of Mind'.

In his *Philosophy of Freedom*, trans. Michael Wilson (London, 1964), although he does not yet name the two principles 'Luciferic' and 'Ahrimanic', Rudolf Steiner discusses the nature of 'experience' as fructified on the one hand by the active life of the intellect and on the other of openness in perception. A man who merely lives in the activity of eyes, ears and other sense-organs would gain little or no intelligible 'experience':

> He loses the objects again when they disappear from his field of vision, because he lacks the concepts which he should bring into relation with them. A man whose faculty of thinking is well developed, but whose perception functions badly because of his clumsy sense-organs, will just as little be able to gather experience. . . . The unthinking traveller, and the scholar living in abstract conceptual systems are alike incapable of acquiring a rich sum of experience. (p. 85)

If we tried to live wholly in the life of the sense and the outer world, we would lose ourselves in the contentless Ahrimanic emptiness; it we were to plunge into the inner life of thought, we should be lost in the abstract Luciferic heaven of the ideal.

As cognising beings we could never achieve real individuality – humanity – but would be perpetually drawn back and forth between these two poles of awareness. Steiner sees the life of feeling as the element which is the ground of our sense of individuality. In practice our subjective being is not a wholly transparent medium where abstract universals subsume the particulars of given perpetual experience. We make idea and perception our *own* experience by our affective response. If in turn, however, we were to attempt to live entirely in our feeling-life, we would soon lose contact with the objective cognised reality around us. But man for Steiner: 'is meant to be whole, and for him knowledge of things will go hand in hand with the development and education of the life of feeling. Feeling is the means whereby, in the first, instance, concepts gain concrete life' (pp. 86–8). Later in the book Steiner develops this Romantic doctrine of feeling as the mediator between man's individuality and the objective absolutes of the Ahrimanic and Luciferic into the idea of a cognition which is permeated by love. Again, therefore, we have an integrated constellation of forces leading out into an expansion of consciousness. Such a kind of thinking – which is exactly what Shelley envisages – is: 'warm, luminous, and penetrating deeply into the phenomena of the world. This penetration is brought about by a power flowing through the activity of thinking itself – the power of love in its spiritual form' (p. 119).

25. Holmes, *Shelley on Love*, p. 71. (*On Love.*)
26. Ibid., pp. 72–3. (*On Love.*)
27. Ibid., p. 106. (*Discourse on the Manners of the Ancient Greeks Relative to the Subject of Love.*)
28. See *A Defence of Poetry*: the 'attack' had been Thomas Love Peacock's article 'The Four Ages of Poetry' in the first (and only) issue of *Ollier's Literary Miscellany* (1820). The texts of both are included in Bruce McElderry, *Shelley's Critical Prose* (Lincoln, NB, 1967) pp. 4–37 and 148–72.

   There have been many discussions of Shelley's *Defence*; more illuminating than any of them, however, is perhaps the independent work of Owen Barfield, *Poetic Diction* (London, 1951), remarkably Shelleyan in much of its thought, though with an emphasis on precision of thought where Shelley was often content to be rhetorical and suggestive. The two works enlighten each other.
29. McElderry, *Shelley's Critical Prose*, pp. 12–13.
30. With Shelley's Romantic version of artist morality it is again interesting to compare the philosophical idea of *moralische Phantasie* in Steiner's *Philosophy of Freedom*, pp. 162ff.
31. 1 Cor. 3:4,7. On the importance of the passage for Shelley see Webb, *Shelley: A Voice Not Understood*, p. 174.
32. Cf. the brilliant discussion in Richard Cronin, *Shelley's Poetic Thoughts* (London, 1981) esp. pp. 104, 128, 142, 152, etc. Earlier, in relation to *Alastor*, Cronin characterises Shelley's ethics as an attempt, in provocatively disposing of the trascendent absolutes, 'to make the language of self-love serve also as the language of morals' (p. 83).
33. Coleridge, *The Friend*, vol. I, p. 253.
34. *Hymn to Intellectual Beauty*, l. 79.
35. *Ode to the West Wind*, ll. 1–14.
36. Ibid., ll. 6–8. The case is different in the traditional Christian imagery of the seed *dying* into the ground, as in the magnificently rhetorical version by Tertullian which forms our epigraph. Shelley was well read in the New Testament and early Christian literature. Can it be that he knew Tertullian's *De resurrectione carnis*, 12? At the very least, it shows Shelley's remarkable proximity in this poem to the forms of the Christian tradition.
37. *Death*, published posthumously by Mary Shelley, was probably composed in 1817.
38. *Ode to the West Wind*, ll. 23–8.
39. Ibid., ll. 29–36.
40. Harold Bloom, *The Visionary Company* (Cornell, 1971) p. 299.
41. *Ode to the West Wind*, ll. 38–42.
42. Shelley's Note to the *Ode to the West Wind*, in *Poetical Works*, ed. T. Hutchinson, rev. G. M. Matthews (Oxford, 1970) p. 577.
43. *Ode to the West Wind*, ll. 48–51.
44. Blake, *A Vision of the Last Judgment*, in *Complete Writings*, pp. 604ff; see also S. Foster Damon, *A Blake Dictionary* (London, 1973) *sub* 'States'.

45. *Ode to the West Wind*, ll. 61–2.
46. Cf. the sweetest song and saddest thought of the *Skylark* ode, and the harmony in autumn of the *Hymn to Intellectual Beauty*. *Ode to the West Wind*, ll. 57–61.
47. *Ode to the West Wind*, ll. 63–70.

NOTES TO CHAPTER 6: RIDERS IN THE CHARIOT

1. Richard Cronin, *Shelley's Poetic Thoughts* (London, 1981) p. 133.
2. *Prometheus Unbound*, I, 21–2.
3. Ibid., I, 827–32.
4. Ibid., I, 120–5.
5. Thus at the end of Act I Prometheus must still say:

> I would fain
> Be what it is my destiny to be,
> The saviour and the strength of suffering man.
> (*Prometheus Unbound*, I, 815–17)

6. Samuel Taylor Coleridge, 'The Prometheus of Aeschylus' (lecture delivered before the Royal Society of Literature in 1825), in *Literary Remains*, ed. H. N. Coleridge, vol. IV, (Pickering, 1836–9) pp. 344–65.
7. G. Wilson Knight is perhaps foremost among those who have stressed the Christ-archetype: see G. Wilson Knight, *The Starlit Dome* (London, 1959) pp. 203–4; also Stuart Curran, *Shelley's Annus Mirabilis* (San Marino, CA, 1975) pp. 54–60; and more generally Timothy Webb, *Shelley: A Voice Not Understood* (Manchester, 1977) pp. 157–90; esp. pp. 162–3.
8. See *Prometheus Unbound*, I, 538 – and the whole episode with the Furies; for Asia see II, iii, 59–61 and the following scene with Demogorgon.
9. Asia comes to understand that Jupiter is the power who torments man with Luciferic urges which cannot be satisfied, and if allowed to work unchecked turns him into a slave;

> And in their desert hearts fierce wants he sent,
> And mad disquietudes, and shadows idle
> Of unreal good, which levied mutual war,
> So ruining the lair wherein they raged.
> (*Prometheus Unbound*, II, iv. 55–8)

Demogorgon, conversely, is an Ahrimanic 'darkness / Filling the seat of power', a sheer negation from whom no positive utterance can be won. After confronting him however, Asia realises that the answers to her questions lie rather in a development of her own inner sense of truth. In Act III the two powers are played off against each other, as if cancelling each other out. Demogorgon tells Jupiter, 'we must dwell together / Henceforth in darkness' (*Prometheus Unbound*, III, i, 55–6). The destructive aspects of the two forces disappear, since the psyche holds them in balance.

10. *Prometheus Unbound*, III, iv, 74–5. The toads, snakes and efts (newts) are *khrafstras* – that is to say, in Iranian, thought-beasts which are harmful or repulsive to man and therefore considered part of Ahriman's work in the creation. Shelley here allows them to cast off their Ahrimanic repulsiveness, perhaps recalling the scene in Coleridge's *Ancient Mariner* where the mariner suddenly sees the beauty of the creatures of the deep and blesses them.

11. *Prometheus Unbound*, IV, 206–35.

12. Harold Bloom, *Shelley's Mythmaking* (Cornell, 1959) pp. 140–1, 231–6. The mediator of the tradition to the Romantics was once more primarily Milton, as Bloom demonstrates. Most scholars have emphasized the extraneous influences on Jewish *Merkavah* mysticism, but I. Gruenwald, *Apocalyptic and Merkavah Mysticism* (Leiden, 1980) is a recent exception, stressing the internal continuity of this development in Judaism. Gershom Scholem also admitted that foreign conceptions were accommodated to the structures of the religion of the Torah; he was surely correct, however, in stressing the Gnostic affinities of the *Merkavah* writings from Talmudic times: see Gershom Scholem, *Jewish Gnosticism, Merkavah Mysticism and Talmudic Tradition* (New York, 1960).

13. Ezekiel 1:4; see Gruenwald, *Apocalyptic and Merkavah Mysticism*, pp. 30–1.

14. Ezekiel 1:19–28.

15. Daniel 7:9.

16. Apocalypse 1:17–18; the *Merkavah* 4:2ff.

17. *Prometheus Unbound*, IV, 236–68.

18. John Milton, *Paradise Lost*, VIII, 79–84; cf. V, 620–5.

19. Wilson Knight, *The Starlit Dome*, pp. 220–2.

20. *Prometheus Unbound*, IV, 269.

21. Cf. Hegel, *Philosophy of Nature*, trans. A. V. Miller (Oxford, 1970) pp. 61–2.

22. *Prometheus Unbound*, IV, 268.

23. See the fascinating study by M. C. Jacob, *The Newtonians and the English Revolution 1689–1720* (Hassocks, Sussex, 1976). God's role in the universe was conceived as that of 'an all-wise governor, a providential deity who governed with supreme order and logic. This formulation of God's relationship to the universe had been an important part of Restoration philosophy and theology as developed by natural philosophers' (pp. 95–6). Newtonian celestial mechanics and the mechanistic chemistry of Boyle rehabilitated the image of the all-ruler. From his Gnostic standpoint, Blake regarded the whole system as purely Satanic:

> O Satan, my youngest born, art thou not Prince of
> the Starry Hosts
> And of the Wheels of Heaven, to turn the Mills day & night?
> Art thou not Newton's Pantocrator.
> (William Blake, *Milton*, 4, 9–11)

24. *The Triumph of Life*, ll. 1–3.

25. Ibid., ll. 26–8.
26. William Wordsworth, *Excursion*, I, 500–2.
27. *Book of Enoch* 14:13. The passage is closely followed by a *Merkavah* vision.
28. *The Triumph of Life*, ll. 79–90; cf. *Prometheus Unbound*, IV, 204–35. Other sources and analogues of the Chariot and the Triumph have been stressed by various critics: Petrarch's *Triumphs*, in particular *The Triumph of Love*; the Car of the Church in Dante's *Purgatorio*; the wild procession of the Indian god Jagganatha (Juggernaut); the 'Chariot of Paternal Deitie', in Milton. On the *Merkavah* aspect, cf. Bloom, *Shelley's Mythmaking*, pp. 231–42.
29. Wilson Knight, *The Starlit Dome*, p. 251.
30. *The Triumph of Life*, ll. 128–31.
31. Ibid., ll. 293–5.
32. Ibid., ll. 211–15.
33. Ibid., ll. 314–20.
34. Ibid., ll. 386–93, 412–14.
35. Ibid., ll. 476–9.
36. Goethe, *Faust* II, Act V, 11574–8:

> Das ist der Weisheit letzter Schluss:
> Nur der verdient sich Freiheit wie das Leben,
> Der täglich sie erobern muss.
> Und so verbringt, umrungen von Gefahr,
> Hier Kindheit, Mann und Greis sein tüchtig Jahr.

NOTES TO CHAPTER 7: THE CHRISTIAN SPIRIT

1. This principle is developed at length in the *Defence of Poetry*, and shows that here too Shelley was verging upon a fully developmental approach to aesthetics, as he was in the 'metaphysics' of mind.
2. *Prometheus Unbound*, II, iii, 93–8. Cf. the discussion in Timothy Webb, *Shelley: A Voice Not Understood* (Manchester, 1977) pp. 172–3.
3. See generally Ellsworth Barnard, *Shelley's Religion* (New York, 1964); Webb's treatment of 'The Christian Mythology' in *Shelley: A Voice Not Understood*, esp. pp. 181ff; and the many shorter discussions in almost every treatment of Shelley.
4. Mary Boyce, *Zoroastrians* (London, 1979) p. 99. For further introduction and orientation in the matter of Iranian influence on early Christianity see for example F. H. Borsch, *The Son of Man in Myth and History* (London, 1967) pp. 84ff. and the literature cited there; fascinating perspectives are also in R. Steiner, *Lectures on the Gospel of Matthew* (London, 1965).
5. Jack Lindsay, *Origins of Alchemy* (London, 1970) p. 134. Particularly important is the work called an *Apocalypse of Adam*, which seems to have originated in a pre-Christian baptising sect, and prophesies the reincarnation of the Illuminator (=Zarathustra) in the 'kingdom of Shem', i.e. among the Jews. See Alexander Böhlig, 'Jüdisches and

Iranisches in der Adam-apokalypse', in his *Mysterion und Wahrheit* (Leiden, 1968) pp. 149ff.

6. Cf. R. C. Zaehner, *Teachings of the Magi* (London, 1975) pp. 139ff.

7. See above, pp. 247ff.

8. The best account of Gnosticism is that of K. Rudolph, *Gnosis* now available in English translation, trans. R. McL. Wilson (Edinburgh, 1984).

9. Goethe in his youth read Gotfrid Arnold's *Unparteiische Kirchen – und Ketzergeschichte*, (1699), and adopted from it a Gnostic system of belief. He too abandoned Gnosticism for a more Christian resolution of imaginative energies in his great poetry; but Alan Cottrell has recently emphasised the importance of Goethe's Gnostic phase for the understanding of his later thought, especially about evil: Alan Cottrell, *Goethe's View of Evil* (London, 1982) esp. pp. 27ff. Baudelaire often breathes a Gnostic–dualistic atmosphere in his lyrics, despite his lack of interest in the construction of an explicit mythology. On the subject of Blake's Gnosticism see: A. J. Welburn, 'The Gnostic Imagination of William Blake', PhD thesis, University of Cambridge, 1980.

10. *Queen Mab*, vii, 106–11; cf. William Blake, *Book of Urizen*, esp. pl. 4, 6ff.

11. See further James Rieger, *The Mutiny Within* (New York, 1967) which contains some interesting insights, though they are not always placed in proper perspective.

12. Athanasius, *De incarnatione*, 54. Similar statements in Irenaeus, *Adversus haereses*, V, praef., etc.; Clement of Alexandria, *Protrepticus*, i (8, 4); Origen, *Contra Celsum*, iii, 28; and so forth.

   It was presumably the fear of humanistic aberrations which fostered that other line of development in Christian thought, which sharply divides faith from knowledge, divine from human. The line reaches from Tertullian's famous 'I believe because it is absurd' to Pascal and to Kierkegaard.

13. Stuart Curran, *Shelley's Annus Mirabilis* (San Marino, CA, 1975) p. 205.

14. Clement of Alexandria, *Stromateis*, ii, 6, 26.

15. See Owen Barfield, *Romanticism Comes of Age* (London, 1966) and the interesting discussion in R. J. Reilly, 'A Note on Barfield, Romanticism, and Time', in the Barfield *Festschrift*, ed. S. Sugerman, *Evolution of Consciousness. Studies in Polarity* (Middletown, CT, 1976) pp. 183–90.

Index

230